PRAISE FOR *SERIOUS EATER*

"How did we all become obsessed with food? The answer might be: Ed Levine. A tremendous writer, eater, and human, Ed has written the hilarious, harrowing, passionate, definitive true story of the birth of Serious Eats, the world's first major food site. This is good stuff. You will eat the pages."

—PHIL ROSENTHAL,
creator of *Everybody Loves Raymond*
and *Somebody Feed Phil*

"The deliciously true journey (with recipes) of one man's adventures in the food business. We all need to eat, but Ed needs (all of us) to eat well."

—SETH GODIN,
author of *This Is Marketing*

SERIOUS EATER

SERIOUS EATER

A Food Lover's Perilous Quest
for Pizza and Redemption

ED LEVINE

Portfolio/Penguin

Portfolio/Penguin
An imprint of Penguin Random House LLC
penguinrandomhouse.com

Most Portfolio books are available at a discount when purchased in quantity
for sales promotions or corporate use. Special editions, which include personalized
covers, excerpts, and corporate imprints, can be created when purchased in large
quantities. For more information, please call (212) 572-2232 or e-mail
specialmarkets@penguinrandomhouse.com. Your local bookstore can also assist
with discounted bulk purchases using the Penguin Random House corporate
Business-to-Business program. For assistance in locating a participating retailer,
e-mail B2B@penguinrandomhouse.com.

LIBRARY OF CONGRESS CATALOGING-IN-PUBLICATION DATA
Names: Levine, Ed, 1952– author.
Title: Serious eater : a food lover's perilous quest for pizza
and redemption / Ed Levine.
Description: [New York] : Portfolio/Penguin, [2019]
Identifiers: LCCN 2019004074 (print) | LCCN 2019005081 (ebook) |
ISBN 9780525533559 (ebook) | ISBN 9780525533542 (hardcover)
Subjects: LCSH: Levine, Ed, 1952– | Food writers—New York (State)—
New York—Biography. | Bloggers—New York (State)—New York—Biography. |
Pizza—New York (State)—New York. | LCGFT: Cookbooks.
Classification: LCC TX649.L479 (ebook) | LCC TX649.L479 A3 2019 (print) |
DDC 641.5092 [B] —dc23
LC record available at https://lccn.loc.gov/2019004074

Printed in the United States of America
1   3   5   7   9   10   8   6   4   2

Book design by Daniel Lagin

Penguin is committed to publishing works of quality and integrity. In that spirit,
we are proud to offer this book to our readers; however, the story, the experiences,
and the words are the author's alone.

The recipes contained in this book are to be followed exactly as written.
The publisher is not responsible for your specific health or allergy needs that may
require medical supervision. The publisher is not responsible for any adverse
reactions to the recipes contained in this book.

For Vicky, the love of my life, who believed in Serious Eats before anyone.
You taught me to love and the meaning of true partnership.
Thanks for helping me stay the course.

For Mike and Carol, without whom there would be no Serious Eats.
Bro, you always had my back, even if you sometimes had a funny
way of showing it. The two of you taught me to trust.

For our son, Will, who has imbued our lives with joy and meaning
from the moment he arrived on this earth.

For my parents, Morris and Sara, who taught me to speak truth
to power at an early age. The beliefs and values you instilled in all four
Levine brothers helped sustain Serious Eats every step of the way.

And finally, for the Serious Eats tribe at World HQ and our community
millions strong, who taught me that anything and everything is possible
with the aid of hard work, a good idea, and a little luck.

CONTENTS

FOREWORD

J. Kenji López-Alt

The first thing I did after I finished reading the last page of the draft of this book was log into my old email account and re-read the first exchanges that Ed and I had, way back in July of 2009.

Actually, that was the second thing I did. The first thing I did was heat up a slice of pizza on the stovetop in a skillet (the best way to reheat pizza). It wasn't just a craving, it was necessary sustenance, as I'd failed to notice the hours that had passed since I started reading.

To read our early email exchange you would have trouble identifying who was the bigger fool. The sheer rate at which it progresses from "Hey, how are you?" to "We will be working together for a long time" surprised even me as I read through it. And I'd lived it.

James Kenji Lopez-Alt <xxxxxxxx@gmail.com>
Tue, Sep 8, 2009, 8:07 PM
to Ed

Hi Ed—are you still up for lunch tomorrow? I could meet you wherever you'd like in the city. Let me know what works best for you.

Kenji

Up to this point, I had written precisely two articles for *A Hamburger Today*, Serious Eats' now-shuttered burger-related vertical. The first was a review of Heston Blumenthal's insanely complex burger recipe (over thirty hours to complete! Thirty-two ingredients!) and the second was a tour of twelve iconic Northeast burger joints, in which I sampled twelve burgers over eight hours. I'd spent a few years writing recipes and features for Boston-area magazines and papers, but those two articles, published on a site I barely knew about, were the most fun I'd ever had researching and writing.

Newly wed, I had recently moved back to New York and was living in a one-bedroom apartment in Prospect Heights with literally no windows. I was supplementing my wife Adri's graduate school income by making ready-to-eat bean burritos and macaroni and cheese for an Upper West Side family as well as the occasional freelance editing and writing gig. I co-"managed" a blog about sustainable eating called GoodEater.org ("Your food . . . and where it comes from." Cringe). We'd recently celebrated having finally hit one thousand page views a day.

On paper, there was no reason for Ed to have much faith in my abilities or potential. I had contacted him a few times over the past few months, hitting him up for some editorial advice or freelance gigs, as I had done with any moderately successful website editor I could stalk. This time Ed had other plans. We finally met face to face on September 9, 2009. (It was over cheeseburgers at a trailer park–themed burger joint a couple of blocks from the Serious Eats office in Chelsea; Robyn Lee joined us.)

I don't remember much from that meeting, but I do remember thinking, *I trust this guy* as we ate some chili-and-cheese-smothered tot-chos (a food trend that has happily started to dissipate). It was because he didn't just order half the menu, he ordered the *right* half of the menu. How could I *not* trust him? I'd had too many interviews with media entrepreneurs who thought business first: Food is only a means to an end. It just happens to be hot right now. With Ed, food, and the pleasure of eating it, *was* the business. Everything else followed.

Later, as we talked about the supremacy of smashed burgers, and what makes them so tasty (that sweet, sweet Maillard reaction):

"You know, Kenji, you should write a food science column for us."

"Hey," I said, "that sounds fun."

I didn't tell him at the time, but I was in shock. You know how sometimes you don't really know what you're hungry for until it's in front of you?* Up until that point I'd never considered the idea of writing about food science. Yet here's this guy whom I'd met just twenty minutes before, dropping my dream job in my lap, as casually as a stray onion ring.

You see, Ed's got this ability to truly understand what people want and what motivates them. Even though this is a rare gift—how many bosses have you had that actually understood your needs?—it might be unfair to call it an ability. You know that thing where sometimes you listen to what people say, but you don't really *hear* them? There's no trick to hearing people: you just have to really, legitimately care. Ed's skill is that he cares about pretty much everyone. He wants to see everyone succeed to their fullest potential. It sounds insanely cheesy (like those tot-chos), but it's true. He cares, and it oozes from every pore of his being and every page of this book.

That night I went home and jotted down some quick ideas for how a food science column could play out. ("It could be like *MythBusters* for food!" or "It's like McGee, but not as smart, and with recipes!")

By the next morning I had this waiting in my inbox:

Ed Levine <xxxxxxxx@seriouseats.com>
Thu, Sep 10, 2009, 9:49 AM
to me

These all sound great, Kenji. We can pay you $30 right from the start. I also have another question for you. I've often thought we had a need for a recipe czar, someone who could look over the recipes we post on the

---

* Let's not kid. It's always pizza.

site and edit out the stuff that is just wrong. It wouldn't take a lot of your time and you could do it remotely.

("It wouldn't take a lot of your time." If only I'd known—ha!)

"Hey," I said, "that sounds fun."

Meanwhile, in my head: *Kenji! What are you doing?! You don't know this guy. You've been to his "office" so you know that the peanuts he's offering you now aren't going to be increasing much in the future. You're not worth much, but you're worth more than this. Do people his age even know what the internet is?*

But it didn't matter. Of course it didn't. I'd spent years working ninety-hour weeks in kitchens earning less than minimum wage, to execute someone else's vision. I loved my days testing recipes for *Cook's Illustrated*, but hated the editorial sausage grinder that turned every voice into the same old dry (but precise!) *Cook's Illustrated* sausage. And here was Ed, telling me I could do exactly what I wanted to do. That my hobby could become my work. The he trusted me to live up to what he saw in me. That is all that mattered.

On October 27, just three weeks after my very first Food Lab column about hard-boiled eggs went live, Ed and I were talking again over more cheeseburgers, this time from Bill's Bar & Burger (they make standout smashed burgers at all their NYC locations). This time Ed said, "Hey, Kenji, you should write a book about food science."

"Hey," I said, "that sounds fun."

And on it went.

"You should write a burger column for us."

"You should interview all the best pizza makers in the city."

"You should be our managing editor."*

How could I say no? It all sounded so fun!

And it was. But man, did it take a lot of faith at the start. Ed, always enthusiastic and cheery when it came to good food, was equally dreary and

---

* This last one was a mistake that I soon transitioned out of. Ed's not *always* right.

difficult when it came to business, as the site scraped by month after month. Ed didn't dwell with us on the finances of the site, but he didn't need to. We—Carey Jones, Erin Zimmer, Robyn Lee, Adam Kuban, and the rest of the editorial team—heard every phone call and saw his deflated form every time he had to start digging around for enough cash to make payroll.

To read his memoirs is like watching a perfectly executed backstory. *Oh,* that's *what was going on then,* I found myself frequently thinking. I'd heard the characters and seen the MacGuffins—Ed's brothers. His early collaborators. That Gusto promo video. (If this all means nothing to you, read on!) But seeing them come to life and understanding the significance they have played in Ed's story is thrilling.

That first holiday season after I started freelancing for Ed, he stopped by my ~~windowless cave~~ apartment one evening and dropped off a hand-written check for two hundred dollars. It's not much, he said, but it's what he could scrape together as a thank-you. If you do the math, he's right. It's not much. A check that size wouldn't even cover the hourly minimum wage rate for half of a typical Food Lab article if I'd been paid by the hour. Yet my boss had trudged down from the Upper West Side, on the subway, through the slushy streets, to deliver a personal thanks. Think about that!

That's when I realized that there was no turning back. I was already on the ride. Not one of those sleek steel roller coasters with smooth bearings, but a seat-of-your-pants, rickety, boardwalk affair. You churn around the track, arms flailing, and as you try to grab a safety bar that isn't there, you realize it's okay. You've got complete trust in the operator, and you might as well see where he takes you.

Am I a sucker for having my trust bought for thirty dollars an article and a two-hundred-dollar check? For continuing to believe in a boss and a business that, on paper, seemed doomed from the start? Probably. I don't regret it. (And for the record, Ed went through superhuman efforts to do right by me every chance he could get.)

From Ed's point of view, you'll find that this earnestness and trust in others will often get him into trouble. From the stories he tells in this book it may even come across as his greatest weakness. I love you, Ed, but you're wrong on this one. Your willingness to trust other people is the best thing you've got going for you. It's what sets you apart. It's what attracted the best people to you. Like ordering from the menu, it's not just getting the people, it's about getting the *right* people. It's what gave Serious Eats the soul it needed to not just weather the crushingly turbulent waters of mid-2000-era publications and blogs, but to come out the other end intact, true to its mission, and more successful than ever.

It's why I worked for you and why I will never work for another boss after you. You've ruined me for all other bosses, Ed.

Come to think of it, that pizza I heated up before checking these emails—I could have eaten that pizza cold, but that would have been a *very* un-Ed thing to do.

One of Ed's basic philosophies for Serious Eats is that it's about *stories*. Whether it's an interview, a recipe, a feature on farmers' markets, or a guide to fast food, the best pieces are the ones that are, at their core, a story, complete with a beginning, a middle, an end; themes to be followed; conflicts and resolutions. In this, he has been wildly successful with his memoirs, which read more like a carefully crafted novel than a real person's life. The nice thing is that, for once, the good guy wins. There are both sacrifices and enemies made along the way, but Ed succeeds despite never once straying from his values, never once taking the easy way, and never ceasing to put us—the ones who recklessly jumped into the ride—and our needs first.

This is a story of generosity. It's generosity that makes Ed the gravitational center of a massive galaxy of writers and chefs and musicians and creators. His strength is not in changing people or molding them into his image, it's in being able to pull them in and slingshot them around at just the right trajectory to help them reach, in his words, onward and upward.

SERIOUS EATER PLAYLIST

B efore I ate for a living, I worked in the music business for twelve years. I love music as much as I love food. I feel very fortunate that I've spent most of my work life doing things I love. Though readers get a glimpse in the book of my life in music, I wish we could have included more. In fact, I wish the book would come with a thumb drive containing my favorite songs. Absent that, I give you the official *Serious Eater* playlist. Listen while you read, before you read, after you read the book, or anytime you want. You don't even have to be eating something seriously delicious while doing so. The songs are either by artists whom I write about or worked with or by musicians whose songs came to mind while I was writing. Kenji chose the suggested songs in the chapter that features him most prominently, "The Great, Slow Pivot to Recipes." So put on your headphones, log on to your favored streaming service, and listen to the soundtrack of my life. Happy listening.

PROLOGUE

"Ain't No Stoppin' Us Now," by McFadden & Whitehead

CHAPTER 1

"(Your Love Keeps Lifting Me) Higher and Higher," by Jackie Wilson

CHAPTER 2

"The Love I Lost," by Harold Melvin & the Blue Notes

CHAPTER 3

"The Thrill Is Gone," by B. B. King

CHAPTER 4

"Ain't Gwine to Whistle Dixie (Any Mo')," by Taj Mahal
"Thoroughbred," by Gil Evans
"The Time and the Place," by Jimmy Heath
"Chuck E's in Love," by Rickie Lee Jones
"Dorothy," by Dr. John
"If You Could See Me Now," by Continuum
"Rainy Night in Georgia," by Brook Benton
"The Real One," by John Doe

CHAPTER 7

"Visions of Johanna," by Bob Dylan

CHAPTER 8

"For What It's Worth," by Buffalo Springfield

CHAPTER 9

"Land of Hope and Dreams," by Bruce Springsteen

CHAPTER 10

"Two Trains," by Lowell George, Little Feat

CHAPTER 11

"Perfect Fit," by Van Morrison

CHAPTER 12

"Everybody Wants to Go to Heaven, but Nobody Wants to Die,"
 by Albert King

CHAPTER 13

"For the Love of Money," by the O'Jays

CHAPTER 14

"Stage Fright," by the Band
"Don't Let Me Down," by the Beatles

CHAPTER 15

"A Hard Rain's A Gonna Fall," by Bob Dylan

CHAPTER 17

"Only the Strong Survive," by Jerry Butler

CHAPTER 19

"A Change Is Gonna Come," by Sam Cooke

CHAPTER 20

"I Can't Help Myself," by the Four Tops
"Keep Me in Your Heart," by Warren Zevon

CHAPTER 21

"Midnight Train to Georgia," by Gladys Knight & the Pips
"Redemption Song," by Bob Marley

SERIOUS
EATER

PROLOGUE

I t was a sunny, bitterly cold day in December 2010, though there was so little natural light in the Serious Eats office that it was impossible to tell once you were inside. The eleven of us were crammed into our funky loft office on one of the last blocks of what was once the thriving Little Italy enclave in lower Manhattan. Actually, to call it a loft would be a stretch. It was a nine-hundred-square-foot, awkwardly shaped studio with low ceilings that our Italian commercial baker landlords had once used to churn out cannolis. The "test kitchen" was a funky island we had bought at Ikea that we had rigged with an induction cooktop. It was so not up to code that we could only hope and pray that the Department of Buildings of New York City would never pay us a visit. It was tight in that office, but it was all we could afford. And we were a tight-knit group anyway.

I was about to ring the cowbell, which I did whenever we earned a major piece of business. And we were celebrating a *major* piece of business: a $500,000 advertising campaign from a huge financial services company. It was a commitment from a Fortune 500 company. It was a big fucking deal. This was going to be the ad campaign that put us over the top, the one that made us a sustainable business after five nail-biting years of me wondering every week if we were good for payroll. We were going to make Serious Eats work as a business. I felt so sure of it, I let myself gloat.

We ordered pizza from Prince Street Pizza to celebrate—specifically, its Spicy Spring, a Sicilian-style pizza with a chili-flecked sauce and crisped slices of pepperoni. A Spicy Spring slice is simply a life-changing slice of pizza. Believe me. I know pizza. I wrote a whole book about it, spending an entire year eating a thousand slices in America and Italy. The pan-baked crust is a gorgeous burnished brown. It is crunchy on the outside and tender on the inside. The crisped pepperoni is the good stuff. It doesn't turn the whole slice orange, though there's plenty of spicy rendered fat on top. Once you have a Spicy Spring slice from Prince Street Pizza it's hard to eat any other slice of Sicilian pizza.

The pizza came, and the celebration was on. We broke out the wine and the beer. Our two resident mixologists, Drinks editor Maggie Hoffman and managing editor Carey Jones, whipped up a cocktail or two. Yup, we were on our way. We were kicking ass and taking names.

The next day our ad sales director got an email from his contact at the financial services company's ad agency. They were canceling the ad buy effective immediately. "Can they just do that?" I asked. "Yup," he replied. "It happens all the time." Five hundred thousand dollars—the $500,000 that would keep us safe—went out the door in a nanosecond. It was gone, and it never came back.

The timing of this particular fiasco couldn't have been worse. We were running out of money. My investor brother had told me, "When you run out of money, you lose control of your business." Actually, in my case, I was just going to flat-out lose my business.

I had been fruitlessly searching for new investors for the previous three months. My old investors were tapped out. I had learned the hard way that just because almost all my investors were people of considerable means did not mean their checkbooks were always open for me. To keep the business afloat, I had taken out a loan from a bank that I had personally guaranteed. Why? Because one of the deep dark secrets of trying to build a small business in America is that you cannot borrow money for that business without personally guaranteeing it.

Of course the bank tells you that the money you get from them in the form of a line of credit should not be used for operating capital. *Good luck with that*, I thought to myself. I had no choice, because there was no other money to use to pay the staff. That's right. I was betting the ranch, or in my case, the apartment we had been living in for more than thirty years.

So the day after my suddenly meaningless cowbell-ringing ceremony, the ball had rolled back down the hill, Sisyphus-style. I tried to put on a brave face, but my lousy poker face made that a doomed endeavor.

How had Serious Eats, the flavor of the month, even the year, the site that the *New York Times Magazine* called the "culinary supersite," that PBS had called the future of food media, ended up in this insanely precarious position? I knew the answer, but I couldn't say it aloud to my employees or even my wife. There was no road map for digital publishing businesses, particularly those that are bootstrapped and undercapitalized. We were all making it up as we went along. And press clippings cannot be used as collateral or to pay the rent. All the great slices of pizza from Prince Street were not going to change that.

Chapter 1

MISSIONARY OF THE DELICIOUS

E dward Philip Levine, get down here," came a thunderous voice from the bottom of the stairs. When my mother used my middle name, I knew I was in trouble. I peeked out of my bedroom over the garage just far enough for her to know that I had heard her.

"Was it really necessary to take a bite out of every chocolate in the box?" she asked.

Boxes of Bartons chocolates had no legend to show what was in each piece. How could I in good conscience tell my friends which chocolate to eat if I didn't taste every one? (The dark-chocolate-covered butter crunch was the clear winner, by the way.)

I was about to mouth a weak apology when the next thunderclap came: "I can't believe that there are children starving all over the world, and my son takes a bite out of every chocolate in the box and then puts them back."

My passion for chocolate had been met by my mother's passion for saving the world.

At my house growing up in the 1960s, the food took a backseat at the dinner table. The pork chops were dry, the pasta was badly overcooked, and the conversation was definitely overheated. With six of us, the only way to claim the floor at dinner was to scream. Partly because our modest, split-level suburban home in Cedarhurst, New York, was directly under the flight path for Idlewild Airport (now JFK). But also because I came from a long line of dreamers who articulated their progressive, "do-gooder" thoughts with a ferocity and focus that was often frightening to nonbelievers.

As red-diaper babies, baby-boomer children of card-carrying Communists, the four Levine boys—my brothers Michael, Jess, and Gil and I— learned early to articulate our views fervently in support of the greater good. We weren't just encouraged to get on a soapbox about things we felt strongly about; we were required.

My mother was a gregarious, charismatic firebrand of a woman. She grew up in abject poverty on the Lower East Side of Manhattan. Her father had flown the coop (he was "a painter of houses and a chaser of women"), and her mother sold pickles out of a barrel on a street corner in Williamsburg year-round. That left my mother and her younger brother to raise each other. That brother, my uncle Abe, dropped out of school in the seventh grade and hustled pool to support the family.

After she and my dad moved to Long Island's south shore after World War II, my mother became a suburban community activist and organizer and then a child psychologist who believed in progressive child-rearing techniques. She wrote a column about the issues near and dear to her heart for the local paper, the *South Shore Record*. When I went to their offices about twenty years ago to dig those columns up, I found headlines like "Let's Do Something About Mass Violence"—from 1960! And one column, titled "Women in Culture," in which my mother wrote that women needed to find satisfying, meaningful work after their children had grown—a full two years before Betty Friedan made a similar argument in *The Feminine Mystique*.

Like many poor Jews in New York in the 1930s, my parents became avowed Communists while attending City College. Family lore has it that they met at a Communist Party meeting on campus.

My soft-spoken dad also grew up dirt poor in Brooklyn. His dad, my grandfather, died when he was an infant. His mother, Ida, was a doting grandmother to us but had been a lousy mother to him. Whenever she would take a lover, she'd place my father in foster care or an orphanage until the affair had run its course. My dad hated oatmeal his whole life because it reminded him of the orphanage food.

I have a photo of my dad addressing a rally of unemployed workers in Union Square in New York City in the thirties; he spent the war years organizing African American workers at weapons factories in St. Louis. Unable to find a teaching job after the war because of his political leanings, he eventually went to work in the lumberyard business for his brother-in-law, my uncle Abe, the aforementioned pool hustler. He wore monogrammed shirts and drove the big cars that the company leased for him.

As adults, my three older brothers would describe my dad as a depressed and frustrated intellectual living his life in suburban purgatory. As the youngest, though, I remember him as the old dad with a smile on his face and a twinkle in his eye. And though he may have made his peace with working for someone else in a job he didn't like, all four of his sons got the message early on that working for other people doing unsatisfying work was no way to roll in life.

Compared with my fractious, argumentative older brothers, I was the easy one—a joyful kid, always smiling and laughing. I could make anyone laugh—my parents, their friends, my friends, even my teachers—though I was not a stellar student like some of my brothers. (I compensated with humor—the laughter formed something of a protective shield around my mediocre grades.) Because I was easy, my parents let me roam freely. I solved my own problems and charted my own course.

And right from the beginning, the course I charted was toward the most delicious food I could find.

My mother, who thought cooking was counterrevolutionary, did so indifferently. But our African American housekeepers, Virgie and later Laila (who basically raised me, as my mom was off saving the world most of the time), filled the house with the sounds and smells of phenomenal southern-style fried chicken. And every Sunday my lone living grandparent, Ida, arrived, mostly to cook for us.

Ida was a tough old bird, but she was also a superb eastern European

Jewish cook who cooked for her grandsons out of love, a love that I received hungrily. Her latkes were crisp and light, just like her blintzes. She made chunky french fries with onion in the frying oil, the pancake-style omelets called matzo brei, and a terrific dense, moist apple cake.

But Ida came only on Sundays, so I ended up making my own forays into the world for food as soon as I could ride a bike.

Harry's Candy Store—a five-minute ride away—was my joint, my corner bar, my Cheers. It had everything I needed and wanted: a big display of packaged candy, ranging from a penny to ten cents; baseball cards for flipping and trading; and, most glorious, a long counter with cherry-red stools that you could spin around on like a top.

What pleasures could be derived from sitting at that counter! Chocolate malts made in a green Hamilton Beach mixer and served in a glass, with the extra in an aluminum cup. I didn't think there was anything better than drinking one of those, knowing that when I got to the bottom of my glass there was more heaven in that aluminum cup. Black and white ice cream sodas. Egg creams. Old-fashioned cherry Cokes made with a squirt of cherry syrup, vanilla Cokes, and tuna sandwiches filled out the menu.

The chaos at Harry's reminded me of the chaos at my house, so I felt right at home there—especially because Harry would extend me credit when I ran out of allowance money.

Very early I understood that not all ingredients were created equal—and that a meal made of the right ones could be far more than the sum of its parts. In fifth grade my lunchtime sandwich consisted of a quarter pound of bologna I would get from Merkel's, the butcher shop a block from my school, and a kaiser roll purchased at Rothenberg's, the small grocery store around the corner from Merkel's. It was simple: the bologna was better at Merkel's, and the kaiser rolls were superior at Rothenberg's. Convenience didn't enter into the equation; serious deliciousness was the only thing that mattered.

I loved the puffy-crusted but still crunchy pizza, topped with both yellow aged mozzarella and white, salty Pecorino Romano cheese, from the local Italian American restaurant, Cairo's, that my parents would serve during the summer with grilled steak (an unusual but surprisingly felicitous combination). But my absolute favorite was the thin, juicy, perfectly formed cheeseburgers at Hamburger Express that arrived at your stool courtesy of a model train that traversed the length of the counter.

The other members of my family rolled their eyes over this food fixation. When we went to Nathan's in a neighboring town, I would drive them crazy by waiting on six different lines to get all the menu items I wanted with the two dollars my dad doled out to each of us: a chow mein sandwich (you heard that right), a lobster roll, those incredible bronzed, irregularly shaped crinkle-cut french fries, a Dr. Brown's black cherry soda, a hot dog or two, and a soft-serve ice cream cone.

Smitty was our local ice cream man, a genial, balding World War II vet. I was a Levine, brought up on my mother's lectures, so of course I shunned the corporate Good Humor man in favor of the independent small businessperson. Plus, Smitty did two things the white-suited guys at Good Humor couldn't do. He sold half ices for a nickel, and he would give me ice cream on credit. He knew I was good for it.

Between the food, the sports I played with my friends nonstop, and our boisterous household, the first twelve years of my life were mostly a joyful blur. I embraced my parents' values but was allowed to find my own way. I discovered my passions and embraced my jester role in the family. It was all good, a perfect *Leave It to Beaver*–like childhood. Until it wasn't.

Chapter 2

THE LOVE I LOST

My dad was always pale and sickly; rheumatic fever as a child had left him with a weak heart and bad kidneys. He also suffered from a bad case of ankylosing spondylitis, a spine disorder. My dad didn't look like the Hunchback of Notre Dame, but I'm ashamed to admit that I was a little embarrassed about his stooped appearance. When he took me to a Yankees-Dodgers World Series game in 1963, I made sure that I walked ten paces behind him on the way to our seats. I didn't want people to see that I was with him, that the slightly hunched man in front of me was in fact my wry-smiling dad.

Hunched over or not, he was a great dad, to me at least. He took me to school every day on his way to work, dropping me off with a kiss on my forehead. He played catch with me on weekends, using a completely flattened glove with no pocket to speak of (my oldest brother Mike's discarded glove; they were the only lefties in the family), even though he winced in pain every time he had to bend to catch the ball.

He was a gentle soul when he was with me, and the two of us stuck together in a house full of shouters. In fact, the only time the decibel level at the table was tolerable was when the two of us ate breakfast by ourselves, sitting at the four-seat counter carved out of the wall separating the kitchen from the dining room. We both had English muffins, which my dad taught me how to fork-split long before Thomas' started doing it at the plant. He always had tart lingonberry jam and farmers' cheese on his, and I buttered mine right out of the toaster so that the butter would melt properly into the nooks and crannies.

He got a huge kick out of his youngest son, because, unlike my three brothers, I never gave him a hard time about anything. Hey, I had nothing to complain about. I didn't rebel, because there wasn't much to rebel against. I was doing exactly what I wanted to be doing, playing some kind of ball from dawn to dusk on our dead-end street or in our driveway, sometimes into the night without any lights. As a result, my parents always knew where I was and what I was up to.

The only recurring concern in our family was my father's health. My dad suffered at least one heart attack that I can remember. I was ten at the time. His health deteriorated after that, and ultimately his kidneys gave out. Finally, two years later, my dad died after a lengthy stint in a hospital in Far Rockaway, a few miles from our house in Cedarhurst. It was right after my twelfth birthday, in March of 1964. I went to see him one last time a few days before his death, but I don't remember much about the visit except that I made it my business to make him laugh. When my dad laughed, it made both of us feel better. We didn't exchange any meaningful parting words, though when I got up to leave, I hugged him as tightly as I could without hurting him. I loved him completely and without reservation.

My dad's death didn't bring my family appreciably closer. In fact, I don't remember talking to anyone in my family about him. My brother Gil still lived at home, but he spent most of his time with his high school friends or playing the bassoon. He would end up a prominent conductor, best known for his friendship with Pope John Paul II (Gil's memoir is titled *The Pope's Maestro*). That relationship spawned numerous televised (on PBS) musical collaborations between Gil and the Catholic Church. My two oldest brothers, Jesse and Mike, had already left for college and beyond. I don't remember one conversation among the four Levine brothers about my dad's passing. We were all silently siloed in our own grief; whatever we were going through we went through alone.

My mom, overwhelmed by her own grief, withdrew. I could often hear her crying in her bedroom. It was a totally understandable and appropriate response to my dad's death. She was grieving, but I was grieving too. Somehow we never shared our grief.

My mom was an incredibly warm and charming woman, who acted as a trusted friend and confidante to many of the people who knew her. She was remarkably perceptive and empathetic. When my friends came over, she would pepper them with personal and even probing questions about their parents, their grades, their thoughts about school in general. Sara Levine was intensely curious because she cared about everyone who was part of her life. That's why I felt her emotional absence so keenly in the wake of my father's death. In many ways I lost my mother the day my father died.

Less than a year after my dad died, my mother started dating Louis, a man she had met at a Parents Without Partners meeting, a support group for people who had recently lost their spouses. They became a couple very quickly, much to my chagrin.

Louis and I had nothing in common. He was a pipe-smoking pseudo-intellectual, a retired French teacher who wrote smut and diet books on the side. Louis had no interest in food, sports, or pop music, my passions at the time. We argued incessantly about the legitimacy of pop music. I remember playing him "As Tears Go By" by the Stones so that he could hear the string arrangement on that track, which I believed (still do) was absolutely masterful. Louis wouldn't even listen. He was utterly contemptuous of popular culture.

We each viewed each other as competition for my mother's attention, and Louis won. It would be easy to say that I was caught in an oedipal love triangle, but that doesn't account for the fact that Louis Golomb was a jerk. The summer a year and a half after my father died, I went on a teen tour, traveling across the country in a covered truck with twenty-five other teenage boys. We pitched tents in a different city every night and received letters at PO boxes in different towns along the way. One day I received a postcard from my mom:

Dear Eddie,

Louis and I got married last week. We had salmon, which Louis had caught in Alaska.

Love, Mom.

When I got back to the city, I found Louis ensconced in my parents' bedroom with my mother. I was hurt and angry, but I never confronted my mother directly. The following two years, eighth and ninth grades, were particularly difficult. I had nothing to say to Louis, and he had nothing to say to me. I had plenty I wanted to talk about with my mother, but somehow we never found the time or the place to say it. I never felt like I could talk to her about the hard stuff. Since my father's death, things had never been the same between us.

I was left to my own devices. I soldiered on, concentrating on my social life, sports, and yes, food.

Food was the salve for my wounds. Overcooked spaghetti drenched in a marinara-like sauce and surrounded by oversized meatballs at Ricci's made me insanely happy. So did the Chinese-style pork roast (it had the telltale red food dye) from the Associated Supermarket; what we called "the dish," bow-tie pasta with ground beef in tomato sauce; and my mother's go-to dinner-party dish, shrimp and rice. Every bite helped me cope with my intense loneliness and increasing sense of isolation.

But all the food in the world could not have prepared me for what happened next. In July of 1966, almost one year after my mother remarried, she fell ill and went into the hospital for some exploratory surgery. Her doctors thought she might need a hysterectomy. But when they opened her up, they discovered cancer so widespread that they just sewed her right back up. There was nothing they could do.

I was away working as a counselor at a summer camp. The doctor told Louis and my oldest brother, Mike, that her condition was fatal but for some reason instructed them not to tell my mother, or anybody else, about the diagnosis. (The fact that I didn't learn about this surgery until more than fifty years later, when I asked my much older cousin's widow about this period, speaks volumes about the dissemination of information in our family.)

I came home from the camp shortly after the surgery. I was surprised to find Mike waiting for me. Why wasn't he in DC working? He and my mother sat me down. She began, "You're so smart, Eddie, as smart as anyone in this family. But your grades don't reflect that." Where was she going with this? My mother and I didn't usually talk about school. But then it got even weirder. "We think going to boarding school will enable you to concentrate on your schoolwork." *Boarding school?* I thought. *Nobody in my family goes to boarding school.* "What? We've never talked about me going to boarding school before." I didn't buy their rationale—my grades weren't great, but it wasn't like I was failing—but it didn't matter. I was headed for boarding school, whether I liked it or not. Just like that. No explanation. In retrospect, my mother and Mike had clearly decided that it was best that I not be home to watch her suffer the indignities of her illness *and* engage in endless fights with Louis.

I ended up at the very proper Hackley School in Tarrytown, New York, an hour's drive from our house. Unbeknownst to my mother and Mike, Hackley was a five-day-a-week boarding school. Everyone except the scholarship kids went home every weekend. Initially, my mother and Mike insisted I stay. After a few weekends shooting hoops with the kids who were left stranded at the school, I made a plea to come home for good.

My mother eventually agreed to let me come home on weekends. But at home I had a front-row seat to her considerable pain and suffering. Both the cancer and her treatments left her weak and wan. Having Louis around was no help, at least to me. Louis turned out to be an attentive caregiver to my mother, but at the time I couldn't admit that.

About six months after her diagnosis, her condition was only worsening. The severity of the prognosis did ultimately spur Mike and his fiancée, Carol, to get married—and quickly. Carol was bright, ambitious, and beautiful. She was an army brat who had escaped an alcoholic stepfather by going off to Duke on a partial scholarship. After college, Carol worked for the government in the Bureau of the Budget, where she met my brother. My mother loved Carol and wanted to see Mike get married, so she was of course thrilled about their decision. They planned the wedding in two weeks.

It was a modest and subdued ceremony for obvious reasons. Though my mom was racked with pain and could barely move, she bought a new dress for the occasion. "How do I look, Eddie?" she asked, coming down the stairs of our house in her elegant blue satin dress. "You look great, Mom." And she did; even in her weakened state, when she swept into the room at the wedding she had everyone enthralled. Sara Levine was always a charmer.

She died two months after the wedding, a little more than three years after my dad. I was about to return to Hackley for my junior year of high school. When she died, I was staying at Mike and Carol's modest apartment in DC; Mike had gone up to Cedarhurst at Louis's behest. At 8:00 p.m. the phone rang. Even before Carol picked up the phone, I knew exactly what had happened. After she hung up, Carol came into the living room, where I was watching TV, lying on the uncomfortable couch that doubled as my bed. She hugged me; I was crying so hard my body shook. "Eddie, I am so, so sorry," she said.

I don't remember much about the days and weeks following her death, except a story Carol told me while we were going through my mother's things. A few days before my mom passed away, she went around the house with Carol trying to put her life in order to prepare everyone for what would be coming next. She articulated her fears and worries about each one of her sons, but when she got to me she said, "I don't worry about Eddie. Everybody loves Eddie." Somehow my usually perceptive and supremely empathetic mother had failed to notice that just because I could make people laugh didn't mean that I wouldn't be devastated by her death. Or maybe she just needed to convince herself that she had one less thing to worry about at that fateful moment.

In the wake of my mother's death, the immediate question for the family, of course, was what to do with me. I was fifteen years old, without parents or a home. (Our house was put up for sale right after my mother died.)

In my mother's will, she had named Mike and my uncle Abe my co–legal guardians.

Abe, my mother's brother, was nobody's idea of an ideal parent. Although he had four kids of his own, and he and I always got along, it's safe to say he was not a natural caregiver or nurturer. So that's how Mike and Carol, newlyweds and grieving themselves, ended up with me.

Because Mike and Carol were living in Washington, DC, at the time and were unsure of their future plans, they decided that I would go to Hackley for at least one more year. I would spend weekends at friends' houses or at my brother Jesse's apartment in New York.

The year after my mom died is mostly a blur, but I really did get by with a little help from my friends. My friend Rob's mother, Pearl, became one substitute parent; my friend Michael's parents, Abby and Mildred, became another set. On weekends we would play basketball for hours at Michael's house and raid the fridge afterward. Sometimes we played truly terrible rock and blues in my friend Stubby's basement. I was the unconscionably bad lead singer. Occasionally I would stay with my brothers Jesse and Gil, who were both living in New York City at the time. On those weekends Morris and Sara Levine's names were never mentioned.

Thanks to the late Fred Neilson, a gruff but kindly English teacher and wrestling coach at Hackley, I learned how to write. I improved my grades. My mother would have been proud.

Amid all the tumult I sought solace again in, what else, food. There were roast beef wedges (Westchester-speak for heroes) with sliced tomatoes, lots of mayo, and just enough salt at Malandrino's in North Tarrytown; surprisingly tender meatball heroes with garlicky marinara sauce on seeded semolina rolls at Arduino's in Tarrytown (I've almost never met a meatball hero I didn't like); and the thin-crusted pizza at Albanese's in Eastchester, gloriously topped with chunks of house-made sweet Italian sausage.

Mike, eleven years my senior, had gotten an offer to teach law at the University of Southern California, and so it was decided that I would move out to Los Angeles with him and Carol and do my senior year of high school there. So after school got out in late June, I flew to Chicago, where Mike and Carol were living. From there we would all drive out to Los Angeles in July, along with my brother Gil.

Mike tried to teach me how to drive so that I could help on the trip, but every lesson was fraught with raw, unrestrained emotion. He was trying to be the best substitute dad he could, but we were both on edge.

One day, as I screwed up yet another attempt at parallel parking, Mike said, "I give up." So Carol stepped into the breach and took over. (It was an act of true heroism: practicing three-point turns at the Museum of Science and Industry parking lot, I managed to knock over not one but two parking meters.) I never passed my driving test in Illinois.

Mike was a newlywed with vaulting ambition, struggling to make sense of his own grief and saddled with a wounded, pissed-off adolescent. Carol was a kindhearted, whip-smart career woman who found herself in the middle of this emotionally freighted situation. I can't imagine that the package deal of Mike and me was the way she'd wanted to begin her married life. And then there was Gil—a nineteen-year-old college student who, like any other nineteen-year-old, desperately wanted to convince the world that he was an independent adult. We were a mismatched quartet with no rehearsal time to figure anything out.

The four of us drove across the country. I can't tell you one thing we ate or talked about on that 2,100-mile journey from Chicago to Los Angeles. Afterward, though, Mike and Carol never tired of the story of our arrival at the Grand Canyon. I hated when they told it—but not because it wasn't true.

We got to one of the most majestic landscapes in the country, and I re-fused to get out of the car. Furious Mike couldn't move me; neither could gentle Carol. "I don't need to see the Grand Canyon again," I told them. "I saw it a couple of years ago and I doubt that anything's changed in the meantime."

Hearing that story over and over again reminded me of that awful time. For me, it wasn't just a matter of getting out of the car to see the Grand Can-yon; it was all I could do to put one foot in front of the other to get through the day. Gil and Mike were intellectual competitors, and they frequently engaged in verbal jousts during that trip. Mike had left the house when I was seven; I hardly knew him, and although I liked Carol very much, I'd known her for less than a year. I knew everyone had my best interests at heart, but it felt like I was being kidnapped.

I have only one photo from that trip: the four of us at the Four Corners Monument, where Colorado, New Mexico, Arizona, and Utah come together. We're each standing in a different state, a metaphor that's not lost on me. We look happy. We weren't.

We made it to California in time for me to start at Fairfax High in Los Angeles, my third school in four years. It's not easy starting at a new high school for your senior year, but mercifully I was adopted by a group of friends in my first week. Matt Spitzer was the son of a USC physics professor and thought doing calculus homework was fun. My friend Andy was my worst angel. He could talk me into doing things I knew were just wrong. I think everyone has a high school friend who fulfills that role. One summer break during college we got a job delivering samples of Dreft diaper detergent to new mothers. Our second day on the job Andy said to me, "Let's go to the beach. We'll just dump all the Dreft into the sewer. No one will ever find out." Great idea, except that a Dreft rep was following us.

Matt, Andy, and the rest of their crew salvaged my senior year of high school. Like my friends in Cedarhurst, they became another substitute family. We went vinyl shopping at Aron's, the used record store across the street from our school. We argued endlessly about who was better, the Dodgers or the Yankees. On our lunch break we went for chili dogs at nearby Pink's, where I invariably asked for extra onions and plenty of mustard on the excellent natural-casing, garlicky, all-beef frank. Pink's didn't sell french fries (at least at the time), so we would often drive another five minutes to get the golden-brown, freshly fried ones with tartar sauce at nearby Pop's. (Tartar sauce turns out to be an excellent condiment for fries.) We made numerous late-night weekend forays to the original Tommy's on Beverly Boulevard. There, eating our messy chili cheeseburgers, which came wrapped in paper with the edge of the burger sticking out, and drinking our milk shakes, which were just small cartons of milk ostentatiously shaken by the counter people (they thought it was funny), we would all complain about our parents. That wasn't an option for me, so I complained about Mike and Carol. Even these classic teenage bitching sessions reminded me of what I had lost.

But at the end of the day, living with Mike and Carol did provide salve for my wounds. The good times with them revolved around food and music. We all loved Little Feat, the Grateful Dead, the Beatles, and the blues. We went to the legendary music club the Ash Grove to see everyone from Mississippi Fred McDowell to the original Firesign Theatre. That Mike and I shared an appetite for food and for life was apparent every time we went somewhere to eat. We ate barbecue at Gadberry's near Mike's office at USC. Gadberry's brisket and coarsely ground beef hot links started my lifelong love affair with Texas barbecue. I also mastered the art of eating the pillow-sized burritos at El Tepeyac without spilling any of the exemplary rice and beans that filled the flaky house-made tortillas, and the modestly sized but perfectly constructed sundaes at C.C. Brown's in Hollywood. I loved those little toy-sized pitchers of hot butterscotch and hot fudge sauce that I got to pour over a perfectly shaped scoop of C.C. Brown's bean-specked vanilla ice cream.

Los Angeles in 1968 was a great place to discover all kinds of revelatory music and food, and that's what the three of us did together. I had never eaten much Mexican, Korean, or Japanese food, and LA had entire neighborhoods devoted to each of them. Musically, clubs like the Ash Grove and the Troubadour introduced me to bluesmen like Sonny Terry and Brownie McGhee and singer-songwriters like James Taylor.

We ate like champions and saw some great shows, but these shared loves were not always enough to smooth the tensions between Mike and me. One of the blowouts I remember best happened at my beloved C.C. Brown's after we'd seen a movie. We were driving there in Mike and Carol's car with Dave and Kaaren Slawson. Dave was a colleague of Mike's at USC's law school. Kaaren was Carol's best friend in Los Angeles. They had no children of their own, so Kaaren had in very short order become my extremely caring foster aunt.

Mike parked the car, yelling over his shoulder to the Slawsons, "Do not give Ed any money for ice cream. He's spent all his allowance, and I'm try-ing to teach him how important budgeting is. In fact, don't even give him a bite of your sundaes. It's the only way he'll learn." I was furious. "Are you kidding me? You're telling the Slawsons not to buy me a sundae or even give me a bite of theirs. Are you insane?" But he wouldn't budge. And he was right. I almost always ran out of allowance money because of my excessive spending on food and records. Hey, what's allowance for, anyway?

So we walked into C.C. Brown's and I sat, glowering at Mike, while the four of them ate perfect single-scoop hot fudge sundaes. I didn't even get to lick the hot fudge residue off the little pitchers it came in. Of course I wanted to storm out, but we were too far away from our house for me to walk.

How did we make it through that year? I don't know, but we had no other options. When Mike and I had arguments, which occurred pretty regularly, Carol functioned as the mediator. Most of the time Mike was right. Like many teenagers, I was careless and irresponsible, prone to goofy mistakes. But sometimes his rage was inappropriate, like when he yelled at me for re-placing the newspaper sections out of order. Mike eventually solved the newspaper problem by getting two copies of the paper delivered to the house, one for him and the other for Carol and me. I still think that's crazy.

When Mike yelled, I would go to my room and slam the door behind me. A few seconds later, Carol would ever so gently knock and come into my room. "Mike doesn't mean most of the stuff he says when he's angry. He loves you very much." All I ever said in return was, "That's bullshit. And if it's true, Mike certainly has a funny way of showing it." The wondrous Carol Stover Levine ended up saving me by summoning up maternal instincts she might not have known she had, providing me with exactly what I needed even though she must have felt caught between a rock (Mike) and a hard place (me).

Mike and I never talked about our parents; back then he never let his feelings show to me about much of anything besides ideas, food, music, and politics. I think he felt he had to be the strong father figure, which meant he couldn't really confront the depths of what had happened to us. Carol has told me that he'd spend hours talking to her about my parents' death. I wish

Hot Fudge à la C.C. Brown's

STELLA PARKS

An authentic hot fudge sundae, the sort Ed was deprived of as a child, is made with real fudge, not syrup or ganache. When the hot candy hits the cold ice cream, it crystallizes in an instant, forming a chewy but tender outer shell. It's a magical thing, and well worth the time needed to make it yourself.

YIELD: Enough for about six monster sundaes (or twelve modest portions)

4 ounces whole milk (about ½ cup)

1¼ ounces unsalted butter (about 2½ tablespoons)

½ teaspoon Diamond Crystal kosher salt (other types of salt may contain additives that cause the fudge to turn grainy)

8 ounces light brown sugar (about 1 cup, firmly packed)

7 ounces white sugar (about 1 cup)

4 ounces 72 percent dark chocolate, not baking chips, roughly chopped (a heaping ¾ cup)

¼ ounce vanilla extract (about 1½ teaspoons)

1. Combine the milk, butter, salt, brown sugar, white sugar, and chocolate in a 2-quart stainless steel pot over medium heat. Stir continuously with a fork until the butter and chocolate have fully melted and the syrup begins to bubble around the edges.

2. With a ramekin of water, wet a pastry brush and wipe all around the sides, wherever you see sugar crystals or splashes of chocolate. Rewet as needed, "washing" the sides until spotless. Be generous! Extra water will not harm the fudge, but sugar crystals will.

3. Clip on a digital thermometer, ensuring it reaches a depth of at least 1 inch, and cook *without stirring* until the mixture reaches 240°F. Remove from the heat and cool to 118°F, then stir in the vanilla extract with a flexible spatula. Keep stirring until the fudge looks thick and dull, about 10 minutes.

4. Scrape onto a sheet of parchment, cover, and set aside for 1 hour to firm, then cut or crumble into pieces and store in an airtight container, up to 3 weeks at room temperature or 2 months in the fridge.

5. To serve, scoop your favorite ice cream into a chilled parfait dish, and freeze until needed. Meanwhile, measure out 1½ ounces (about ⅓ cup, crumbled) fudge for every serving, and microwave in several 15-second bursts. Stir briefly between each round, but don't overdo it (excess stirring will resolidify the fudge). When the mixture is melted, gooey, and thick, pour over a scoop of ice cream in a well-chilled parfait glass, and allow 30 seconds to set.

Dad's Old-Fashioned English Muffins

STELLA PARKS

Whether you prefer these smeared with butter like Ed, or topped with a spoonful of tart lingonberry jam like his father, these yeast-raised muffins are the perfect weekend treat.

YIELD: Twelve 3½-inch muffins

16 ounces unbleached bread flour, such as King Arthur (about 3⅔ cups, spooned)

1 ounce white sugar (about 2 tablespoons)

¼ ounce salt (volume will vary by brand; about 2 teaspoons Diamond Crystal kosher)

⅛ ounce instant dry yeast such as SAF, not rapid rise (about 1¼ teaspoons)

16 ounces whole milk (about 2 cups)

2 ounces unsalted butter, melted (about 4 tablespoons)

Polenta, grits, or farina, as needed

Oil or bacon fat, as needed

1. Whisk the flour, sugar, salt, and yeast together in a large bowl, then stir in the milk and melted butter with a flexible spatula. When well combined, cover with plastic wrap and let stand at cool room temperature (between 60° and 70°F) until spongy and roughly tripled in volume, 10 to 12 hours.

2. Cover a half-sheet pan in a very thick layer of polenta, grits, or farina. Use a ⅓ cup measure to divide the spongy dough into 12 portions, and drop each onto the prepared baking sheet. With wet fingers, pinch the dough as needed to tidy their shape, then cover loosely with plastic wrap and refrigerate overnight or up to 24 hours.

3. Preheat an electric griddle to 350°F, and brush generously with oil or bacon fat. Gently transfer the puffy dough to the griddle by hand, stretching each portion to a width of about 3½ inches.

4. Cook until the muffins are golden brown along the bottom, about 8 minutes. Dab the tops with oil, then flip with a spatula and griddle as before. Cool 10 minutes on a wire rack, then immediately split by hand. Toast before serving.

he'd shared some of those thoughts with me. I didn't even know that I needed somebody. I was just a sixteen-year-old kid, trying to figure out a way to survive.

All three of us did, in fact, survive. By the end of that year we were something approximating a family. Unbreakable bonds had been established, but they would be tested in the years to follow.

Chapter 3

GRINNELL COLLEGE: WHERE EVERYTHING SEEMED POSSIBLE

s Professor Levine in?" I asked one of the USC law school faculty secretaries.

"He's teaching a torts class right now. May I take a message?"

I said, "When he gets out of class, please tell him to call his brother. I'm at the Poweshiek County jail."

I made my one permitted phone call to (who else?) Mike from the county jail in my college town, Grinnell, Iowa—the result of my first entrepreneurial venture, even though I ended up smoking up most of the profits with my friends. A high school friend, Anson, would send me pounds of pot to sell and smoke in packages addressed to my nom de pot, Bob Scronson, c/o Ed Levine, via Greyhound Bus freight. The bus stop in Grinnell was in a gas station a block from campus in the middle of the tiny town. When I went to the station and asked if there were any packages for Scronson, two policemen dressed as mechanics informed me that I was under arrest.

Mike called an hour later. "For the record"—one of Mike's favorite expressions—"what are you doing in jail?" he asked in a surprisingly calm voice. I started to tell him the whole sordid story. He immediately interrupted me. "Don't tell me now. In fact, don't say another word to anybody. First we need to get you out of jail. Then we need to find you a lawyer." I had my own ideas about that. "I want the same lawyer that defended the Panther Ten in Des Moines," I said defiantly. Mike said, "I'm not so sure that's the way to go here. Let me call my friend Gary Bellows from law school. He had a law school buddy who grew up in Iowa."

Mike wired me bail money. Through Gary he found me a local lawyer who was intimately acquainted with the Poweshiek County legal system. It was an unusual case. The police in Grinnell generally had a hands-off policy when it came to the college. The only reason they'd busted me was that the pot had crossed state lines, so the FBI tipped the Grinnell police off about this Scronson character.

While I awaited trial, my lawyer told me to "keep my nose clean." I couldn't tell if he understood the irony of that particular cliché. All three of my brothers came to visit me at Grinnell, just to show support. Mike was shockingly cool. He and I shared a joint with the great Chicago blues guitarist Buddy Guy and his harmonica-playing musical partner, Junior Wells. My brother Jesse came with me to party at a house off campus and demanded we leave when he saw people smoking pot. My brother Gil took the intermediate approach. He didn't partake with me, but he realized it was an exercise in futility to avoid pot smoking at Grinnell College in the early seventies. So he sort of looked the other way at certain moments on his visit when he really had no choice.

Thankfully my local lawyer didn't get wind of any of this, and he continued to work the system with Mike's careful oversight. It was touch and go for a while. My lawyer was having difficulty explaining away the note telling me to sell the "lids" for fifteen dollars.

Ultimately, white small-town justice prevailed. I had to plead guilty to what they were calling an indictable misdemeanor, but if I stayed out of trouble, the conviction would be expunged from my record. Mike's wry comment: "Maybe you can stay out of trouble at Grinnell. I suggest you cut off the deliveries to Scronson from Anson." Mike was beyond chill through all of this. We weren't in LA anymore. Despite all our bruising battles, Mike always had my back. I took his advice, and I did manage to avoid further run-ins with the Grinnell Police Department.

It was Mike who'd suggested Grinnell to me in the first place. "Grinnell is a really good small school," he'd said. "It's in the middle of nowhere, rural

Iowa to be precise. But the students come from all over. Lots of professors' kids go there." *Hmm,* I thought to myself. *I'm not a professor's kid. Or maybe I am. I'm at least a professor's something.* At that moment I didn't even know how to describe my relationship with Mike. It was some weird amalgamation of brother and son.

Scronson antics aside, Grinnell College turned out to be the perfect place for me to be in the tumultuous years from 1969 to 1973. Located in central Iowa in the middle of some of America's richest farmland, Grinnell was a first-rate academic institution that was both progressive and permissive. Would-be poets found a haven there, as did actors, writers, teachers, and activists. The air at Grinnell was always pregnant with possibility; with only 1,200 students, there were increased odds of getting a lead in a play or a column in the student newspaper. That feeling of endless possibility was what I loved most of all about it, and when I started Serious Eats nearly forty years later, that was the air I wanted everyone who worked there to breathe.

Because of its small size, Grinnell was an easy place to find your crew. The tightness of the community fostered intimacy and experimentation. I found mine almost immediately—a cadre of jazz and American music lovers. One of my friends, Gary Giddins, went on to become the longtime jazz critic at the *Village Voice.* Another, Peter Keepnews, became the managing editor of *Jazz Magazine* and an editor at the *New York Times.* They schooled me every day, turning me on to records like Miles Davis's *In a Silent Way,* B. B. King's *Live at the Regal,* and John Coltrane's *My Favorite Things.* Close friends Ron Stanford and Fay Hazelcorn were both gifted folklorists and musicians who exposed me to artists like guitarist Doc Watson, country singer Merle Haggard, and bluegrass virtuoso Bill Monroe. I was an American music major, but my real musical education happened in the apartments and dorm rooms of my friends.

Gary, Peter, and Ron were in charge of bringing the music to campus. I couldn't believe they were being paid (albeit modestly, a hundred dollars a semester) to book these great musicians. As soon as I heard about it, I knew I was going to find a way to get that job.

Eventually I did become the concerts chairman. I loved turning people on to music that deserved to be heard, my experiences with Louis to the contrary. No commercial concerns were considered; I had carte blanche, as every concert was paid for by the activities fee that was part of tuition. There was never an admission fee at a Grinnell College event.

As a result, the list of musicians we brought to Grinnell reads like a who's who of American music: Count Basie, Duke Ellington, Muddy Waters, B. B. King, Buddy Guy, Bruce Springsteen (the year after I graduated), Jefferson Airplane, and the Jackson 5, who played at Grinnell when Michael Jackson was only ten years old. They were a "local" band from Gary, Indiana.

We booked live music just about every weekend, whether it was a folkie like John Prine or a rock band like the Steve Miller Band or an avant-garde jazz pianist like the late Cecil Taylor. Almost every practical thing I learned at Grinnell was in the service of producing those concerts: negotiating fees, dealing with creative people, mastering the details of concert production. Things never fell apart; Grinnell was a catastrophe-free environment. Maybe that's why I loved it so much.

But not everything was perfect. Grinnell was a great place for music, but it was severely lacking in the food department. Still, the sausage sandwiches at the Longhorn were pretty damn fine, and so were the onion rings. There were other good indigenous Iowa dishes to be had as well—to this day I have never met a pounded and fried pork tenderloin sandwich with mayo and pickles I didn't love. Maid-Rite loose meat sandwiches, basically a sloppy joe without the ketchup-tinted slop, also made the cut. So did fresh-out-of-the-fryer cake doughnuts we fetched at 2:00 a.m. from the Danish Maid Bakery in downtown Grinnell (all four square blocks of it).

Grinnell turned out to be an ideal place to lick my wounds and find myself. I survived, even thrived there. Mike used to say he was thrilled that I chose Grinnell. He would chortle, "I figured the worst that could happen is that you would drive your car into a cornfield in the middle of the night."

I left Grinnell with a BA in American music and a mission to make a difference in the jazz world, and there's only one place to do that, right?

NYC, here I come.

Chapter 4

TRYING TO HOOK ALL THE SHIT UP

need someone who can hook all the shit up—record contracts, tours, publishing, press, everything. Can you two hook all the shit up?" Wynton Marsalis asked. He was posing this question to my artist management company partner, Jim, and me, in the closet-sized dressing room/office of Seventh Avenue South, the jazz club I was booking at the time.

It was an unseasonably warm day in April of 1983, so the tiny room was stiflingly hot. Wynton had just burst onto the scene as the young-gun virtuoso trumpet player in Art Blakey's Jazz Messengers and was looking for a manager. He was, as usual, impeccably dressed: tailored gray suit, red tie, matching handkerchief, and perfectly pressed dress shirt. Jim and I seemed to be dressed for another meeting, in jeans and button-down shirts. Dresswise, that was our A game.

Why had he even agreed to meet with us? I had given Wynton one of his first gigs as a leader at the club (I still have the contract—we paid him and his quintet $2,750 for four nights, and we lost money), and Jim had worked for years in the jazz department at Wynton's record label, Columbia. I'm sure Wynton intended the "hook all the shit up" question as a rhetorical one, assuming the answer was that we couldn't. But we responded, "Of course we can." We even had a gussied-up presentation to help convince him; hey, we were professionals too.

Unsurprisingly, we didn't get the gig.

Ever since my friends had introduced me to the pleasures of jazz in 1969, my freshman year of college, New York had become a symbol of hope and possibility and opportunity. Every Monday I would go the Grinnell College library to read the pop and jazz writing, the ads for concerts and club engagements that I was missing, and the restaurant reviews in the *Village Voice*. The *Voice* and all the other newspapers were put on those sticks at the library that successfully functioned as primitive antitheft devices.

When I was at Grinnell, Mike would ask me what I was going to do after college, and I would tell him I was headed for New York and the jazz world. Every time, he would try to talk me out of it by telling me how impractical it was, but eventually he gave up trying to convince me and settled for cutting me off: "You can do what you want, but financially you're on your own."

As planned, after graduation I headed to New York with my portable KLH stereo, a record collection of a couple of thousand pieces of vinyl, two pairs of jeans, two work shirts, a bunch of music-related T-shirts, and some socks and underwear. I had a little money that my parents had left me, enough to tide me over until I found a job in the city. I wanted the musicians I loved to get the recognition and compensation that American culture had denied them and "the music," as true jazz aficionados called it. Ever since rock and roll and rhythm and blues had supplanted jazz as America's popular music, in the forties and fifties when Charlie Parker and his fellow beboppers took over the scene, most jazz musicians had struggled to make a decent living.

I found a job at the NYC Department of Cultural Affairs producing concerts in the city's parks and museums, thanks to my friend Bob Rosen's sister. The Rosens became the next family to informally adopt me. Bob's late parents, Ruth and Jesse, already had three kids, but they didn't hesitate to take in a stray.

I couldn't believe how cool New York was. Where else could I see Sonny Rollins at the Village Vanguard three times in one week without getting in a car? I became enough of a regular there that the Vanguard's late owner Max Gordon's cook, Elton, would make me a hamburger in the tiny kitchen/ office in the back of the club, off-limits to everyone except musicians.

I liked Elton's thickish juicy burgers, cooked medium no matter what and never adorned with cheese, but what I really loved was feeling accepted by all the musicians I had dreamed about meeting ever since Grinnell. Ten years later, Max Gordon called me up and asked me to come talk to him about taking over the Vanguard when he retired. I'm sure he was just posturing for his wife, Lorraine, whom he was usually fighting with, but I felt honored nonetheless. Lorraine did in fact end up taking the Vanguard over when Max died in 1989, running it until she passed away in 2018.

New York also offered a seemingly inexhaustible number of gustatory pleasures. I couldn't afford much on my $111-a-week salary, but I could spring for two perfect slices of pizza from Sal's Pizza at Ninety-Fifth and Broadway. Sal's slices were classic thin-crust beauties. They were a little crustier and doughier than a classic New York slice, but the sauce wasn't too sweet and there wasn't too much cheese—perfectly balanced. Sal died in 2009, but his pizza lives on at Sal and Carmine's, located seven blocks north of the original location.

Then there was Tom's Pizzeria at Eighty-Fifth and Columbus. Tom made dark-crusted, chewy slices with browned cheese that was a combination of mozzarella and Romano. Tom was a prickly dude, and he had a strange way of adding up checks. If your bill was $3.25, he rounded it up to $4.00. No explanation was ever given, his prickliness prevented anyone from questioning his math, and the food was so good that I never protested. If I was feeling flush at Tom's, I would have one of his incomparable meatball parmigiana heroes. His meatballs were light, the melted mozzarella was oozy and creamy, and the hero roll got just crunchy enough in the pizza oven.

When I was feeling lonely or homesick, I would go down to Russ & Daughters on Houston Street. The wait was always long, but I didn't mind. I would take a number and look at all the smoked fish in the case while listening to the wisecracking counter people's repartee, which sent me hurtling back to memories of my mom sending me to Rothenberg's for smoked salmon, bagels, and cream cheese. Mark Federman, the owner, and his daughter Niki became one of the many families that eased my transition to New York. Mark gave me an oral history of his family's involvement in the Lower East Side that in some ways mirrored my own. Mark's great-grandfather started the business selling smoked fish out of a pushcart at the turn of the twentieth century. Niki resisted going into the family business for the longest time. But eventually she and her cousin Josh took over in the early 2000s, and they've modernized and expanded it while somehow managing to maintain the store's emotional connection to its customers.

But I had come to New York to "save" the jazz world, not to talk smoked fish with the Federmans, though that was in fact extremely pleasurable as well. Shortly after arriving there in 1973, I programmed a jazz concert series at the Studio Museum in Harlem called Uptown Conversations. I was still working at the NYC Department of Cultural Affairs at the time.

One of the musicians I booked for that series is arguably the greatest jazz tuba player of all time, Howard Johnson. Howard is smart, funny, joyful, with a million-kilowatt smile. He effortlessly traverses musical boundaries. As a sideman, Howard has played with everyone from the Band to Taj Mahal to the great jazz composer-arranger Gil Evans to the Saturday Night Live Band. His own band, Substructure, is a twelve-piece band featuring six tubas and a rhythm section that at times included Paul Shaffer, who went on to become the leader of the David Letterman band.

When Howard asked me to be Substructure's manager, I was flattered and immediately said yes. Of course I had no idea what being a band's manager meant—especially when six of the band's twelve pieces were tubas. And so I became the band's booking agent, publicist, and road manager. (There was certainly no money to pay anyone else to do any of that.)

I was sure there was money to be made booking and managing Substructure, but we never got there. All I had to show for my efforts were the memories and a couple of gorgeous Substructure T-shirts. It didn't matter one bit. I was having a ball and doing what I loved to do—trying to get recognition and compensation for people who deserved both.

I noticed that all the musicians in Howard's band cobbled together a living any way they could. One taught music at a junior high school. A couple of others played in Broadway pit bands. Another played with a trio in Central Park every weekend during the day and passed the hat.

Multitasking, I discovered, was the way most jazz musicians survived. And it was the way I learned to survive as well. In my first ten years out of college I did everything from help jazz aficionado, historian, and DJ Phil Schaap create ID cards for Columbia students every fall (as a result, I was allowed to play basketball at the Columbia gym), to road-managing the New York Pro Musica (a short-lived gig—I dropped a centuries-old viola da gamba at the Kennedy Center in Washington). I once made a list of every gig I've ever had. When I got to a hundred I stopped counting.

One rainy night in 1974 I went to Boomer's, a now-defunct club on Bleecker Street in the West Village, to hear a few of the musicians I had booked for Uptown Conversations. The band featured saxophonist Jimmy Heath and three brilliant musicians sadly no longer with us: Cedar Walton, a phenomenally lyrical piano player; timekeeping swing machine bassist Sam Jones; and drummer "Smiling" Billy Higgins, who played the drums with more dynamic sensitivity than any other drummer I have ever heard.

I had a few drinks, which was a few more drinks than I should have had. I am the world's cheapest drunk. The alcohol enabled me to go up to Jimmy between sets and say, "Hey, Jimmy. You guys sounded great. I have a question for you. Do you give saxophone lessons?" He replied, "I do teach advanced students. Who are we talking about?" "Well," I said, "would you consider teaching someone who has never picked up a saxophone before?"

Maybe he felt sorry for me, or needed the money, but he agreed. The next week Jimmy Heath went shopping with me for a saxophone. This is the equivalent of Eric Clapton taking a neophyte guitar player shopping. We ended up finding a gorgeous used Selmer Mark VI, the Rolls-Royce of saxophones and the kind that Jimmy and virtually every jazz saxophonist of note played. I still have that horn, though I stopped playing years ago.

Every week I would drive out to the modest two-bedroom apartment in Corona, Queens, that Jimmy shared with his extraordinary schoolteacher wife, Mona, and two of his children. The walls were covered with concert posters and photos of many of the great musicians Jimmy had played with: Dizzy Gillespie, Charlie Parker, John Coltrane. These jazz giants were Jimmy's heroes and inspiration, and they became mine as well.

The lessons were hard—endless exercises done to the relentless beat of a metronome. Jimmy practiced constantly, and he expected his students to do the same.

One thing about convincing a legend to give you lessons: you're motivated to practice. And just being in the room with Jimmy was an education, my PhD in jazz culture and history. Over the course of a few years I became a decent practice player. Jimmy would encourage me to go play in the local Jazzmobile workshops in Harlem, which he sometimes led. "Ed," he would say, "you sound good in my crib, but playing in my apartment is not really playing. But if you really want to learn how to play like your man Sonny Rollins, you have to actually go play with other people. Get your ass kicked. Charlie Parker did it, and if it was good enough for Bird, it's good enough for you."

I never went. I was scared to get my ass kicked, I guess. I also realized I enjoyed the time I spent talking and hanging out with Jimmy more than I liked playing.

I learned from him just what the creative struggle entailed. Even the great Jimmy Heath had to hustle: playing gigs as a sideman and leader; teaching (he ended up a chaired and tenured professor at Queens College in New York City); giving private lessons; applying for grants; touring by himself and picking up local rhythm sections to play with both here and abroad; and receiving commissions from academic institutions to compose and arrange.

Beginning in 1975, I managed and booked the Heath Brothers, a band featuring Jimmy and his brothers, the late bassist Percy (of Modern Jazz Quartet fame) and drummer Albert, or "Tootie," for three years. Fighting the suits to get Jimmy the recognition and money he deserved became my mission. I was also the road manager (we couldn't afford one), so I ended up traveling around the country with three of the smartest and funniest jazz musicians ever.

One time the Heath Brothers and I were in Southern California to play four nights at the Lighthouse in Hermosa Beach. Mike and Carol invited us for dinner at their gorgeous house in Pasadena overlooking the San Gabriel

Mountains. I wondered how the evening would go, but I shouldn't have. Mike and Carol had been wowed by the Heath Brothers recordings I had sent them. And they loved the Modern Jazz Quartet, so having the great Percy Heath over to their house for dinner would give Mike a lot of cred at both Caltech and USC's law school, where he was teaching at the time.

It was a great night. Carol served us perfectly medium-rare grilled steak with roast potatoes. The conversation at the dinner table was far-reaching and inclusive. As we were leaving, Percy said to Mike, "Don't worry about your little brother. He is so into the music, and he works his ass off for us." Jimmy then followed up with more soothing words. "Ed is doing just fine. You have a lot to be proud of." Mike and Carol had just received a glowing progress report on their former ward turned jazz missionary. What could be better than that?

I'm happy to report that Jimmy is still going strong and playing well at ninety-two. Through all his struggles Jimmy has never lost his sense of humor, his incredible grace and humanity, or his resolve. To this day, the twinkle in his eyes remains. One night in 2016, I went up to his tiny dressing room at the Blue Note in New York City, where he was celebrating his nine-tieth birthday with a weeklong big-band gig. After I exchanged warm hugs with him and Mona, Jimmy introduced me to another well-wisher, saying, "This is Ed Levine. He used to be our manager and booking agent, and then he left us to become a big-time food critic." I laughed off his compliment (Jimmy couldn't care less about food) and changed the subject: "The band sounded great, Jimmy." Jimmy shook his head and said, "Come on, man, you know better than that. We were not tight at all. You should come back later in the week. We'll be tighter by then, especially on the new tunes." This ninety-year-old saxophonist and bandleader was still writing new music—and maintaining his inordinately high standards. I take great pride in my nearly fifty-year friendship with Jimmy.

While managing the Heath Brothers, I went to work for a concert pro-duction firm called New Audiences. It produced just about all the jazz and blues and folk concerts in New York at that time. New Audiences' princi-pals, Art Weiner and Julie Lokin, would have liked to book some rock concerts, but promoter Ron Delsener had a stranglehold on the New York rock concert scene at the time. The talent agents for the David Bowies and Rolling Stones of the world wouldn't even take our calls. And there was a promoter like Ron Delsener in every major market. The country was divided up into mob-like territories, and no amount of money could alter the situation.

That meant we had to be more creative in putting together packages of musicians that could sell out the halls we could rent, like Carnegie Hall in New York, the Kennedy Center in DC, and Symphony Hall in Boston. I relished the opportunity to be creative in the underdog role I loved.

We produced life-changing shows by Tom Waits, Sonny Rollins with Wynton Marsalis as a guest soloist, Charles Mingus, Nina Simone, and Miles Davis at these venues. Perhaps my favorite bill of all time was the late Ray Charles and the Staple Singers, featuring the late Pop Staples and the thankfully still-with-us Mavis Staples. They practically tore off the roof of Carnegie Hall.

New Audiences' office was the second floor of a brownstone Art Weiner owned on West Eighty-Second Street. There were great options for lunch: Linda's Deli, where a Russian immigrant couple served the most incredible turkey sandwiches carved off a big bird they would put in the window every morning, or the minestrone soup at Al Buon Gusto. The lunch decision was a topic of serious discussion, almost as momentous to me as whom we should book for a concert.

My ultimate fantasy in the music business was to produce records. Miraculously, at least in my eyes, I got to produce or coproduce four records that still sound as good today as when I produced them. My friend Jack Heyrman owned Clean Cuts Records, a small independent jazz and rock label in Baltimore. I had done publicity for a couple of Jack's records after a brief stint in the late seventies as a publicist at Warner Bros. Records, where I worked with many musicians I loved, like the Talking Heads, the B-52s, and Rickie Lee Jones.

Jack and I met through a mutual music journalist friend. We would talk music for hours over pizza at John's in Greenwich Village, one of New York's original coal-oven pizzerias. We discovered we had similar tastes and shared sensibilities when it came to music of any kind, as well as pizza. Jack asked me to coproduce a Dr. John solo record.

Mac Rebennack, aka Dr. John, was between labels and struggling with many personal demons at the time. When we scheduled the recording sessions in the summer of 1981, Mac would often show up an hour or more late and—we thought—in no condition to play.

Then he would sit down at the Steinway piano in the makeshift rehearsal studio that we had rented in New York's flower district, and magic would emanate from the keys. We recorded two albums' worth of material, which became *Dr. John Plays Mac Rebennack* and *The Brightest Smile in Town*. When the first album came out in 1982, *Time* magazine called it "one of the best albums of the year." Both records are still available as *Dr. John, the Legendary Sessions* (volumes one and two). If you're a fan of joyful, soulful, syncopated New Orleans piano playing, do yourself a favor and listen to them.

New York had the best music to offer, and the best food. But the city's greatest gift to me was neither of those things. No, Gotham's greatest gift to me was my wife, Vicky.

Though of course both music and food figured in our meeting.

New Audiences was producing a Sonny Rollins concert at Carnegie Hall that night, so I was late for a dinner party I'd been invited to. I did show up for dessert, though, because I had heard that there would be homemade ice cream.

As soon as I walked into the party, I found myself staring at a stunning, slender woman with piercing hazel eyes and a swan-like neck. When I got up the nerve to talk to her, I realized she was articulate, smart, funny, and classy. I'd never met anyone like her.

Emboldened, I told the group my favorite Sonny Rollins story. I had called Sonny one day to see if he had heard back from bassist Stanley Clarke, a much younger musician he had asked to appear as a guest soloist at one of his concerts at Carnegie Hall. "No, I haven't heard back from him," he said, "and I'm not calling him again. Fuck Stanley Clarke and fuck you." And with that, my hero Sonny Rollins hung up the phone.

Sonny then called my bosses Art and Julie and told them that he no longer wanted to deal with me. But since there was still much more work to be done and nobody else to do it, and I had never met Sonny, we decided that I would disguise my voice when I talked to him and identify myself as Bob Scronson, my nom de pot at Grinnell.

That's the story that made Vicky laugh, and the sound of that hearty laugh was what made me fall in love with her. (It brings me joy to this day.)

We both stayed at the dinner party until 2:00 a.m., well after the homemade ice cream was gone. The more I learned about this incredible creature, the more smitten I became. She was an editor at Oxford University Press and seemed to have read every book worth reading. She was a third-generation Manhattanite as well. Who knew that there were people who had grown up in Manhattan?

It had already been snowing for a few hours when I arrived at the party, so by the time I got up to leave, there must have been a foot of snow on the ground. The city was snow-white and blissfully quiet and clean, the way it gets when snow first accumulates. Vicky and I left together; I lived across the street, and she lived four blocks away, but like a nitwit I said good night without offering to walk her home.

Even after that flub, I floated home. Boy, was I smitten.

A few days later I dialed Vicky's number, which I'd gotten from the dinner party host. She answered the phone in her unique, inimitable style: "Hel-loe." Both Vicky and her late mom have a two-octave hello, the warmest, most welcoming hello I've ever heard. We made a dinner date.

I was so desperate to impress Vicky that I made a reservation at Butler Terrace, a restaurant on the top floor of a Columbia University residential building, with spectacular views in every direction. It had been favorably reviewed in the *Times*, which noted the romantic, gorgeous views of both the George Washington Bridge and the Triborough Bridge from just about every table.

At dinner I had the mustardy rack of lamb and Vicky had the perfectly rare duck breast with all the fat rendered, and I discovered that she had come back to New York after college to be a modern dancer, which explained her extraordinary grace. Over what Vicky called our "divine" soufflé desserts (I had never heard anyone use the word "divine" before), she explained that when her career as a dancer had proved impractical, she'd followed her first love—books and writers—to a career in publishing.

Vicky had endured the loss of her father when she was seven, so incalculable loss was something else we shared. Values, too: at Oxford University Press, she was advocating on behalf of writers and their writing, just as I was doing for musicians.

When the check came, I practically choked on my last bite of chocolate soufflé. The bill was over a hundred dollars for the two of us, before tax and tip. That bill represented almost 50 percent of my weekly income at the time. I tried to hide my dismay, but Vicky noticed it right away. To spare me any further embarrassment she immediately said, "Let's just split the check." Her incredible generosity of spirit revealed itself in that moment. At the end of that magical evening I knew that this indeed was the woman for me.

After that first date I immediately realized two things. I was punching way above my weight class, and I had to do everything in my power not to let this extraordinary woman get away.

Our courtship was a joyride of seriously delicious meals, much laughter, and lots of conversation. And forty-one years later, I can still say that Vicky is the most decent, compassionate, and generous-spirited person I have ever met. Oh, how my mom and dad would have loved her!

We got married in 1982, but we started living together six months after we met. When I told my friend Bob that we were engaged, he marveled, "Holy shit. How did you pull that card trick off, dude?" I wondered about that myself. The only answer I could come up with became the advice I give to anyone contemplating marriage: "Marry up and hang on for dear life." It's worked for me for thirty-seven years.

Fat, Diner-Style Burgers à la the Village Vanguard's

J. KENJI LÓPEZ-ALT

This burger is the kind you'd get if you hit a twenty-four-hour diner early enough that the last orders from breakfast are still leaving the flattop (or if you hit it late enough at night that the early birds are already eating breakfast). The flattops at places like this are invariably kept at a cooler temperature than those at dedicated burger joints that aim to sear and serve as fast as possible. This means that a thicker burger patty has plenty of time to pick up flavor from the clarified butter used to fry the hash browns and eggs and the bacon grease that coats the griddle as the outside slowly browns and the center reaches a perfect medium rare.

A slice of gooey American cheese (or some sharp cheddar if you're feeling fancier), some onions (sliced pole-to-pole to maximize onion flavor while minimizing pungency), some slices of dill pickle, and a smear of mayo are all this burger needs to achieve beefy nirvana, but you can top it up any way you choose.

Note: When shopping for ground beef, look for a fat content of at least 20 percent (80/20 beef). Plain old ground chuck will do. For a superior burger, combine 50 percent ground sirloin with 25 percent ground fatty short rib and 25 percent ground brisket. To clarify butter, place it in a small microwave-safe container and microwave in 15-second increments until fully melted. Skim off the white scum from the top surface with a spoon and discard. Carefully pour off and reserve the yellow butterfat, discarding the milky white liquid at the bottom. The yellow butterfat is your clarified butter.

TOTAL TIME: 30 minutes   **ACTIVE TIME:** 30 minutes   **YIELD:** Two 6-ounce burgers

12 ounces freshly ground beef (see note)

Kosher salt and freshly ground black pepper

6 strips thick-cut bacon

3 tablespoons clarified butter (see note)

2 slices American or cheddar cheese (if desired)

2 soft white hamburger buns

Toppings and condiments as desired

1. Form the beef into two 6-ounce patties about 5 inches wide and ¾ inch thick (it should be about 1 inch wider than your bun). Season heavily on all sides with salt and pepper.

2. Heat the bacon strips in a large cast-iron skillet and cook over medium heat, turning occasionally, until crispy on all sides. Transfer to a paper towel–lined plate. Use a spoon to carefully remove any large bits of debris left in the pan from the bacon.

3. Add the clarified butter to the skillet and increase the heat to medium high. Add the hamburger patties and cook without disturbing until a deep crust develops on the first side, about 1½ minutes. Lower the heat as necessary if the fat starts to smoke excessively. We're aiming for slow and steady browning over a hard dark char here.

4. Flip the burgers, top with cheese, and continue to cook until the second side is browned and the center of the patty registers 125°F on an instant-read thermometer for medium rare or 130°F for medium. Transfer the burgers to a plate and set aside to rest. Scrape the skillet out into the sink, removing any gunk but leaving a thin sheen of oil in the bottom.

5. Toast the buns in the now-empty skillet, turning them gently for even browning.

6. Construct your burgers, topping as desired, and serve immediately.

Chapter 5

FROM JAZZ GUY TO AD GUY TO *NEW YORK EATS*

How do you walk, Ed?" asked my ad agency mentor, Jerry, clad in his Brooks Brothers suit and yellow power tie.

I thought Jerry had called me into his palatial office to discuss my professional development. "I've never really thought about it," I replied, confused. Jerry stared at me intently and continued: "People tell me you amble."

I stammered, "I've never thought about how I walk before, Jerry. I guess I do amble. I'm always thinking about lots of things, I guess."

His eyes were boring a hole in my own yellow tie. "You can't amble around here. When you're walking in public areas where one of our clients might be, you have to stride purposefully, like you know where you're going at all times."

He wasn't kidding.

"I'll work on it," I told him.

But how do you relearn to walk when you're thirty-three? By the time I got back to my own cubicle, I had come to the inescapable conclusion that my attempt to grow up had failed. Which was a problem, because I had gone to work at J. Walter Thompson to do exactly that.

Seventh Avenue South, the jazz club I'd been managing when Vicky and I got married, had closed in June of 1983, exactly a year after our wedding. It had never been profitable to begin with, and co-owners and ace studio musicians Randy and the late Michael Brecker's bad habits had caught up with them.

I got an MBA at Columbia in 1984, with the idea of becoming a securities analyst covering the media business. "You know more about that business than just about anyone," Mike had said encouragingly. I did have a passion for media, but I had no aptitude for or interest in financial analysis.

My grades were mediocre, but somehow I graduated on time. My classmates even elected me class speaker. Unfortunately, the dean had heard that I was a bit subversive (at least for a business school student), so he declared the election null and void. That really pissed off my classmates, who proceeded to elect me nearly unanimously the second time around.

The speech I gave was a fairly conventional one about the role of ethics in business, but the conclusion was not so conventional. I paraphrased something the cattle wholesaler character said in the 1948 classic Howard Hawks western *Red River*: The wholesaler had acquiesced to a request for a cash advance made by Montgomery Clift, who had just driven hundreds of cattle on a perilous journey from Kansas to Abilene, Texas. "Absolutely, son. There's three times in a man's life when he's allowed to howl at the moon. When he gets married, when his children come, and when he finishes something he never should have started in the first place."

I looked up from my speech and announced, "I guess we can all howl at the moon right now." The dean was behind me, but Mike told me he turned purple when I said that.

After graduation in 1985, I started working at J. Walter Thompson. Even though the career counselors at the business school had convinced me that it was the perfect job for a creative-minded MBA, I hated being an account executive from the very first day. I worked on campaigns for Listerine and Anusol, a hemorrhoid medicine. I had certainly come a long way from Jimmy Heath, Wynton Marsalis, and Sonny Rollins. When my mentor told me I had to walk differently to succeed at the agency, I knew my tenure at J. Walter Thompson would be brief.

I got laid off after fifteen months, which would have been a tender mercy except that the timing was terrible. When I got home, not exactly anxious to break my news, Vicky was all too excited to share hers: "I'm pregnant!"

I couldn't bear to tell her that I didn't have a job anymore. So I did what any cowardly husband would do. For the next three days, I put on my Paul Stuart suit, grabbed my briefcase, and left the house. I'd spend the day on a park bench or in a Greek coffee shop.

Three days of that charade came and went before I broke down and told Vicky. She was supportive but nonetheless worried about our future. Going mainstream—getting an MBA and an advertising job—clearly hadn't taken.

My next job, at a hybrid ad agency–production company, wasn't much better. It was the advertising agency for MTV Networks, which was pretty cool, but in the end it was just another advertising job.

On July 8, 1987, our son William was born. I was besotted from the moment he appeared on this earth. I resolved as soon as I took his tiny hands in mine that he would never suffer through what I did as a kid. Thirty-one years later, I am still just as besotted. Will is as smart, funny, and perceptive as his mother. He is seemingly just as unflappable too, so unlike his excitable dad. And he has always been his own person. Will was five when we were in the two-story Barnes & Noble at Eighty-Second and Broadway. On the escalator up I asked him, "So what do you think you want to be when you grow up?" He shrugged. I said, "Maybe you'll be a writer like your dad." Will wasn't having any of that: "That's you, not me." Sensible.

Fatherhood struck a very deep, almost primal chord with me. I finally had a family to call my own. I much preferred to be with Vicky and Will than at work. Unfortunately my employer's business was not really set up with parenting in mind, so Will's arrival made life even more difficult for me there. And it wasn't easy to begin with.

"You look miserable," Vicky told me as I opened the door to our apartment after another unsatisfying, not-fun-at-all day of work. "I can tell just by the way you put your key in the door how unhappy you are. You need to write something, create something, anything, that's yours and yours alone, that takes your mind off work."

She was right, of course. (Vicky is just about always right.) I started thinking about writing a book. The fact that I had never written a book before didn't faze me in the least. While doing the music business hustle, I had written dozens of newspaper and magazine articles about jazz and pop for the *New York Times* and *Rolling Stone* (among many other publications), so I figured that writing a book would be just like writing fifty feature stories and some connective tissue to tie them together.

With Vicky's encouragement, I decided to write a food lover's book about New York, focusing exclusively on nonrestaurant food.

Chasing deliciousness was one of the only things that made my life at work tolerable; I'd read an article in the *New York Times* or *New York* magazine about an Italian sandwich shop in Brooklyn or a slice joint in Manhattan and make a pilgrimage the next day.

The year before, I had fallen in love with *The Food Lover's Guide to Paris*, a book by Patricia Wells, an American food writer who lived and worked in France. Wells wrote about chefs and restaurants, but she also wrote evocative portraits of artisanal food purveyors. In her loving profiles of chocolate makers and bread bakers, she was not only introducing us to the good stuff but also telling us why we should care about both the food and the people who made it.

I also greatly admired Calvin Trillin. In books like *Alice, Let's Eat* (part of his *Tummy Trilogy*), Trillin played the funny, discerning fresser in search of the great indigenous foods America has to offer. Barbecue, fried chicken, crawfish, and boudin sausage were his gustatory sweet spots. In the process, he let his readers get to know the people who made those foods as well.

I wrote a few extremely opinionated sample entries one weekend and showed them to Vicky. To my surprise and delight, she liked them. I put together a formal proposal for a book I called *New York Eats*, which Vicky—by then a literary agent—sold to a wonderful editor, Barbara Anderson, at St. Martin's Press. That it was for a modest advance didn't deter me in the slightest. A publisher was paying me to eat and explore. What could be better than that?

Every weekend, I'd set out for a different New York neighborhood armed with a subway map, a shopping cart, yellowed clippings from newspapers and magazines, and tips from friends who had grown up nearby, which gave my explorations some shape. If the food was any good, I tried to engage the shopkeepers in a conversation about their work.

I was pleasantly surprised that the purveyors were so willing to share their stories with an unknown writer. I didn't realize at the time how happy they were that a writer was interested in the kind of food they made or grew or sold. It helped that I could put them at ease and make them feel I was on their side, a gift I'd gotten from my mother. And in fact, I was on their side.

I discovered Georgie's Bakery in Harlem, where the yeast doughnuts were so good that even southerners, who believe that yeast doughnuts are their birthright, thought so. The gorgeous burnished-brown clouds of fried dough would come out of the fryer at one thirty, so a line of lawyers, cops, and street hustlers would form at one o'clock—and by 3:00 p.m. the doughnuts were gone. A box of them became my calling card at business meetings; nothing melted resistance to new ideas like a Georgie's doughnut.

I learned how Mary Lou Cappezza made chicken parm and eggplant parm sandwiches to order at the Corona Heights Pork Store. (More than a decade later, I took Calvin Trillin there for a story he was doing for the *New Yorker*; in it he called the eggplant parm "sublime.") The immaculate shop was in the old Italian neighborhood of Corona Heights, across the street from a park with a bocce court, where middle-aged men in tracksuits hung out and drank espresso all day. The forty-five-minute wait for a sandwich gave me an opportunity to get to know Mary Lou and her husband, Frankie. They also became part of my New York family, and I became part of theirs.

Frankie made world-class mozzarella and soppressata in the small kitchen at the back of the store. Whole legs of prosciutto hung from the ceiling, with a name tag attached for each person who bought one. When the health department told Frankie that he couldn't make his pork sausage and mozzarella in the same place, Frankie spent thousands of dollars he really didn't have to create a legal setup. The fact that he didn't make both at the same time and that he scrupulously scrubbed the area clean between uses was lost on the health department bureaucrats. Ultimately Frankie and Mary Lou tired of the fight and closed the store, and I thought of the great

Bob Dylan lyric "To live outside the law you must be honest." I still mourn their store's loss.

I devoted a whole chapter to greenmarkets, eating my way through the Union Square Greenmarket and getting to know many of the farmers. The Kents have been growing crisp and juicy apples and pears at Locust Grove Fruit Farm for almost two centuries. For a story for the *New York Observer*, I slept on the family's couch after packing a truck bound for the greenmarket at dawn. Wall Street traders can talk about risk all they want, but farmers understand and tolerate risk in a much more personal way. It begins and ends with something they absolutely cannot control: the weather. And while the assumption in business school is that the only rewards that matter are financial, small farmers prove that to be false. Even farmers who sell baby arugula for twenty dollars a pound make a fraction of what a first-year associate would pull down at an investment bank. For farmers, growing delicious things, being careful stewards of their land, and feeding people while they provide for their family are the yardsticks of their success.

I hadn't expected to love the research and writing as much as I did. I was traveling around the world with a subway token for a passport. I'd come home full and exhausted, and I'd write up my findings between 6:00 and 8:00 a.m. before heading off to work. It was cleansing and downright exhilarating.

By contrast, the office was less and less happy. Most of the revenue was derived from the ad agency division, and company founders Steve and Bart and I all hated the advertising business. The two principals couldn't fire themselves, so I was in a vulnerable place.

Instead of waiting to get fired, I quit right before the book came out. Leaving without another job may have been the right thing to do, but it wasn't the easiest: our son Will was just three, and though Vicky's literary agency was already successful, we needed my financial contribution to make things work.

New York Eats came out in 1992. It could have sunk like a stone, except that chef and cookbook author Rozanne Gold had been given the bound galleys by the one person I knew in the food establishment, Chinese food expert and restaurateur Ed Schoenfeld (who now owns my favorite Chinese restaurant, RedFarm). Schoenfeld had taken me around Chinatown for a sidebar in the book, "The Adventures of Chop Sooey Looey." Rozanne loved the book and asked if she could show it to some of the folks she knew in food media.

A few days later, Florence Fabricant of the *New York Times* left a message on my answering machine asking if I would take her to some of my favorite places in the book for a feature in the *Times* Dining section. When I heard the message, I was convinced that it was really one of my friends punking me. But it was indeed *the* Florence Fabricant. Rozanne Gold had shown her the galleys.

Flo Fab, as she's known, and I ate our way through Manhattan, Queens, and Brooklyn: doughnuts at Georgie's and fried chicken from the M&G Diner in Harlem, both long gone now. (The M&G Diner also had the best jazz, R&B, and soul jukeboxes I had ever come across: Brook Benton's "Rainy Night in Georgia," Miles Davis's "All Blues," and Marvin Gaye's "Sexual Healing," all there waiting for me to drop a quarter into the slot.)

I took her to Carroll Gardens in Brooklyn for buttery rugelach at Margaret Palca Bakes and to Red Hook for roast beef, mozzarella, and fried eggplant heroes at Defonte's. (Go! They're both still there.)

The piece came out on the day the book was published, with the headline "The Homer of Rugelach." At that moment I felt that I was the luckiest man on the planet. "No one should come to New York to live unless he is willing to be lucky," E. B. White wrote in 1939. I was willing, and lucky too.

I appeared on the now-disgraced Charlie Rose's talk show, then on PBS, with a tray of Georgie's doughnuts. Clearly uncomfortable eating on camera, Rose took a bite at my insistence before asking his next question; before I could answer, he said, "God, that's good." After that, Rose and his socialite then-girlfriend, Amanda Burden, became regulars at Georgie's. I found out from Georgie himself. "That nice white fella on TV just picked up a dozen doughnuts. Thank you for sending him."

My book was the number one nonfiction bestseller for a few weeks at my neighborhood local bookstore, Shakespeare & Co. I would walk into my favorite food stores and find the "As Seen in *New York Eats*" laminated posters that my publisher distributed. My little book had become a big deal, at least as far as I was concerned. A joyride was sure to follow.

Chapter 6

ONE SMALL THING

N ew York Eats was truly a godsend. It gave me a place at a table I had long fantasized about being at, next to writers and editors like Johnny Apple, Ruth Reichl, Calvin Trillin. It was so much fun I could barely believe it was happening.

In 1997 I published *New York Eats (More)*, an expanded and updated version of *New York Eats*. This time I took then–*Times* restaurant critic Ruth Reichl on a multiborough food adventure. She noted admiringly that my itinerary was too ambitious for one day. (It was only ten places!) We managed to hit Badoo International, then the best jerk chicken joint in East Flatbush, Brooklyn; Philip's Candy, a place in Coney Island (it's now in Staten Island) where they still made their oversized lollipops by hand; the aforementioned Sullivan Street Bakery; and Esposito's Pork Store in Carroll Gardens, Brooklyn, for the porkiest soppressata ever.

Finally, baker Jim Lahey also introduced Ruth to the joys of pizza bianco, a puffy, focaccia-like "pizza" topped with rosemary and sea salt, so good it needs no sauce or cheese, at his original Sullivan Street Bakery location. In the story Ruth called Jim's bakery a "church of bread." He also makes dark loaves of pugliese bread that many people think are burned. "That's the way the bread is supposed to be," Jim tells any customers who complain. "If you want bullshit, cottony Italian bread, go to the supermarket. They have plenty."

Her story in the *Times* called me the "missionary of the delicious." Ruth described what I did better than I ever could: "Mr. Levine is on a crusade to see that the people who make food get the recognition they deserve. He sees them as creative artists waging a losing battle against mechanization, and he cheers them on."*

The recognition was a narcotic, and I certainly appreciated Ruth's turn of phrase, but I still couldn't afford the drugs. Recognition as the head artisanal food cheerleader may get you an extra bagel in your bag, but it doesn't pay the rent, and it was no way to make a living.

That was where media consulting came in. Using the skills I'd honed as a marketer, I helped Harriet Seitler, a friend who had been my client at MTV, to define the branding of *SportsCenter* and ESPN 2. I did similar work for many cable networks: Bravo, SportsChannel, TLC, AMC, and the Travel Channel, to name a few.

I liked the work itself, which was intellectually stimulating and satisfying in its own way. I learned how to sell, how to articulate and defend an original point of view, and how to get my clients to buy in. I liked the problem-solving aspect, and I enjoyed working with super-smart, talented, and focused media executives, but I wasn't emotionally invested in it the way I wanted to be in my work. I wanted to put this skill to work on something I loved and believed in and had created myself.

Luckily, the *New York Eats* books had also led to well-paying glossy-magazine work: *Gourmet, Bon Appétit, Businessweek, GQ.* Alone, those writing fees weren't quite enough to make a living. But add them to my consulting income, and I was doing okay.

In 1996 I applied for the only CEO job in the world I might have been qualified for—at the Food Network, which was then owned by the Providence Journal-Bulletin Company.

I knew it was a long shot, but I sent my résumé to the white-shoe headhunting firm handling the search. I did streamline it, figuring the hundred or so "jobs" I had had would not serve me well in the pursuit of a CEO position at a media conglomerate.

---

* Ruth Reichl, "Critic's Notebook; On an Odyssey with the Homer of Rugelach," *New York Times,* November 12, 1997.

The headhunters were intrigued by my rather unusual combination of cable television and food media cred and experience. And I was passionate about my mission, to spread the gospel of seriously delicious food on television by telling the stories of the people who make and grow it. I wanted to tell the stories of my favorite peach grower, Art Lange of Honey Crisp Farms outside Fresno, California; Paul Spadacenta, the best (and I'm sure the only) one-armed pie man of the long-gone Paul's Apizza in East Haven, Connecticut; and my old friends the Cappezzas at the Corona Heights Pork Store.

The finalists were me and a woman with a much more conventional media business résumé. We were both flown up to Providence to meet with the board of directors. I still have the fancy suit and shoes I bought for the occasion.

I articulated my vision for the network, full of confidence and brio, right down to the new show schedule I had devised. Each board member nodded affirmatively at all the appropriate moments. They even laughed at my jokes.

On the way to the airport I stopped at Al Forno for a quick dinner of sublime grilled pizza, rich baked penne made with cream and five cheeses, and a buttery, flaky, baked-to-order crostata. I couldn't stop telling the chef co-owners, husband and wife George Germon (who tragically died in 2010) and Johanne Killeen how well the interview had gone. George drove me to the airport in the pickup he used to transport produce from the farm he and Johanne maintained; the whole way there, I could barely contain my excitement.

Alas, I found out a few days later that the Journal-Bulletin crew was negotiating with the other finalist. I called the acting CEO to ask what had happened. "Can I be honest here? You scared a lot of people in Providence," he told me. "You were so sure of yourself. You seemed so confident and had so many ideas."

That was difficult to swallow. I had no idea that being confident and having a lot of ideas were disqualifying characteristics when it came to a CEO job.

They were right, of course. I *was* a loose cannon who had no idea how to get anything done in a corporate environment. I would have had no interest in creating programming just for the sake of ratings, which would have meant weekly if not daily clashes with my board of directors in Providence. I would have flamed out fast.

A year later, they called asking if I would consult for the network. I demurred, the old cliché in my mind: "Why buy the cow when you could have the milk for free?" Or, in this case, for cheap.

I did get some food-consulting assignments, which were interesting at the very least and more remunerative than my writing gigs. In 1997, for Northwest Airlines/KLM, I sampled more than a hundred coach airline chicken entrées in one sitting, searching for the two or three the airline would ultimately serve. I would fly to Amsterdam on an overnight flight, shower at the Amsterdam airport, sample the entrées at the KLM catering kitchens at the airport, and then jump on the two o'clock flight back to the States. Mike, who was then working at Northwest Airlines, had put me up for the job.

I created a consulting chef team for Northwest Airlines, which meant eating my way through all of NWA's hub cities (San Francisco, Los Angeles, Boston, Minneapolis, and Detroit) and finding chefs to work on all classes of airplane food. I am still friends with many of those chefs today, including Nancy Silverton of Pizzeria Mozza in LA (if you go, and you should, make sure you finish your meal with the butterscotch budino—it will change your life) and Seattle's Tom Douglas.

For ten years that was my life: slaloming back and forth between food and media consulting and my writing. I loved what I did—I just needed to figure out how to make it pay.

In 1998 I did a local cable TV show loosely based on *New York Eats*. Its producer, Ron Fried, had come up with the idea of pairing me with then–*Vogue* food critic Jeffrey Steingarten and actress and comedian Susie Essman (later of *Curb Your Enthusiasm*). Ron figured that Jeffrey's knowledge of high-end food would play nicely off my egalitarian approach, and Susie would handle the hosting responsibilities, since it was going to be shot live to tape.

Before we shot the pilot, we all had lunch, and Jeffrey, whom I didn't know very well, seemed even more nervous than usual. I tried to calm him down. "Jeffrey," I said soothingly, "I find that the people who succeed on TV are the ones that come across as likable and believable. It's as simple as that." Jeffrey, without missing a beat, replied, "You take care of the likable and I'll take care of the believable."

The show lasted two seasons, which was about the normal shelf life of one of my gigs.

It was a sublime two seasons. We interviewed chefs like Gabrielle Hamilton, Tom Colicchio, and Alice Waters, and had them cook for us; we reviewed restaurants; and we did rigorous taste tests in search of everything from the best ketchup to the best bagel.

In 2001 I created *Dish*, a radio show on the public radio affiliate in New York, WNYC. *Dish* was my dream show. I took a few interesting people to lunch and miked each one of them.

At a Chinese banquet, surrounded by Ruth Reichl and Calvin Trillin, Nora Ephron explained that she loved location scouting because she got to sample local specialties at each place she went. At Lombardi's, Joel Coen explained that experienced moviemakers knew that the place to go on movie sets for the best cup of coffee was craft services and not the catering truck. Over short ribs at Craft, Wynton Marsalis and Gabrielle Hamilton had the following exchange: "Man, when I meet a young trumpet player I can tell by the way he or she holds her horn whether she can play or not." Gabrielle chuckled knowingly and replied, "For me it's the same thing with young cooks. I can tell by the way they hold a knife if they can cook or not." In the end *Dish* was canceled, even though I did everything—raised the money, booked the guests, wrote the show, and coproduced it. To this day I don't know why.

Then I got lucky again. Another dream came true when I started writing regularly about food for the *Times*. Sam Sifton, then the Dining section editor (now the food editor for the entire *Times* operation, the founding editor of NYT Cooking, and a columnist for the *New York Times Magazine*), was a big fan of the *New York Eats* books. So in 2002 we developed a format for front-page food-section stories that sent me in search of the best iconic American and New York foods: hamburgers, hot dogs, cheesecake, pastrami, pizza, ice cream. I was getting prominent bylines and loads of space in the greatest newspaper in the world. And my late, great mother-in-law could finally tell her friends what I did all day.

I often think about the month the *Times* sent me all over New York in search of the best burger. I hipped folks to the burger Peter Luger's served at lunch using dry-aged steak trimmings; the great bar burger at the Union Square Cafe, which still has a perfectly charred and seared exterior that gives way to juicy innards in each bite; and the burger at the now-shuttered Prime Burger, where for seventy-four years the properly sized four-ounce burgers were made out of prime meat in a huge salamander broiler.

Prime Burger was right across the street from St. Patrick's Cathedral, so when it was open twenty-four hours a day, a sign above the door read, "The Gates of Heaven—Never Closed." The burgers were brought to your table for one (they looked like grade-school desks, with swivel tops) in the most elegant fashion by dignified servers in spiffy white coats. I always skipped the mediocre frozen french fries and opted for the far superior onion rings, a tangle of sweet fried onions battered ever so lightly. It was de rigueur to finish with a piece of apple crumb pie made by Eddie Adams, Prime Burger's octogenarian pie baker, who is unfortunately no longer with us.

Sam also sent me looking for New York's best ice cream, a quest that led me to Greenwich Village's Siracusa, helmed by an eccentric Sicilian gelato master, Gino Cammarata. His pistachio gelato was so good, and tasted so purely of the finest Sicilian pistachios, that one bite reduced me to tears. Alas, Siracusa closed, and Gino ended up making his transcendent gelato in a tanning salon in Bensonhurst. Tans are not permanent, and neither was Gino's stay there. I do hope he's out there, making gelato somewhere.

What could be better than all this? Perhaps more money and maybe some health insurance? That almost happened. In 2003, after a couple of years of blissfully writing for the *Times* as a freelancer, I heard that they were looking for a staff writer and reporter. I told Sam that I was definitely interested.

Sam and I went out to lunch. "I'm not going to give you the job," Sam told me. "If you were on staff, I would have to send you out on stories that you didn't care about to fill space in the section. You would hate it, and you would end up hating me. I know you're going to be pissed at me for not giving the gig to you now, but believe me, you'll thank me in the end." He was right on both counts, but I thought, *Hey, it was worth a shot.*

Life was good. Vicky and I were beating the system, my brother Mike would often say admiringly. We were doing (mostly) what we loved without the encumbrances and constraints of working for a single corporate entity, dealing with a boss, or having an office to show up at every day. In my case, New York City was my office. How sweet it was.

But Mike also used to say we were operating without a net. And no matter how many risks he took in his work life, Mike always had a plan B, namely a tenured position at a major law school. There was no plan B, no version of tenure, in my universe. Anyway, I think I had convinced myself that the net, the relative safety and security a corporate gig offered, was an ephemeral one.

Though I did have some inkling of what was coming. As the digital age descended on the world of food media, I tried to adapt. Right after the first book came out, I created a *New York Eats* content area for AOL's Digital City online city magazine venture. Big fun, not big money. Then for the early online service Prodigy in 1996, I developed an all-encompassing food content area—a mix of reviews and recipes—called Yum. That seemed like a dream gig: Prodigy was to supply the startup capital (the company was a joint venture among CBS, Sears, and IBM, so money was not a problem), and I was going to earn a handsome salary and own a pretty significant chunk for creating and maintaining it.

It was exhilarating to be ahead of the curve, to be innovating and leading the pack. Weeks of expensive negotiations produced an agreement, except that the agreement in principle failed to become an agreement in fact.

In the meantime, the freelance fun continued unabated. And people were—unbelievably, it felt—taking note. Nora Ephron, another one of my writing heroes, turned out to be a fan. In December of 2005 she wrote in a *New York Times* op-ed about how she turned to me in her search for cabbage strudel, a story that was included in her bestselling collection of essays, *I Feel Bad About My Neck*. Nora wrote, "I dropped Ed Levine's name so hard they heard it in New Jersey." The idea of Nora Ephron dropping my name instead of the other way around still makes me laugh. (But if you read the essay, notice that she didn't initially get the cabbage strudel.)

Years later, after Serious Eats launched, Nora would show up to participate in our pastrami and store-bought-biscuit taste tests. She appreciated the fact that I asked a friend to be my pastrami "mule," smuggling Montreal smoked beef into the United States for said pastrami taste test. She also asked me to be an extra in *Julie & Julia*. If you freeze a certain frame in the film, you can catch the back of my head when Amy Adams is shopping at Dean & DeLuca. On second thought, don't bother.

I spent one glorious weekend hanging out with the *New York Times*'s legendary political reporter and food explorer R. W. Apple Jr. ("Johnny" to his legion of friends all over the world) and my own fressing and food-writing hero Calvin Trillin at the Southern Foodways conference in Oxford, Mississippi.

I loved every second of that weekend: eating incomparable catfish and hush puppies at the Taylor Grocery; chowing down on an all-pie breakfast made by one of our greatest pie bakers, Karen Barker of the dearly departed Magnolia Grill in Durham, North Carolina; sampling Ed Mitchell's whole-hog barbecue and Big Bob Gibson's barbecued chicken, the only barbecued chicken I have ever loved.

But mostly I loved listening in while Johnny and "Bud," as Trillin is known to his friends, swapped Kansas City barbecue lore and war stories from their reporting days (Apple had, in fact, covered the Vietnam War). To give you an idea: they'd both last been in Oxford when they were covering James Meredith desegregating the University of Mississippi in 1962. On the trip back to the Memphis airport from the conference, I convinced Trillin, New York über-restaurateur Danny Meyer and one of his chefs, Michael Romano, to make what I told them would be a quick stop at the original Gus's World Famous Fried Chicken in Mason, Tennessee.

Romano, who'd made his reputation at Meyers's Union Square Cafe, made the mistake of going back to the kitchen at Gus's to see how Gus made his chicken. "Stand back; don't take one more step" were the words he was greeted with. "I'm not kiddin'," Gus continued. "Nobody outside the family gets to see how I make my chicken." Michael was escorted back to the tiny dining room.

And although we almost missed our flight home waiting for our chicken (worth it, I thought, although Danny Meyer seemed less sure), it was a miracle. Somehow, in his talented, floured hands, Gus manages to achieve what I call the "cosmic oneness" between the batter and the skin in every burnished-brown piece of chicken he sells. We sped to the Memphis airport. I tossed the keys to the rental car onto the Avis desk with Gus's grease still on my fingers. But we made it onto the plane with seconds to spare.

My pieces for the *Times* allowed me to really dig into a subject, like cheesecake or burgers. But some topics deserved more—and so in 2004 I researched and wrote an entire book on pizza, *A Slice of Heaven*, for which I ate a thousand slices of pizza, all over the country, in a year. On one call home, my ever-wise (or do I mean wiseass?) fifteen-year-old son Will asked me, "How's the 'work' going, Dad?"

Of course, he was right. It was hard to believe this was a job.

When the book came out, I got pizza-related hate mail. I had written: "At best Chicago pizza is a good casserole," and *Chicago Sun-Times* columnist Mark Brown urged his readers to defend their native pies. A freelance food writer collects no hazardous-duty pay, but when it comes to pizza I can take the heat. No bodily harm came to anyone in the end.

Italophiles were equally dismayed when I declared in the same book that the best pizza in the world could be found in Phoenix, Arizona, at Pizzeria Bianco. It was pizza blasphemy to not bow at the altar of Neapolitan pizza greatness. Even after eating at more than fifteen Naples pizzerias in a week doing research for the book, I still stand by my review. Chris Bianco's crust is just thin enough, puffy and crisp on the outside and softer and chewy on the inside, with hole structure like great bread. His mozzarella, made in-house every morning, is creamy and slightly tart. The sauce, made from his own brand of canned tomatoes, tastes like the ripest tomato in concentrated form. His sausage tastes of fennel and pig, with just the right meat-to-fat ratio.

When I went out to Phoenix to try his pizza for the first time, Chris and I ended up hanging out 24-7 for three days, eating pizza, meeting the farmers who supplied the restaurants, and talking about food and life nonstop. We both loved music, sports, and, yes, pizza. More important, I realized that we both had the same missionary impulse to spread the gospel of great handcrafted food.

One night, after the pizzeria had closed, we were sitting at the counter facing the domed pizza oven sharing Chris's transcendent "Rosa" pizza, made with red onion, Parmigiano-Reggiano, Arizona pistachios, and fresh rosemary.

As usual, our conversation was far-reaching and filled with laughter, but all of a sudden it took a serious turn. Chris told me, "My menu might be small, but to me it's the biggest thing in the world. Pizza inspires me, fascinates me, and gives me hope."

This was obviously something he'd thought long and hard about. He took a bite of pizza before continuing, "I have invented nothing, but I'm on a mission. I have a responsibility to do something with integrity and dignity. I'm just trying to do something—one small thing—right."

Chris's words landed with me, and I've thought about them countless times over the years. That same statement could have come from almost any of the dedicated, obsessive food makers I talked to in the course of writing the two *New York Eats* books. At the same time, I could also have said them about myself.

I'd gone from being a disillusioned ad exec with a weekend lard-bread habit to someone who got paid—handsomely, for a freelancer—to chronicle the food stories I cared about most deeply. But for all my hustling, for all the accolades and pizza hate mail, I still couldn't make the money work, so that I could do what I loved and make a New York living.

"You're like a kid in a candy store," one of my editors teased me as I pitched him a deep dive on my passion of the week. She was right, but for the first time I wondered: was that really where I want to be at fifty-two years old, with a kid in college? I was no longer ten years old drinking chocolate malts at Harry's.

Chapter 7

GUSTO: THE MEAL TICKET THAT WASN'T

A lot happens at a New York power lunch. Some of it's good, some of it's bad, and some of it's both. One gorgeous spring day in 2004 I found myself at a catch-up lunch with my friend Hamish (not his real name). In one way we were the original odd couple—he was a slick-suited senior executive at MTV Networks, a cable network company with a huge office in the sky in Times Square, and I was a jeans-clad, knish-loving food writer working out of a home office.

But when we had first met fifteen years earlier on that great New York equalizer, the basketball court, we had been in different places. He was a midlevel executive at a cable network, and I was the managing director of the ad agency that created on-air identities for iconic cable channels like MTV, Nickelodeon, and Nick at Nite.

When it's time to pick a restaurant, people tend to defer to me. So I eagerly suggested Esca, an inspired and original Italian seafood restaurant on the edge of the theater district in New York City. I had gotten to know and love the fisherman, chef, and co-owner there, Dave Pasternack.

Hamish and I had barely settled into the thick leather banquette before Dave appeared at our table with a plate of thinly sliced striped bass, drizzled in rosemary-infused olive oil and finished with crunchy grains of gray salt, telling us the story behind our dish in a New York accent thicker than the morning fog that envelops the house he and his family live in a few blocks from the ocean.

"I caught this striper yesterday ten minutes from my house, right before we were about to give up and come home. Beautiful, isn't it? Like my friend Mike says: I hate fishin'; I love catchin'. The stripers have been huge this year."

I casually mentioned to Ham that I'd long harbored an ambition to launch a cable network that recognized America's heightened interest (some would call it an obsession) in every aspect of food culture. Actually, the mention wasn't that casual. I was hoping that Ham would put two and two together and decide he had to have what I was then calling EATv for his stable of cable channels.

I explained that EATv would be a channel devoted to telling the food stories I loved to tell. I had learned how to tell those stories on television, on radio, in print, and online. I reminded Hamish that I had cohosted a beloved (at least by some) *New York Eats* TV show with Jeffrey Steingarten and Susie Essman.

Ham knew about all the content I had created, as well as my overall cable television and food media chops. I was hoping that Ham would see that I was the right guy, the only guy, the perfect guy, to launch a cable network about eating for his company. Of course, I had no experience running a P&L. In fact, I had no relevant corporate experience, and no financial management skills whatsoever. *Details*, I thought to myself.

To my astonishment, Hamish loved my idea. I was so used to having my passion met by executive indifference. Maybe it was the bright-coral Alaskan salmon adorned with Sicilian olive oil and sea salt, or the scallop crudo with tangerine-infused olive oil Dave had sent out next, but Ham slapped the table and said, "Let's do this together. I'll pay you to develop it for us. And if it goes anywhere, you'll get to run it and retain a small piece of equity." At least, that's how I remember the conversation.

That sounded like a capital (pun intended) idea. This could be my family's path to security, financial and otherwise, something I had belatedly started to think about. A small piece of equity in a cable network could be worth a substantial sum of money. Plus, I knew that given my inability to flourish in a conventional business environment by working my way up the corporate ladder, this would be my only path to being the president of anything.

Yes, let's do this. Please let's do this, I thought to myself.

It was on. Ham put together a SWAT team of people to work with me on what I was now calling Gusto. (My good friend Bob Rosen came up with the obviously superior name.) Though none of them had any knowledge or experience in the food world, they all had expertise in the media business. Some, unlike me, even knew their way around Excel spreadsheets and Power-Point. And most of them liked to eat. We began honing the concept at weekly meetings in a fancy all-white conference room on a high floor in Hamish's company's Times Square corporate headquarters.

The first meeting was at 9:00 a.m. I needed us to get off on the right foot. I decided to cater the breakfast myself to set the tone for the project and, truth be told, to make sure the food was seriously delicious.

I practically danced up to Absolute Bagels, my favorite bagel bakery. Absolute looks like every other mediocre bagel shop in New York, including the cold case featuring every cream cheese spread imaginable (many of which should not be a reality): bacon, blueberries, cheddar. But the bagels—if you get the perfectly proportioned minis—are crunchy and chewy and not too dense. Bagels are all about texture.

Mrs. Thongkrieg, the matriarch of the Thai family that owns Absolute, was behind the counter as usual. I got four everything, four sesame, two poppy seed, and two egg bagels the glorious color of saffron. Egg bagels are an endless source of controversy among bagel freaks, but I'd made converts before. My next stop was Barney Greengrass the Sturgeon King, to pick up some meaty, almost beef-like smoked sturgeon and some scallion cream cheese. Three generations of the Greengrass family had been selling sturgeon in the same location for almost a hundred years. The waiters there had perfected the art of putting your food on your table and simultaneously walking away, a form of ballet exclusive to the store's idiosyncratic staff.

This "stroll" was thirty blocks out of the way, but when had that ever stopped me? Often my wife would put the kibosh on this sort of thing, but Vicky wasn't going to be at the meeting.

I loved every item I bought for the meeting. They were all uniquely delicious. But I loved the stories of the people who made them just as much. These were the stories people were going to see on Gusto.

Catering the breakfast was a perfect setup. When I got to the meeting, I explained to the Gusto team the provenance of each item on the breakfast menu. They nodded appreciatively, but I don't think I won any converts to my cause. My food cred clearly needed to be supplemented by my business cred. I did know the ins and outs of the cable business and made sure to show it.

Still, they weren't going to green-light Gusto and spend hundreds of millions of dollars on it because I had brought the best bagel spread in New York to the meeting. But it did make our meetings a helluva lot more fun (not to mention delicious) than anybody else's.

Ham and his crew were also developing a number of other "lifestyle" channels, one about cars, one about luxury goods (it was nicknamed "Bling"), and one about wellness. Not all of them would be green-lit. Gusto was the only one with a firmly entrenched and fully distributed competitor, the Food Network. So Gusto was, to put it mildly, the underdog.

The weekly meetings mostly consisted of the entire group questioning the wisdom of Gusto going up against the Food Network. One of the SWAT team members would say the same thing at the start of every meeting: "We all appreciate your passion and enthusiasm, Ed, but in and of themselves they are not enough in the current environment to build a business." It was a simultaneously exhilarating and discouraging time. I was chasing a dream—for once, one that was tantalizingly close. But so many people doubted the validity and viability of my idea.

I would come home deflated. "These people just don't get it," I would tell my wife. Vicky urged me to persevere. "You were born to do this," she would tell me. "Do not let them pull the plug." Armed with my wife's steadfast support and encouragement, my own stubborn, completely irrational "refuse to lose" mentality kicked in with a vengeance.

MTVN gave each team $200,000 to produce a "sizzle" reel (a sales tape) that would give prospective viewers an idea of what they might find on a given network. For Gusto's sizzle reel I came up with the idea of assembling and shooting a dinner party attended by interesting, funny, smart people talking about—what else?—food and life, and what Gusto meant to them. We found a beautiful loft in lower Manhattan that we could rent for a couple of days with a gorgeous kitchen and a fabulous view.

I carefully created a guest list: Susie Essman, because with her love of food, her smarts, and her wicked sense of humor, Susie was the essence of Gusto; Pete Wells, then my editor at *Details* magazine and now the *New York Times* restaurant critic, who is insanely intelligent and knowledgeable and has a wonderfully droll sense of humor; and badass, fiercely intelligent and talented Prune chef-owner Gabrielle Hamilton, who had been on the TV show I had done with Steingarten and Susie.

Rounding out the guest list was Nobu über-restaurateur Drew Nieporent. Drew is a bon vivant and raconteur of the first order who is as much of a food enthusiast as I am. A few years earlier, he and I had partnered on yet another entrepreneurial food idea of mine, a weekend-long seminar called "How to Open a Restaurant and Make It Last." We did it a few times in New York and always made money. But when I wanted to expand it to other cities, Drew demurred. He decided that he had too many other things on his plate (pun intended) that he wanted to do more.

I can still taste that meal fifteen years later: rare, dry-aged, bone-in rib eye steaks from chef-favorite meat purveyor Pat LaFrieda, vine-ripened summer tomatoes, mozzarella (from Di Palo's, of course) and basil salad, and strawberry shortcake and lime melt-away cookies for dessert.

For the tape we shot a minipilot for a reality show called *The Protégé*, in which my old friend Jeffrey Steingarten looks for his next assistant. The first shot is of Jeff in his white terry cloth bathrobe on the phone. The next shot has Jeff explaining, "Training an apprentice is a matter of breaking down her or his ego step after step after step until they are blubbering jelly." He was joking, but you wouldn't immediately think so given his stentorian delivery and patrician manner.

Calling in every favor I could, we also shot short "Gusto" vignettes with everyone I knew who was even the slightest bit well known. Our friend, neighbor, and serious eater Frances McDormand gave us fifteen minutes of her time to shoot her in her kitchen rhapsodizing about eating a baguette topped with butter and jam. One take was all she had time for, and boy, did she nail it.

What else was in the sizzle reel? There were snippets and screen shots of a faux video blog and a website that would be part of Gusto, which was supposed to have a major interactive component. There was a shot of a person making a restaurant reservation on his phone, three years before OpenTable introduced the first restaurant reservation app.

The suits at MTVN dubbed Gusto a 360-degree network because it could be accessed anywhere. There would be a linear cable channel, video on demand (VOD), and of course a major interactive digital component on the web.

I wish I could say I took a deep dive into the blogosphere at this juncture. But I didn't. Blogs were just something we put into the presentation to make ourselves seem like digital media mavens. In fact the faux blog on the sales tape was a user-uploaded video snippet of two laughing young women spilling flour all over their kitchen while baking something. We even got the URL wrong: gusto.blog. If it had really been a blog, it probably would have read either "gusto.blogspot" or "gusto.blogger," the two blogging platforms available to the public at the time.

We missed a huge opportunity here, because the blogosphere had already exploded by 2005. One study released that year said that thirty-two million people read blogs, but unfortunately not one of those thirty-two million folks was on the Gusto team. Some terrific, seminal food blogs were already up and running, including former Chez Panisse pastry chef David Lebovitz's eponymous website (which many people call the first food blog).

Nor did we notice the now-famous, made-into-a-book-and-movie *The Julie/Julia Project*. It began as a blog by aspiring writer Julie Powell on Salon.com in 2002. *The Julie/Julia Project* was basically an online diary chronicling Powell's attempt at cooking her way through Julia Child's

Mastering the Art of French Cooking to counteract the effects of a mind-numbing day job. My only excuse is that Powell had an obsessive cooking gene, while I had an obsessive eating gene.

Truthfully, the cable executives I was pitching didn't care about the blogosphere or any of the other exciting food websites popping up. The only reference to any food website in our final Gusto presentation was to Epicurious, which was described as being "the world's largest recipe database, launched in 1999 and owned by our marketing and content partner, Condé Nast." When in doubt, I had learned by then, when you're pitching an idea to a big media company, always mention other big media companies as potential partners. Spread that risk around, baby.

We shot and edited the Gusto sales tape in three weeks. They were three weeks of pure joy fueled by the greatest adrenaline rush ever. For me it was the ultimate magic carpet ride. The end result was something to behold: my take on food in five glorious minutes of videotape.

Our sizzle reel was a big hit with focus groups in Philadelphia and Chicago. In Philadelphia I fed the groups cheesesteaks from Jim's, at the time my preferred cheesesteak joint. Later on I discovered Dalessandro's and John's Roast Pork, which do make the best classic cheesesteaks in the City of Brotherly Love. In Chicago I brought Italian beef sandwiches from Mr. Beef, double-dipped in pan drippings, to the research facility. I don't know if my catering influenced the focus groups, but I figured it couldn't hurt to feed folks seriously delicious food.

When we showed the sizzle reel to the company's executive committee, they were blown away. Maybe it helped that I brought a great Turkish lunch from Akdeniz, a casual restaurant with seriously good mezze and kebabs a few blocks from the skyscraper all the execs inhabited. It might as well have been a hundred blocks away. Akdeniz was not a restaurant most of these execs would have been caught dead in. And for dessert, some Junior's cheesecake to clinch the deal. I practically danced out of that meeting. To get buy-in on Gusto from such a seasoned group of executives was no small feat. It really felt like Gusto was going to happen.

Comcast was going to be the distribution partner. Everything was proceeding according to plan. The summer of 2005 was becoming my greatest summer ever, careerwise. I couldn't believe my good fortune. Alas, when it came time to negotiate my equity agreement with MTVN, my buddy Hamish claimed that he had never offered me equity in the channel. I was furious. In retrospect I realized that my friend was merely protecting his own future at the company, that he had made a promise to me that his bosses told him he could not keep.

I got my lawyer involved. Because I never delete emails, we had some pretty compelling evidence to work with. A summit was arranged for all the relevant parties and their lawyers. I told my version of events calmly and assuredly. Hamish told his. My story was apparently much more convincing. The MTVN lawyer called mine the next day to say that they would draw up an agreement acknowledging that I was indeed entitled to a piece of equity in Gusto. We had gone toe to toe with a bunch of MTVN suits, execs and lawyers, and won. I was ecstatic.

I went out to dinner at Jean-Georges Vongerichten's restaurant Perry St with the exec who was going to be in charge of these new networks. With the company's resources at our disposal, Gusto's creative possibilities were endless. We feasted on Jean-Georges's scallops with capers and raisins, one of my all-time favorite dishes. The exec, no foodie to be sure, agreed with my assessment.

We went over a launch schedule and shook hands on a compensation scheme. It was all good. There was a mention of the channel in the *Wall Street Journal*. This sucker was going to happen.

Until it wasn't. The day after Columbus Day in 2005, I got a call. "Ed, hey, it's Ham. I know you are not going to believe this, but we're not going to move forward with Gusto. Comcast has pulled out as the distribution and financial partner, and the powers that be here have decided we don't have the wherewithal to do this by ourselves. I know we shook hands on a deal to do Gusto together, but as of now we are putting Gusto on indefinite hold. I'm really sorry. Nobody believed in Gusto more than I did. I hope you know that. Anyway, let's stay in touch. I'll have my assistant get lunch on the calendar soon."

Magic Bagels

STELLA PARKS

It was a little hair raising to present Ed Levine with a bagel for testing, but earning his seal of approval was worth the stress. My approach isn't traditional, but it ensures the bagels have a thin, blistered crust and chewy interior, along with a near-magical shelf life so you can keep them around for days.

YIELD: Eight 3½-inch bagels

For the Flour Paste:

6 ounces water
(about ¾ cup)

3½ ounces bread flour
(about ¾ cup, spooned)

For the Dough:

12½ ounces bread flour
(2½ cups, spooned),
plus a pinch for dusting

½ ounce white sugar
(about 1 tablespoon)

⅓ ounce salt (volume
will vary by brand;
about 2½ teaspoons for
Diamond Crystal
kosher salt)

⅛ ounce instant dry
yeast such as SAF, not
rapid rise (about 1¼
teaspoons)

3½ ounces water
(about ½ cup minus
1 tablespoon)

To Boil:

6 pounds water
(3 quarts)

1 ounce malt syrup
(about 2 tablespoons)

1. In a 10-inch skillet, whisk the water and flour together over medium heat, cooking until the mixture comes together in a thick, mashed potato–like paste, about 2 minutes. Scrape onto a plate, spread into a 1-inch layer, and cool to approximately 75°F.

2. Place the flour, sugar, salt, and yeast in a food processor fitted with a metal blade, and pulse once or twice to combine. Add the remaining water and the prepared flour paste, then process until silky smooth, about 90 seconds. Scrape dough onto a lightly floured surface, and divide into eight 3-ounce portions. Shape each into a smooth, tight ball. Cover with plastic wrap and rest 15 minutes.

3. With lightly dampened hands, press your thumb through the center of each ball and gently stretch until about 2¾ inches across. Arrange on a lightly greased baking sheet, cover with plastic wrap, and refrigerate for 24 to 30 hours.

4. Adjust an oven rack to the middle position and preheat to 450°F. Combine the water and malt syrup in a large pot and bring to a boil. Working two at a time, boil the bagels for 60 seconds, flipping them from time to time to ensure they cook evenly on both sides. Drain on paper towels for a few moments, then transfer to a parchment-lined half-sheet pan.

5. Place in the hot oven and immediately reduce the temperature to 400°F. Bake until the bagels are blistered and golden brown, about 25 minutes. Cool on a wire rack at least 15 minutes before serving. Once cooled to room temperature, the bagels can be stored up to 48 hours in a paper bag, or wrapped loosely in parchment.

After I hung up, I couldn't breathe. I was gasping for air. I felt like I was in a malfunctioning elevator that had just hit the basement floor. A year of insanely hard work had evaporated. The dream had, in one split second, turned into a nightmare.

On some level I knew that Gusto was just "business," but I took the outcome personally and felt betrayed. I couldn't really process this all-too-brief exchange. Ham's voice sounded normal, like this was just another conversation between friends and colleagues. But he had to know how devastated I would be. He did sound disappointed, sort of like the way a drama teacher tells a high school student he didn't get the lead in the school play. But it was clear from his voice that after he hung up the phone he was going to keep going down his to-do list checking off boxes like "Call Ed and tell him that Gusto is a no-go."

Remarkably, we stayed friends and basketball buddies both immediately after the fact and to this day. I think we both realized that there might come a time in the not-so-distant future when we would need each other again.

But at that moment I realized my personal risk meter had been pinned to the red. I had poured everything I had except money (which I didn't have) into Gusto's development. All my dreams for creative fulfillment with the promise of financial security at the end of the rainbow had been dashed. All I was left with was a bitter taste in my mouth that I was all too familiar with. If Gusto was a fight, I had been knocked down. And, oh yeah, I had been out of the consulting game for two years, and the point of reentry did not immediately reveal itself to me. I had risked a lot more than I thought.

Chapter 8

THE SIREN CALL OF THE BLOGOSPHERE

Fuck MTVN. You don't need them or their money. You're going to start blogging right here, right now. You're a brand in the food world, and we're going to blow your brand up online. And it's not going to cost you a cent, except for your food. Blogging is the future of media, and for you, Eddie, the future starts now. It's gonna be great."

I was in my old boss Steve's (not his real name) office. After working with me on and off for twenty years, he recognized my "things are fucked forever" look.

It was a few days after the fateful call from Ham. The October air was crisp and bracing, but I was still walking around in a self-flagellating daze. Steve was giving me a pep talk in the corner of his bright, cheerful office space, decorated with music and animation posters. He had allowed me to work there when I started developing Gusto. Steve had also been involved in MTVN's "lifestyle" channel initiative.

Steve and I knew about brands. Between the two of us we had as consultants helped develop the on-air look and feel of some of the most successful cable networks: MTV, Nickelodeon, Nick at Nite.

On my own of course I had worked with ESPN developing the on-air look and feel of ESPN 2 and *SportsCenter*. Of course, Steve and I had done all this valuable work with these large media companies assuming all the financial risk. The only thing we risked was losing the confidence of our consulting clients, and the resulting loss of income.

We were interrupted by my phone ringing. It was my editor at the *Times*. I had been trading phone calls with her about what my next freelance assignment was going to be. No matter how many stories I had written for the paper, pitching them never got easier. I'd call all excited about my latest food discovery, which I knew I always had to turn into a trend story.

"I had this amazing cheese Danish at G&M Pastries on Madison Avenue. I think cheese Danish is making a comeback," I would say excitedly. "I don't know," she would say. "I think I saw something about cheese Danish in *New York* magazine. What else you got?"

This time she wasn't calling about a story. "Ed," she said without a trace of emotion, "our budgets got cut. We can't pay you two thousand dollars a story anymore." I was indignant, but she was following orders and her bosses were just following the money. Freelance food writing and content producing in general was going to be no way to make a living.

By 2005 my byline started appearing less frequently in high-paying magazines. I couldn't help but notice the migration of food media online. Freelance food writing and content creating on the web were most assuredly not a growth industry from a monetary standpoint. The digital migration created many more creative opportunities and many more outlets to contribute to, as Steve was pointing out. But as I had learned firsthand when I created a *New York Eats* content area on AOL's *Digital Cities* initiative five years before, those opportunities were paying decidedly less. I think I was making a hundred dollars a week to update my AOL site. It was nothing compared to what the *Times* had—until now—been willing to pay.

The financials certainly didn't add up. But I was weary of the freelance hustle. I wanted to own something. Yes, I was good at finding work, and a lot of it I enjoyed, but to what end?

So when Steve sat me down in his chair behind his desk and helped me set up *Ed Levine Eats*, I was ready to be schooled big time. "This whole thing is going to take five minutes to set up, and then you'll be good to go," Steve said in his unflaggingly confident voice. He logged on to Blogger.com, the free blogging site. We picked out a template and a color scheme. "What color do you want?" Steve asked. "I like that one," I said, pointing to a washed-out fatigue green on his monitor. "Green it is. Now it's all you, Ed."

And it was. And I loved it. *ELE*'s first post was in October of 2005. Here's what the tens of readers of *Ed Levine Eats* were greeted with when they came to my home page: "I'm writer, radio and TV host* Ed Levine, AKA 'The Missionary of the Delicious' (at least that's what Ruth Reichl called me in the NY Times). My idea of a perfect day is wandering the streets anywhere in the world looking for the perfect bite. If that's yours, or you just figure that since you have to eat, it might as well be good, come on board Ed Levine Eats."

Posting on *Ed Levine Eats* was the ultimate tool of liberation: no gate-keepers (aka editors), all creative freedom and joy. I was finally in control of my own creative fate. The only person I had to pitch was me. "I want to do a post on what I call the fried clam belt," I imagined saying to myself. "Great idea," I would respond. "Do it." If I wanted to write five thousand words on the greatest clam shacks in Connecticut, New York State, and Massachu-setts (with a spot in southern Maine thrown in for good measure), there was no one to stop me. There was no one to cut my complaint about how even good fry shacks fail to properly salt their batter, or to take a red pen to my long-held belief that clams hold up better on a plate than in the iconic bas-ket, which traps heat and makes the bottommost clams soggy.

I loved everything about blogging. I loved the soapbox that it gave me, allowing me to proselytize about the food and the purveyors I felt so pas-sionately about. Blogging was my emancipation proclamation.

I really enjoyed interacting with the folks who somehow found their way to *Ed Levine Eats*. My conversational writing voice was made for inter-active media. The fried clam post was a perfect example. I opined, I refer-enced and linked to other things I had read, and I encouraged readers to fill in the blanks. "Great list, Ed," wrote one commenter. "But have you checked out the fried clams at Giordano's in Oak Bluffs, Massachusetts?" I was doing

---

* I should have put the word "former" before "radio" and "TV."

my missionary thing, having a spirited conversation about food with other serious eaters at a digital cocktail party. What could be better than that?

On a great day, Google Analytics (the seminal internet-audience-measurement tool) told me, a thousand people were reading my stuff. But on an average one, the readership would be a couple of hundred intrepid folks, at least fifty of whom were family and friends. Still, those people were super engaged. The comments indicated as much. Not everybody commented (those who didn't were known as "lurkers" in the trade), but enough people did to make me think I was building a community of like-minded people passionate about food. And though some comments were snarky, most were supportive, even if they disagreed with me.

Between my feature writing, restaurant criticism, and food commentary, not to mention writing about and linking to other people's stories, I was publishing up to three posts a day. Conventional wisdom in the blogosphere at the time was that multiple daily posts were required to give readers a reason to come back again and again.

I worked eighteen hours a day on *ELE*, but it felt like minutes. My appetite was inexhaustible. I had finally found a place in the media universe that utilized all my talents, a place that I could own and control. The blogosphere was every journalist's dream.

I totally immersed myself in digital publishing. I started reading food blogs, websites, and online message boards and forums, both to familiarize myself with the genre and to scout for talent. Steve had succeeded in putting a bug in my ear.

Blogs gave hope to journalists like me with business aspirations. In theory, blogs gave us the opportunity to control our own destiny by scaling what we did more cost-effectively than any old-media company could do.

And the old-media companies really were asleep at the wheel during the formative years of the blogosphere. They were afraid—existentially terrified—that they would lose the ad revenue derived from magazines, newspapers, radio, and even TV. But they were doing very little to protect themselves. In my head, I was a new-media David, slaying the many Goliaths I was doing battle with. That fantasy fueled my ardor.

As did the business press, which declared the internet and the blogo-sphere to be the future of media. I remember reading an interview with Time Warner CEO Richard Parsons in the *Financial Times* in April 2006: "The internet is going to be like television of the 21st century and the ad-supported model is going to be the core for content businesses."* Yeah, baby. Tell him, Dick.

In short order I concluded that the blogosphere was my passport to starting a business based on my passions without enlisting financial or op-erational support from a big old-media company. Prodigy and Yum had been strike one in that regard; Gusto and MTVN were strike two. At my age I couldn't afford to swing and miss a third time.

I told Vicky all about the business potential of the blogosphere for cre-ative types with an entrepreneurial bent. "All the advertising money is mi-grating to the web. This blogging thing is going to be great. Trust me," I told her one night, portioning out the roast pork egg foo yong, no sauce, I had brought home from my local Cuban-Chinese restaurant, La Dinastia. (This egg foo yong will change your life. It has a dark brown, slightly crunchy ex-terior that gives way to an eggy interior studded with sautéed onions and roast pork chunks.)

"It's going to be great" eventually became my standard answer/rationale/explanation when I was articulating the promise of *Ed Levine Eats* and the blogosphere to prospective investors, prospective employees, and prospective vendors, even banks I was trying to borrow money from. Some entrepreneurs had tons of data backing their assertions. "It's going to be great" and a bunch of clippings from the *New York Times* were my calling cards.

I had started to do some back-of-the-envelope calculations (the only kind I knew how to do) for a blogging network business. I quickly realized that the only way to scale and significantly monetize a blog-based business was to sell ads for other blogs I liked that were having trouble monetizing because their readership wasn't large enough. With more content and more

* Aline van Duyn, "A Cool Hand in the Heat of Battle," *Financial Times*, April 2, 2006.

readers, I thought that I could earn a living more quickly. Otherwise it would have taken me years on my own with *ELE* to make even a thousand dollars a month from my single blog.

When my Gusto team had run the numbers on what it would take to launch a new cable network, they had calculated that it would take $500 million and five years to break even. There was no way a first-time entrepreneur like me, with no track record, could raise anywhere near that sum. Running the numbers on an internet-based business, I figured (wrongly, it turned out) that I could move the decimal point over three places. That's a lot of decimal points.

I convinced myself that a measly million dollars would get me to break-even on a blogging network brand. That would cover hiring a managing editor and a general manager, paying for server costs (servers are where data and information and content on the internet live), and securing the necessary technological expertise.

Distribution would be free (God bless the internet); the bloggers I would bring into the network would share in the ad revenue; content would, in classic blog style, be aggregated and produced really inexpensively; and we could market and promote our blog for free by trading links—linking to bigger blogs and hoping they would link back to our stories. Blogs represented the collectivization of media; my Communist dad would have been so proud!

Of course, those calculations stayed on the back of the envelope for six months. I was too busy having a blast blogging.

A lot of people were food blogging, but not many of them saw it as a full-time job. Deb Perelman had launched her terrific *Smitten Kitchen* blog, but she wisely kept her day job for a few years. The blogosphere's Martha Stewart, Ree Drummond, aka "Pioneer Woman," started her blog as a hobby. Somehow I didn't get the "blogging is not a full-time job, it's a hobby" memo. People were calling digital media the future, but it sure wasn't the present if you wanted to make any kind of living. I was making a pittance off my blog's tiny audience; Blogger did accept Google AdSense ads. But because my traffic was so tiny, I ended up making in the high two figures in a good month.

I kept going by telling myself that the newspaper and magazine articles were right. We were in the middle of a media revolution, and I was on the right side of history.

Not everyone was persuaded by "It's going to be great." "Have you lost your mind?" Jeffrey Steingarten asked rhetorically over an orgy of Korean barbecue we were enjoying at New Wonjo, one of the only restaurants in New York's Koreatown still using buckets of live charcoal for grilling instead of gas. The buckets are brought to your table with great fanfare and dropped into a slot in the middle of your table—enough of a fire hazard that you have to check your coat so it doesn't go up in flames as the buckets pass behind your chair.

He continued incredulously, "You're not going to write for the *Times* anymore? How are you going to make a living?" Both legitimate questions, for sure. I actually wrote one more piece for the *Times*, on chicken soup, after I started blogging. But as a nascent publisher, I couldn't afford to give the *Times* my best stuff anymore.

"Blogs are the future of publishing," I told Steingarten with total conviction. "The money will follow, Jeffrey. This is not a suicide mission."

From his perch at *Vogue*, writing ten pieces a year for a very healthy salary and an equally healthy T&E budget that allowed him to fly to China to write about Chinese food, this sounded like career suicide and the ravings of a madman. No matter what Dick Parsons said.

I could understand his reaction. Jeffrey had at that point never read a blog, food or otherwise, in his life. Old-school *Vogue* dispensed fashion intel (and, in Jeffrey's case, food intel) to its readers from on high. Jeffrey's impeccably elegant and flat-out hilarious prose style and refined tastes were well suited to a publication that showcased $15,000 dresses and purses.

The best bloggers, on the other hand, were interested in dispensing informed opinions on our blogs in the hope of starting a dialogue with our readers. The comments were almost as important as the story.

I convinced myself that my tiny audience and lack of monetization were a temporary state of affairs that would soon change. I had no data to back that assertion up. My desire for blogging to be my one "small thing," in

Chris Bianco's parlance, obscured all rational thought. Eventually, I told myself, the mainstream food culture would see the light.

One miraculous day, it felt like the establishment had finally taken notice. I had a reservation at Per Se, an upscale American restaurant informed by classic French culinary technique. It is the sister restaurant of the French Laundry in Yountville, California, and I had once referred to it as the church of its chef-owner, Thomas Keller. It celebrates both local ingredients and iconic American combinations, like the whimsical take on coffee and doughnuts on its tasting menu. At that moment it was the epicenter of the mainstream food culture. I had agreed to meet some friends there for lunch to celebrate a birthday. I decided to chronicle the entire episode for *Ed Levine Eats.*

The morning of my visit to the restaurant, I wondered online if my Per Se lunch could possibly be worth $210 before wine, tax, and tip (now it's even more expensive). I calculated that for the same amount of money I could eat seventy-seven Gray's Papaya Recession Specials (two excellent hot dogs and a medium papaya drink) at my favorite local hot dog joint. That meant that I could eat lunch for two and a half months at Gray's for what I was spending on a single lunch at Per Se.

Midway through the meal our server brought out a beautiful silver tray topped by a gleaming cloche. With a flourish she removed the cloche to reveal a perfectly grilled hot dog in a brioche bun. I started to crack up, as did my server. Someone in Keller's organization had obviously been reading my blog, someone with a sense of humor. Our server asked us to accompany her to the kitchen. Thomas Keller himself appeared out of nowhere. "Are you having fun at church, Ed?" he asked.

The entire episode was life-affirming, or should I say blog-affirming. Food blogs were going to change the world of food media one post at a time. If Thomas Keller was paying attention to my tiny blog, then I really was David smiting Goliath. I was stoked. The food blogosphere was upsetting the staid world order of food media. The gatekeepers were headed for the exits. The whole world would soon be reading blogs, and the money would follow. The days of high-two-figure monthly blogging income would surely be coming to an end. My lunch at Per Se was proof positive that it really was going to be great.

My wife was happy to see me emerge, crawling, from the wreckage of Gusto. And now I was fully and passionately engaged in an enterprise that could possibly have a future!

It never occurred to either one of us that launching an undercapitalized startup in a nascent business category with no proven route to financial security was a business, career, and life Hail Mary.

Belief, passion, and willful naïveté are the first-time entrepreneur's best friends. Somehow, some way, at that moment, the air in our light-filled apartment seemed pregnant with possibility, the same way it had back in Grinnell or when I first arrived in New York. As soon as I raised the money and put together a business plan that proved *Ed Levine Eats* could scale, it really was going to be great.

Chapter 9

NEXT STOP STARTUP-VILLE

My investing in Serious Eats is not a given. I'm not going to just give you this money for a blogging network, whatever the hell that is. I'm going to treat this like any other investment Carol and I make. Do your homework, write a business plan, and then, when you think it's good enough, bring it to me and we'll go through it line by line."

Mike and I were sitting at the bar of the old Union Square Cafe having a burger. Actually he was chomping contentedly on his superb bacon cheeseburger, and I was practically choking on mine. Before the burgers, I had convinced myself that getting Mike to invest was somehow going to be a linear, quick, and anxiety-free process. Then why was I having trouble breathing, much less eating a cheeseburger?

Mike picked up one of the perfect burnished-brown fries before continuing. "And you'll probably get mad at me, because I am going to ask a lot of questions. You're going to need money from other people as well, and they're going to want the same answers that I do. Pretend you're getting a doctorate and you're defending a dissertation. You want other people's money, this is the deal. People don't part with their money easily, no matter how much of it they have, especially if you're asking them to invest in something so risky and so new that they don't even really understand what you're talking about."

I was counting on Mike's investment for Serious Eats. And I was even counting on him to school me in the ways of business as he knew and had learned them, first as president of the now-defunct shuttle-like New York Air, then as dean of the Yale School of Management, and finally as the chief marketing officer of Northwest Airlines.

I was also counting on Mike's counsel, which I had depended on for a long time when it came to career and money matters. Mike had serious business chops. Northwest Airlines was in real trouble when it recruited Mike to be its chief marketing officer in 1992. His innovative pricing, marketing, and route strategies saved the company from bankruptcy. But Serious Eats was a content- and technology-based startup, and those were not Mike's areas of expertise.

Mike was first and foremost an ideas person, another missionary Levine up on a soapbox. Before diving into the airline business, he had been a teacher and scholar, an academic whose field of interest was airline deregulation. He even got to practice what he preached. When the Carter administration deregulated the airline industry in the seventies, economist Alfred Kahn, the Civil Aeronautics Board head, brought in Mike as the price controls director at the CAB to help design and implement the deregulatory changes.

That he ended up making a fair amount of money in the airline business was in some ways a happy accident, a product of someone in a boardroom in rather desperate straits giving him the opportunity to put his ideas into practice. Don't get me wrong. Mike enjoyed the life his newfound money afforded him. There was always at least one sports car in his garage; Krug champagne at occasions big and small; and expensive stereo equipment in the living rooms at his abodes in Manhattan and outside New Haven. But he had also enjoyed his life of the mind on an academic's salary.

I admired Mike for his fierce intelligence, his passion for his work and his family, and the gusto with which he lived his life. The man ate a one-pound Carnegie Deli pastrami sandwich in four bites, six tops. He in turn admired me for blazing my own path, for pursuing my dreams, and for being able to work with all different kinds of people. Our mutual admiration society in the years after my parents' passing had drawn us quite close, the inevitable disagreements notwithstanding.

That was how I convinced myself that it was okay to mix family with money and business. That conclusion was certainly not drawn from my father's experience managing a lumberyard for his brother-in-law, my uncle Abe. My dad didn't much care for my uncle or his job, and he wasn't very good at it.

Mike had seen for himself the ugliness that punctuated my father's work life, so I can't imagine he was positively predisposed to this idea.

I convinced myself that he would be amenable because I *had* to (I wasn't all that confident about other financing possibilities for Serious Eats) and also because I thought that no matter how bad things might get, when push came to shove Mike would never pull the rug out from under me. I had heard and read so many stories about investors, usually VCs, pushing out founders when things didn't go according to plan. Tumultuous as our relationship could be, I knew that Mike would never do that.

My relationship with Mike was solid but painfully built after our parents died. I knew he could be difficult, demanding, even unintentionally hurtful, but I figured that I had learned how to handle and manage him as well as anyone could. His daughters Anna and Sara regularly told me, "You are Dad's favorite child." My response: "That's a scary proposition." Mike was tough on just about everyone, but maybe the circumstances that brought us together, the early deaths of both our parents, enabled him to cut me a tiny bit more slack.

I was going to try to raise the startup capital I needed from other sources, but I hoped against hope that if all else failed Mike would come through. Though, optimistically, I didn't think it was going to come down to that. In 2006 investment money was flowing freely to content sites and blogs. Venture capital firm Greycroft Partners' Alan Patricof, a seminal tech investor who had provided early-stage investment for companies like Apple and AOL, put money into ContentNext Media, a blog publisher whose blogs included *paidContent*. His rationale: "I look at blogs as the hyper-interactive magazines of the future, only with far greater ability to create communities and expand into new areas."*

Shortly after Alan Patricof made his move, the seminal political and general-interest blog the *Huffington Post* announced that SoftBank Capital was making a $5 million investment in what was at the time a year-old site that mostly aggregated and curated content rather than creating it. It was launched in May 9, 2005, by Andrew Breitbart (yup, *that* Breitbart), Arianna Huffington, former AOL communications honcho Kenneth Lerer, and Jonah Peretti. The latter two went on to cofound *BuzzFeed*.

Peretti, an MIT Media Lab graduate, was obsessed with the question of what kind of online content went viral. So *HuffPo* and later *BuzzFeed* were both dedicated to that proposition. His devotion to engineering viral content paid off. In 2006 *HuffPo*'s traffic had grown like kudzu on the side of a gardening shed in Mississippi. How much kudzu? By Christmas, eighteen million people were logging on to *HuffPo* every month.

How did *HuffPo* do it? It was a combination of first-mover advantage; access to big names like Nora Ephron, who blogged for free in exchange for a small piece of equity; using an army of unpaid contributors in search of a larger audience of their own; and, perhaps most controversial, walking right up to the edge in terms of aggregating, summarizing, and publishing other media outlets' stories before linking. Many of its competitors thought it in fact stepped over the edge.

Was this practice ethical and legal? Many people had their doubts. *HuffPo* had (accidentally, according to Jonah Peretti) published *and* linked to entire concert reviews from the *Chicago Reader* on *HuffPo*'s new Chicago site. In a story in *Wired* magazine Peretti defended the practice in general by claiming, "The Huffington Post's intention in aggregating other publications' content is to send traffic their way." Peretti said, "You tease, you pull

---

* Mark Sweney, "Digital News Websites Win Cash Injection," *The Guardian*, June 26, 2006.

out a piece of it, and then you have a headline or link out. Generally publishers are psyched to have a link."*

A New Orleans–based journalist begged to differ in that same story: "In other words: professional newsgathering organizations have paid professional writers to do professional work, and then Arianna comes in, creates links to their creations, and sells ads on her own page. How progressive."

In the *New York Times* in 2011, then–executive editor Bill Keller weighed in on this issue: "Aggregation can mean smart people sharing their reading lists, plugging one another into the bounty of the information universe. It kind of describes what I do as an editor. But too often it amounts to taking words written by other people, packaging them on your own Web site and harvesting revenue that might otherwise be directed to the originators of the material. In Somalia this would be called piracy. In the media sphere it is a respected business model."†

In any event, the marketplace settled the dispute instead of the courts. The blogosphere's currents had simply become too strong to fight, even for the likes of the *New York Times*. The *Huffington Post* was eventually sold to AOL in 2011 for $315 million dollars.

Ad dollars were starting to migrate from print, TV, and radio to the web. In 2005, according to the Interactive Advertising Bureau (IAB), marketers spent more than $12.5 billion advertising on the web. And that number was growing by at least 30 percent a year.‡ I had researched this revenue migration while trying to launch Gusto.

This content and revenue migration to the web spelled trouble and caused major agita for even the best of the old-media publishers, like the *New York Times* and Condé Nast. They were befuddled by the internet, and rightfully so. Their reasoning seemed solid. Why should they give away their content on the internet for free when consumers were still willing to

---

* Ryan Singel, "The Huffington Post Slammed for Content Theft," *Wired*, December 19, 2008.
† Bill Keller, "All the Aggregation That's Fit to Aggregate," *New York Times*, March 10, 2011.
‡ IAB Internet Advertising Report Industry Survey.

pay for magazines and newspapers? It is a question that is as vexing now as it was then, especially for sites like Serious Eats, which has no paywall.

Food news seekers were starting to turn to early food news blogs like *The Food Section* and *Sauté Wednesday,* which aggregated and curated the food news of the day and linked to the source material in a generally more responsible way than the *Huffington Post.*

Recipe seekers went to sites like Condé Nast's Epicurious, the would-be Gusto content partner that was mostly a repository for all the recipes generated by its magazines; Allrecipes, a user-generated recipe site started by a few cooking-obsessed technologists in Seattle; and a rapidly proliferating array of cooking blogs. The result was that food information seekers could find just about everything and anything they wanted free and fast.

Content was king, or so the pundits said, and the rush was on to seize the crown. A friend of mine in finance told me, "The capital markets are flush with cash sitting on the sidelines looking for content companies to invest in. There's a lot of easy money out there." I very quickly learned that it's only easy when you don't need it. Furthermore, the only people telling you about easy money are folks who aren't trying to raise it.

I needed a business plan pronto, for me, for Mike, and for anyone else who might invest in Serious Eats. I bought half a dozen books on how to write a business plan. My favorite for obvious reasons: *The One Page Business Plan.* I still have that book, but it didn't turn out to be all that helpful. The one thing I learned from all those books was that, by year three, your revenue had to hit some all-but-unattainable number to entice investors. Aggressive but plausible, as Mike would say.

I had the incredibly slick hundred-page Gusto deck to use as a model. But the difference in the Gusto days was that I'd had MBAs on my team who actually knew how to use Excel to do financial projections. Even today my Excel skills are nonexistent. When I started Serious Eats it was just me, a knish-loving journalist and accidental MBA who barely made it through introductory accounting and finance courses.

In fact, in business school, my bow-tie-clad professor in what was called "Baby Finance" pulled me aside after a few weeks and said, "You wrote down on your class questionnaire that you were planning to be a double major in marketing and finance. If I were you, Mr. Levine, I would seriously reconsider the finance concentration." I guess he had noticed my eyes glazing over while he explained the capital asset pricing model. I just couldn't get excited about it then—or now, for that matter.

To mitigate the risk for potential investors and prospective employees, and to fill in the many holes I had in my digital media game, I knew I needed to put together a crew of experienced digital publishers, thinkers, technologists, and business folks to work on Serious Eats. Blogging for fun and a few extra bucks for an individual was one thing. A lot of people could do that and were in fact doing it. Making a living as an individual food blogger, like *Simply Recipes'* seminal food blogger Elise Bauer, required a much higher degree of computer literacy than I had or could even develop over time. Elise had gotten an MBA from Stanford before working for Apple and then starting her recipe blog in 2003. I had eaten a thousand slices of pizza in a year and written a book about it. Talk about two different skill sets. I may have been naive, but I knew I needed a team that knew how to do what I didn't. Steve came to the rescue again. He knew a kick-ass coder who had collaborated on various projects. The fact that said coder, David Karp, was barely old enough to drive didn't worry me that much. In fact, David got his license a few months after we met. He then bought himself a Lexus, and he could very well have paid for it in cash.

Sure, he was a high school dropout (his teacher mother did make him get his GED, I told myself), but by the time he turned sixteen he had already made his first quarter of a million dollars as the chief technology officer of online parenting forum UrbanBaby, after its sale to CNET. Before that he had spent a year in Japan on his own working for another technology company. That was some serious cred as far as I was concerned, as it was $250,000 more than I had made from any enterprise, digital or otherwise, and I'd never been to Japan for any reason.

I agreed to pay David a monthly retainer when I found the funding. In the meantime he worked for the burgers I bought him at Shake Shack, which had just opened in Madison Square Park. The line at Shake Shack was our de facto conference room. And what a conference room it was, filled with incomparable Shack burgers, with their great crusty, almost-caramelized exterior; Chicago-style hot dogs with neon-green relish made with sport peppers; and fantastic eggy soft-serve that made the Carvel I had grown up with seem like custardy Play-Doh. Shake Shack pro tip: order a coffee malt and ask for extra malt powder. It will be the best malt you'll ever drink.

Over a couple of perfectly browned Shack burgers and two of those blessed coffee malts, I agreed to make David chief technology officer of Serious Eats, which of course didn't exist yet. Hell, I was thrilled to have a CTO, even if I didn't have the money to pay him (not wanting for cash, David was willing to wait until I had raised money) and wasn't sure what he was supposed to do. Didn't matter. I was putting together my crew.

Other members of the soon-to-be Serious Eats team were also readily available in Steve's office. I solicited Steve himself. "Of course I'm in," he said when I asked him. "Whatever you need. I just want you to be successful." I was gleeful to have a silver-tongued futurist like Steve on my side. He was and is a provocative contrarian and a masterful media idea salesperson. Steve had once convinced MTV that the great then-septuagenarian singer Tony Bennett should be the star of its new ad campaign. Tony Bennett selling MTV? That's some serious salesmanship.

Bill (not his real name) had also hooked up with Steve. He was Steve's hard-core business colleague and right-hand person at an animation studio Steve had run for a couple of years. Bill had the proper swagger of a new media executive. He spoke with absolute authority about anything and everything concerning new media. He certainly convinced me of that. Of course, I was a pretty easy mark.

I thought I was sitting pretty. I had the beginnings of my dream team, three people who could supply business chops, new-media expertise, and clear-eyed objectivity to go along with my food cred, old-media chops, and passion.

I still needed to get my own digital media rap down cold, both for my own edification and for my prospective investors. After all, I was going to be the front man, the face of Serious Eats. I took a deep dive into the blogosphere in general and food blogs specifically.

Eater launched on July 21, 2005, as part of the Curbed network of blogs. It began publishing at almost exactly the same time that Gusto crashed and burned. Its welcome screen and initial post: "Welcome to Eater. The paint is just about dry, the banquettes arrived last night from Budapest (customs is a real bitch), and it looks like the chef is done experimenting with the menu. So, come in. Can we take your coat?"

Eater was founded by Lockhart Steele and Ben Leventhal, neither of whom was a food writer. Steele had been the editorial director of the Gawker network, one of the first blog networks launched as a business. He even kept that job for a while after *Eater*'s launch. The Curbed network was named after Steele's first for-profit blog, a real estate blog that grew out of his personal blog about his New York City neighborhood.

Leventhal, now the cofounder of the restaurant reservations site Resy .com, had started a blog/online newsletter, *She Loves NY,* where he gave restaurant and nightlife tips. But he still kept his day job, which was working at the cable network VH1. He and Steele were entrepreneurial technologists first and restaurant aficionados second. And they were twenty years younger than me.

Eater's subject matter was the restaurant scene and its celebrities, not the food that came out of the kitchens. As Ben Leventhal told me at the time, "*Eater* was all about creating heroes and villains. Nothing more, nothing less." And, oh yeah, it was all about business. At that point *Eater* was resolutely opposed to opining about food or even offering restaurant recommendations. All it cared about then was what's hot. I couldn't care less about what was hot—in fact, I preferred undiscovered gems. All I cared about was what was seriously delicious.

But Lock—as he liked to be called—already knew his way around the blogosphere businesswise, thanks to his experience at Gawker. Even before Gawker he'd already had a failed startup under his belt—a learning experience. "Fail early and often" is a Silicon Valley mantra that I never heard until it was too late. Actually, it didn't matter that I never heard that mantra. At my age I had one shot. Failed digital content entrepreneurs over fifty were not perceived favorably.

Lock had also learned a ton at the feet of the original blogger/businessman, Gawker founder Nick Denton. One thing he learned: a blogging network should include many different subjects or verticals. Why? Different verticals gave you a bigger pool of potential advertisers to pitch. At any given moment Denton had a minimum of six blogs going, covering everything from gadgets to sex to media gossip to travel. Lock had real estate (*Curbed*) and food (*Eater*) and later shopping (*Racked*). Me? When I eventually launched, I had pizza and burgers and New York victuals, which were actually all part of the same vertical, food.

Denton started his career as a journalist in London. His coverage of technology led him to digital media entrepreneurship. He was able to self-fund Gawker because he had sold his first two digital startups, First Tuesday and Moreover Technologies, for a reported combined $89 million, according to the *New York Times*.* So he had no outside investors to worry about.

Eater and Gawker shared a similar smart, confident, and snarky voice. They had the same mission, creating heroes and villains. But a few other business-savvy folks saw the financial promise of blogs. In September 2003 Jason Calacanis, the founder of defunct trade magazine *Silicon Alley Reporter*, founded Weblogs, Inc., a network of up to ninety niche blogs, with the help of a few outside investors, including Dallas Mavericks owner Mark Cuban. The only one of his blogs I paid attention to was *Slashfood*, which was not known for its journalistic excellence or rigor. The blog that put him on the digital map was his gadget and tech blog *Engadget*. Calacanis and Denton were fierce competitors. How fierce? Calacanis stole Peter Rojas, the editor of Denton's most profitable blog, *Gizmodo*, by offering Rojas a huge piece of equity. That piece of equity turned out to be worth millions.

Two years later, in 2005, just as I was launching *Ed Levine Eats*, Calacanis sold Weblogs, Inc., to AOL for a reported $25 million. On one level this occurrence gave me pause. AOL had lots of resources to put behind *Slashfood*. On another level, it would be a favorable comparison to put in our investor deck.

* David Carr, "A Blog Mogul Turns Bearish on Blogs," *New York Times*, July 3, 2006.

But I was mostly focused on *Eater*, just because it seemed to have the mechanics of food blogging down pat. One of *Eater*'s best-known series was "Death Watch," in which the editors tried to predict the demise of certain restaurants. I respected the hell out of *Eater* (I still do), but I was repulsed by "Death Watch." Why? It was doing a play-by-play on people's dreams. I was much more interested in keeping deserving restaurants and food shops and food purveyors' dreams alive.

Serious Eats was not competing with *Eater* at this time. In fact, in the years after the launch of Serious Eats, Lock and I would often have lunch to exchange notes, along with *Apartment Therapy* founder Maxwell Gillingham-Ryan. There was of course a limit to how deep the note exchanging went. Certain trade secrets were not shared. After teaching at a Waldorf school for a few years, Maxwell had started *Apartment Therapy* in 2004 with his new-media executive brother Oliver. Its mission: "saving the world, one apartment at a time."

Maxwell unsuccessfully tried to start blogs in other verticals but did succeed along with his now-former wife, Sara Kate Gillingham, in launching the food blog *The Kitchn*, which mostly focused on simple, homey food that could be prepared with minimal fuss and prep time. Eventually *The Kitchn*, by dint of its huge audience and slick design, did become one of Serious Eats' greatest competitors.

But in April of 2006 there was no one doing anything on another blog or medium that scared me. This was probably irrational bravado on my part. The thought that I would finally have my own soapbox to climb on, armed with my own megaphone, obliterated all the rational concerns I should have been thinking about.

In the meantime I had to keep feeding the *ELE* beast. I was told I had to have *ELE* growing sufficiently to have "proof of concept," as they say in the money-raising trade. *ELE* was the business petri dish for Serious Eats, which of course didn't exist yet. On *ELE* I blogged about my favorite pies in New York, including Yura Mohr's incomparable pumpkin pie, with its buttery, crisp crust and custardy filling. Yura is one of New York's great unheralded bakers and purveyors of elevated comfort food. The day after my post went live, my phone rang. It was Yura. "What did you do, Ed? Out of nowhere there was a line around the block for my pumpkin pies." *Ed Levine Eats* was moving the needle. More and more people were reading it. I put the Yura anecdote in the business plan.

Labor Day weekend of 2006, six months after the Union Square Cafe burger meeting, Vicky and I stopped at Mike and Carol's outside New Haven on our way home from Martha's Vineyard. Along the way, we had gone to Frank Pepe Pizzeria Napoletana, known as Pepe's, to pick up a large clam pie and a large sausage and mushroom.

(Mike was firmly in the Pepe's camp, but not because of the pies. He knew that Sally's Apizza was consistently better, except for its clam pie, made with canned clams, but he hated the fact that Sally's regulars could skip the line if they had the very private reservation number.)

It was a gorgeous late-summer day. Carol's garden was positively resplendent. I thought the flowers were a sign from the heavens that something good was about to happen, that Serious Eats was going to bloom. I hoped the scent of the flowers would cover up my sweat-ridden angst. Mike summoned me to the back porch of their rambling colonial house. I felt like one of those guys in *The Godfather* about to ask Don Corleone (Marlon Brando) for a favor on his daughter's wedding day. Like all those guys, I came bearing gifts, the boxes of pizza I set down on the table.

He had a copy of the business plan in his hand. "I still have a lot of questions about this, and frankly I don't understand much about the internet, much less the blogosphere, but I'm going to invest $500K in your business, which you clearly have great passion for. I don't know if I'll ever get any of it back, but I've talked to Carol and it's something we want to do. This is your shot, Ed. We will put the money in a separate checking account, and anytime you think you need some money, you'll have to come over to our apartment and sign a ledger sheet."

Holy shit. I had $500,000 for Serious Eats. I was so excited I was practically vibrating like a tuning fork. I couldn't believe that Mike had enough faith in me to invest that much money. I calmed myself down by telling myself that even if I failed, the money that Mike and Carol had lost wouldn't cause any change in their lifestyle. But that was before I understood a fundamental truth about individual investors: just because someone has made enough money to invest in a speculative venture like Serious Eats doesn't mean they won't be upset if they lose it. That goes double if they are family. People who have made money usually didn't make it with a casual attitude about money in general.

I didn't fully think through the ramifications of having to go to my brother's apartment to sign out money. All I knew was that I had the cash. Maybe, just maybe, that moment on Mike and Carol's sun-filled porch was really going to be the start of something great.

When you raise the first tranche of money for your startup, you feel a great sense of accomplishment, like you completed an arduous journey. And it is in fact a real achievement. But then you realize that the money just gets you to the starting gate, not the finish line.

Nevertheless, I had everything I needed. I had my team. I had my brother's blessing, which was the hardest thing of all to earn. We were in business.

White Clam Pizza

J. KENJI LÓPEZ-ALT

This recipe makes a poufy dough with a sturdy, crusty underbelly of the kind you'd see at Zuppardi's in West Haven, Connecticut. That sturdiness is a structural requirement for both their voluminous fresh sausage and mozzarella pie, and for their best-in-class clam pie, which features clams shucked fresh to order directly over your pizza so that every drop of delicious clam liquor seeps into the dough as it bakes.

Like any good pizza dough, this one requires a little planning. You'll need to make it at least 24 hours in advance for a chance at decent flavor through slow fermentation. A solid 48 to 72 hours is even better. After that it'll start to degrade. If you don't have a food processor or stand mixer, you can make it using the no-knead method: Simply combine the dough ingredients as directed in a regular bowl using your hands. Once the dough comes together in a shaggy ball and no lumps or pockets of dry flour remain, place the dough ball back in the bowl and cover it tightly with plastic wrap. Let it rest at room temperature for 12 to 18 hours. Form the dough into a ball, and refrigerate it for up to 3 more days before proceeding as directed in step 3.

This recipe calls for a few pieces of special equipment. It lists only mass measurements, as mass is the only way to accurately measure dry, powdered ingredients for baking. A decent digital gram scale is essential for any baking project. You'll also need either a baking steel or a baking stone to place in your oven. An oyster knife or a clam knife will make shucking a few dozen clams easier and safer than using a butter knife. (Make sure to grasp the clams with a folded kitchen towel to protect your hands either way!) A single metal pizza peel will work, but having a separate wooden pizza peel specifically for constructing and launching pies makes the job much easier as dough doesn't stick to wood nearly as much as it does to metal.

Finally, this recipe calls for an oven with a built-in broiler element at the top. If you have an under-the-oven style broiler, you'll need to separate the baking and broiling steps into two phases. First, bake the pizza on the stone in the oven until the base is crisp and lightly charred. Transfer the pizza to a broiler pan and place it 3 to 4 inches under the broiler, rotating it occasionally until the top of the pizza is browned and charred in spots.

TOTAL TIME: At least 2 days and up to 4

ACTIVE TIME: 1 hour

YIELD: Two 15-inch pizzas, or three 12-inch pizzas, serving 3 to 4

For the Dough:

200 grams water

3 grams instant yeast

10 grams olive oil

335 grams bread flour

7 grams salt

For the Toppings:

36 live littleneck
clams

6 tablespoons extra-
virgin olive oil

6 garlic cloves, finely
chopped

1 tablespoon dried
oregano

6 tablespoons finely
grated Pecorino
Romano

Kosher salt

Red pepper flakes
(optional)

Handful chopped
fresh parsley

Lemon wedges

1. To make the dough, whisk together the water, yeast, and olive oil in the bowl of a stand mixer fitted with a dough hook attachment, or a food processor. Let rest for 2 minutes. Add the flour and salt. If using a mixer, mix on low speed for 7 minutes (dough should clear the sides of the bowl and just stick to the bottom). If using a food processor, process until the dough ball starts riding around the blade, then continue processing for 30 seconds.

2. Transfer the dough to a lightly oiled container at least twice its volume. Cover and refrigerate for at least 24 and up to 36 hours, folding the dough back onto itself a few times per day.

3. Three hours before you are ready to bake, remove the dough from the refrigerator and divide into two even balls for two 15-inch pizzas, or into three even balls for three 12-inch pizzas. Store each ball in a lightly oiled sealed container at least twice the volume of the ball. Let rest at room temperature for 2 to 2½ hours.

4. Meanwhile, place a baking steel or baking stone on a rack in your oven 4 inches below the broiler element. Preheat the oven and the stone to 550°F (or as high as your oven will go) for at least 1 hour before baking.

5. To top and bake, shuck the clams, reserving the clams and juices together in a small bowl. In a separate bowl whisk together the olive oil, garlic, and dried oregano.

6. Flour one dough ball and turn out onto a lightly floured surface. If using two dough balls, stretch each into a rough circle about 15 inches wide (for three balls, stretch each into a circle 12 inches wide), forming a rough edge by pinching up the border. Transfer the dough to a lightly floured pizza peel.

7. Working quickly and shaking the pizza peel occasionally to ensure the pizza is not sticking, brush the dough with a little of the olive oil and garlic mixture, leaving the outer ¾ inch of crust bare. If making two pizzas, top with half the toppings. If making three pizzas, use a third of the toppings. Start with the shucked clams and drizzle with some of the extra juices in the bowl. Drizzle the clams with additional garlic oil. Top with Pecorino Romano, a pinch of salt, and a pinch of red pepper flakes (if desired).

Recipe continued . . .

8. Transfer the pizza to the preheated pizza steel or stone by gently shaking the back lip onto the stone, then rapidly pulling back on the peel while shaking back and forth. Switch on the broiler and bake for 1 minute. Using a thin metal pizza peel, retrieve the pizza, rotate it, and return it to the broiler. Continue baking for an additional minute. Check its progress and continue baking, rotating as necessary until the pizza crust is crispy underneath and deep brown with lightly blackened edges on top. Transfer the pizza to a cutting board.

9. Sprinkle the pizza with chopped parsley, cut into slices, and serve with lemon wedges.

10. Repeat steps 6 through 9 for remaining dough balls.

Chapter 10

TEAM SERIOUS EATS

t came to me last night. This is what we should do: hire a photographer to take pictures of the storefront of every food establishment in New York. Even every McDonald's, because not all McDonald's are created equal." My newly appointed nineteen-year-old chief technology officer, David Karp, was once again schooling me at two o'clock in the afternoon (David's morning) in the ways of digital media. David poured forth ideas like a waitress dispensing coffee at a diner. He was on a roll: "That will give us the metadata we need to cover the entire city."

"What the hell is metadata?" I asked incredulously. "It's data about other data," he replied, as if everyone else in the world knew what metadata was except me. He paused, not to take my order but to let his words sink in, before continuing. "Whenever you write about a place, we will have the metadata we need for the post: a photo, a time stamp, a location. We can use it in the tags." "What the hell are tags?" I asked. David smiled and replied, "Tags indicate what should be displayed on the screen when the page loads. They are the basic formatting tool used in HTML." What the hell is HTML? "Hypertext markup language. You'll use it to format each post." I was looking for the perfect bite, and David was looking for the perfect byte.

Three days after my meeting with Mike at his house, I was back in my office. It was one of those rare, glorious summer days in New York that doesn't require air-conditioning or an oxygen tank to breathe on the city's sticky, airless subway platforms.

My euphoria had been short-lived. It had given way to panic and anxiety. Now I had to turn the "It's going to be great" rap into reality. Armed with Mike's money, I knew it *was* time to make my move. The first order of business? Marshal my forces, namely David, Steve, and Bill.

For the most part, David and I got along well. Was David full of himself and a know-it-all? Damn right he was, but he knew a helluva lot about all kinds of stuff I didn't. And he *was* juiced by my enthusiasm. So I was thrilled to have a CTO, even if I didn't have the money to pay him a salary until launch. Didn't matter. I was putting together my team, and David was my first draft pick.

Steve and I had a complicated relationship during the almost five years in the late eighties and early nineties that I worked for him at his ad agency. I learned a tremendous amount from him. He was my work Mike, a substitute dad schooling me for my own good. There were some good times and accompanying good feelings sprinkled in those five years. Our thinking and strategizing had helped create billions of dollars of market value for MTV Networks.

There were also a lot of dark moments. I knew Steve and his partner, Bart (not his real name), could feed my ego one day and starve it two days later. It was steak on Tuesday and bread and water on Thursday. The day after Will was born in 1987, I actually went back to work (Vicky was not exactly thrilled with that decision), only to be greeted by a torrent of criticism from Bart. "I don't give a shit what's happening in your life. You screwed up a media buy. Now fix it!"

When I finally left my job in 1991, right before *New York Eats* was published in 1992, it was an acrimonious exit. Steve was setting me up for a fall because the company was failing. I was the designated scapegoat. Beating him to the punch, before he fired me, I told Steve I was leaving and that if I didn't get a fair severance package, all accounts at the agency were in play. Two days later Steve presented a reasonable offer that I quickly accepted. It was most assuredly not a graceful exit.

But the bad feelings dissipated in the ensuing years. Steve even referred me to my first big independent consulting client.

And of course Steve was the person who sat me down in his office chair
and helped me set up *Ed Levine Eats* after the Gusto debacle. He even lent
me $25,000 to get Serious Eats going months before Mike invested.

But in this instance Steve was always going to be the demanding dad
and I was always going to be the desperately-trying-to-please son. Steve
would giveth in the good times, and Steve would taketh away in the bad. Yet
somehow I always managed to convince myself that he was like a strict,
hypercritical father who was, in the end, looking out for me and my best
interests.

I was living out George Santayana's famous pronouncement, "Those
who cannot remember the past are condemned to repeat it." So when Steve
said he was in, I ignored the flashing hazard lights. "We are going to kick
some serious ass this time," I said, high-fiving him as if my life depended on
it. My life did, but his didn't.

I had no history with Bill, but Steve offered him up to me as a package
deal. I mistakenly thought that with his business bona fides Bill would
bond with Mike. "This sounds cool," Bill said. "I'll help you write the business plan and raise the money. It shouldn't be hard to raise the money.
There's plenty of capital out there sitting on the sidelines looking for a
home."

Bill did say one thing that turned out to be prescient: "It may take you
a while to get to launch, but once you do, everything starts coming at you
like a freight train. Decisions have to be made at warp speed, and you don't
have the time to ruminate. These businesses change at the speed of light."

Bill also issued another warning that turned out to be true. "People like
you who start passion-based businesses do so because they want to spend
90 percent of their time doing the stuff they love to do and 10 percent of
their time doing other stuff. The sad truth is that when you are running
your business those percentages are in fact reversed."

But after a very short honeymoon period, Bill turned into the team-
mate from hell. In fact, he and Steve would often join forces and attack me,

just to make themselves feel superior. Over a phenomenal beef rib lunch at Blue Smoke they told me, "You really don't know how to lead, Ed. Which is a major problem for us and everybody else on the team. People are going to start bailing on you right and left if you don't get it together. We're telling you this for your own good."

In one sense they were right. I wasn't projecting the strength and confidence a founder should, like, say, my teenage CTO, David Karp, did. That's because deep down I was scared shitless. To make matters worse, I have always had the world's worst poker face. You really need a Mount Rushmore–like poker face in startup-ville.

On the other hand, I was never going to be a top-down boss. My strongest management skills were people skills. I considered myself an astute judge of character and talent. I've always been able to excite any group I'm working or playing with through my enthusiasm and passion. That's my jam. Yet I abandoned those instincts with Bill and Steve, because I had no other alternative at the time and because I *needed* them to like me.

Bill was smart enough, but he wasn't passionate about food, and he most assuredly did not share my values. Somehow I overlooked all those things at that moment. I thought I could live with Bill's shortcomings if he helped me get Mike and other potential investors on board. Every fiber of my being should have told me otherwise, but my neediness trumped everything else. Whatever the holes in your emotional and psychological game are, they will be exposed over and over again when you build a startup.

I considered chucking Bill from the team just about every week, but I didn't have the cojones to do so (see above). Plus, he spoke startup-ese much more fluently than I did, which really came in handy in potential investor meetings. Phrases like "discounted cash flow" and "run rate" practically danced off Bill's tongue. And Bill was going to help me raise money, if for no other reason than that he wanted to get paid.

Surely, I thought, Mike would be impressed by Bill's skills and business fluency. But it turned out he wasn't. I mean, he *really* wasn't. Once Bill dialed into a conference call we were having at the Serious Eats offices with

Mike in attendance. Bill launched into an elaborate explanation of our expansion and funding strategies and timing.

I could tell right away that Mike wasn't feeling it at all. He was glaring into the phone. His legs were flapping like a bird's wings, which I knew was a sign that he was waiting to pounce. Finally he screamed, "Are you finished yet?" Bill stopped talking, and I stopped listening. But he remained on the team for the time being.

I should have realized that I hadn't assembled the right team for Serious Eats. The ultimate tell should have been that my three partners really didn't care that much about food. How did I overlook that? For years, no matter what restaurant Steve and I went to, he ordered the most simply prepared chicken on the menu for lunch and an unbuttered English muffin and a plain yogurt for breakfast. His standard request to any server: "Could you put the sauce on the side?" That's an indictable offense as far as I'm concerned. I regarded every restaurant meal as both R&D and pure pleasure. Steve regarded lunch as fuel. David and Bill liked to eat (who doesn't?), but food was most assuredly not their passion.

Despite my serious, continued misgivings, I had made a deal with all of them to come on board the Serious Eats train as consultants and equity stakeholders. The consulting fees would be paid when I raised a million bucks (my brother's $500,000 plus another $500,000 from potential investors that I had already been pitching). I thought that sum would get me through the first seven months, which is when I naively thought I would break even. Their equity would vest at the same time.

We started meeting almost every day. Bill would blather on about how many cities we should be in within three years. I thought we should start by getting one city, New York, right. Outwardly I was all smiles. Inside my eyes were rolling like a 45 rpm single.

David, being the youngest and, ironically for nineteen, the most experienced, had the most ideas. Like a young trumpeter soloing at a jam session, he felt the need to show us how much he knew every time he expressed himself. The least malevolent character of the bunch, he wanted a lot of the Serious Eats content to be user generated. He was building Serious Eats' content management system to make it easy for users to post a photo, text, illustrations, and ultimately even video à la YouTube. He called it tumble-blogging. Serious Eats was going to be the first blog with tumble-blogging as its chief organizing principle, though eventually David's plan was to license his tumble-blogging software to other noncompetitive blogs. I was willing to allow users to tumble-blog post some of their own content, but my vision for the site was that experts would host each "channel" and create much of the content.

Meanwhile I was out trying to raise more capital. I needed more than Mike's money to launch. Bill arranged a meeting with Spark Capital, a very successful Boston-based VC firm that had been an early investor in Twitter, Warby Parker, and Foursquare. Bill knew one of the partners. If Spark invested, my faith in Bill would be restored. I stayed up two nights writing and rewriting the Serious Eats pitch. We flew up to Boston and took a cab to Spark's spare but casually elegant offices in Back Bay.

Our cab passed by the distinctive Santarpio's Pizza sign right outside Boston's Logan Airport. Excitedly I told the team, "Let's get some pizza at Santarpio's. We should also get some of the sausages they cook over an open fire in the restaurant. We could be in and out of there in twenty minutes." David, Steve, and Bill were not at all interested in that kind of pit stop. Patting me on the head like a puppy, Bill said, "We don't have time. We have business to attend to. Maybe we can stop on our way home." *Yeah*, I thought to myself. *Eating pizza is in fact my business, but clearly not theirs.* Another warning sign I missed. The Spark offices reeked of arrogance and money and faux casualness. I didn't realize then that almost all VC offices do. Why? Because VCs have what all startups require, capital, lots of capital. They have all the leverage, unless you happen to be a Silicon Valley darling headed up by someone who had previously made a lot of money for VCs. We gave what I thought was a compelling pitch:

> Serious Eats is the first digital network for eaters, connecting food
> lovers to each other and to leading food experts. The company's
> strategy is built around five pillars: original and unique content

(static and video); community focus on connecting and empowering
food lovers; "save time" search tools; an eating blog ad network;
and a proprietary platform based on open standards that focuses
on ease of use, content portability, and community participation.

It was a veritable kitchen sink of ideas. It was absolute folly to think
that we could build a proprietary search tool and do everything else in that
paragraph for a million dollars. But the combination of my passion and belief and focus and everyone else's desire to get paid allowed all of us to drink
the same Kool-Aid and get drunk off it.

The Spark guys asked a lot of questions, some obvious to me and some
not. They of course asked the question that every VC I have ever spoken to
asked (they all practically stage-whispered in unison): "How could Serious
Eats scale or grow in such a way that we could get a minimum of between
five and ten times our investment back in three years?"

VCs are not interested in singles or doubles. They want to invest in
home runs. Grand-slam home runs, in fact. I may not have understood their
MO, but I knew my way around baseball metaphors. We knew that they
were going to ask it, and I thought we had a good answer for them, a slide
that showed Serious Eats becoming the go-to food-review website in the
twenty-five largest cities in the world. Yup, Serious Eats was going to go na-
tionwide and worldwide. A lovely fantasy, for sure.

Their ears really pricked up when we got to the financial projections
slide: Year one net profit, $1.1 million. Year two net profit, $10.7 million.
Year three net profit, $38.6 million. And we put forward these numbers
with a straight face. Those numbers were beyond a shot in the dark, and way
beyond "aggressive but plausible," which is what Mike had told me that
numbers in a business plan had to be. They were fiction, numbers you had
to put in when you were seeing VCs. Of course they were absurd, but we had
convinced ourselves otherwise. My partners knew how VCs think. They
need these kinds of silly numbers to justify investing their investors'
money. And maybe they're not actually silly, because there are a lot of very
rich and successful venture capitalists out in the world.

But here was the real problem with those kinds of numbers. You needed them in Startup-ville because you wouldn't get the money otherwise. But on some level I knew that I was really trying to raise money for a small business so that I could pursue the things I loved and get paid for them. You can't raise money from VCs or even friends and family for a small business trying to do "one small thing right" (as Chris Bianco described his pizza making) that gives its founder his dream job. It would be like raising money for a dry-cleaning store from venture capitalists. They would turn you down cold unless you presented them with a disruptive proposition or idea that every dry cleaner in the country would have to use. That's what they call scale. In retrospect, perhaps I shouldn't have even tried to scale Serious Eats with VC money—or any institutional money for that matter. Perhaps the more prudent and less problematic way to go about building my business would have been to scale organically using minimal outside investment. But I was too old to do that, because scaling organically and sustaining that growth takes years. It also takes more money than I personally had. Also, I didn't have the technology chops to be a one-man shop, so I needed a staff. And staff costs money. Plus, I had caught the startup bug that was going around at the time, and conventional wisdom dictated going after VC money. In the end, I turned out to need every hard-fought cent I found.

We left after three hours with a promise from the Spark guys that they would get back to us quickly, that they were not like all the other VCs out there, who string people along endlessly because they fear saying no only to find a rival successfully investing in that same business. I didn't know at the time that every VC tells you the same thing: that they are not like all the other VCs, that they're there only to offer expertise and guidance.

On the plane home I was feeling pretty confident about the Spark pitch, and so was everybody else on the team. I bought a round of drinks for everyone at the airport to celebrate, though we didn't stop at Santarpio's. "Not enough time," Bill told me. We drank to Serious Eats' success. Not so fast, as it turned out.

A few days later Bill wandered over to my desk and said matter-of-factly,

"I just got off the phone with the Spark guys. They're not going to invest in Serious Eats right now. They love you, they love your passion, they love the team you've put together, but they're not convinced that Serious Eats can scale."

"Well... well... what else did they say?" I asked, unsuccessfully trying to hide my craven disappointment. "Not much. At the end of the call the Spark guy said, 'Good luck. Keep in touch.' And to let them know what happens." I hate that kiss-off line. It is the height of disingenuousness. I have heard it a hundred times in creative and business pitches of all kinds. The person who says it doesn't really mean it, and even if they do, why the hell would I let them know what happens?

Then, a couple of weeks later, Spark called Bill back with the news that they would invest $8 million dollars—in Next New Networks.

Unbeknownst to me, my three partners had hatched an idea for another startup that had nothing to do with Serious Eats. They were calling it Next New Networks (NNN), a group of a hundred micro–television networks that would serve audiences like car enthusiasts and comic book fans. Not only that, but they had already had plans to pitch Spark this new idea when we were in Boston to pitch Serious Eats.

I was beyond furious. I railed at Steve and Bill. "How could you guys do that? You went to Boston to see Spark again behind my back? To pitch them another business? You're my partners. Partners don't treat one another that way."

I might as well have substituted "family" for "partners." Almost in unison Steve and Bill said, "Don't worry. Serious Eats could very well be one of the micro–television networks we're going to build. And if SE does become part of NNN, we will invest in it. Don't worry so much. You're paranoid."

I was justifiably paranoid, as it turned out. Just about everything Steve and Bill said turned out to be a lie, as I was slowly starting to realize. And yet I still couldn't cut them loose. I didn't have other options. If I got rid of them, I thought I'd be back at square one.

A week later Bill wandered over to my desk. "We're going to need the space you're sitting in for some of the new company's hires. Don't worry, though. There's a spot for you on the floor below us. No window, but it's still nice enough."

Not only had my team deserted me, but they were also succeeding at the very things I was trying to do. And let's face it: Like Spark Capital, David, Bill, and Steve hadn't done anything inherently evil. They were merely making business decisions. It was just business the way most define it. Here's the problem: For me Serious Eats wasn't just a business. It was a crusade that defined who I was.

So why did I keep the original team intact long after I recognized their unsuitability as partners? After all, I knew deep down that Bill was 95 percent bad news and Steve was a mixed bag at best. My strengths, my abilities to judge character and spot talent who shared my values, were overwhelmed by my compulsion to be liked at any cost. I thought that if I listened to everything David, Steve, and Bill said, they would like me more. If they liked me more, they would jump in my foxhole and never leave. They would take care of me. Most important, they would have my best interests at heart.

I was crushed. I was starting to lose hope. I didn't know where else to turn, or who else to turn to. I was going to flush a half a million dollars of my brother's hard-earned money down the drain. Maybe Serious Eats was just not meant to be.

I took a ferry to meet Vicky, who had gone up to see her ailing mother on Martha's Vineyard. As soon as she saw me trudging off the boat, Vicky knew that all was not well with me and Serious Eats. I angrily explained, "They screwed me, they totally screwed me. They got some Spark money for another new company they're starting. I got nothing. And they moved me out of my office." Vicky listened intently (as she always did) and said, "The hell with those guys. You don't need them. Serious Eats is a great idea. It's what you were put on this earth to do. Do not give up now."

Vicky was right. She and Mike were the first two members of the real Serious Eats tribe—the honest and true Serious Eats tribe. But I needed other tribespeople to actually get the site up and running. And at that moment I didn't know where to look.

Chapter 11

TRIBE SERIOUS EATS

M eg practically invented blogging," explained yet another Next New Network partner Tim Shey. There were a lot of partners at NNN, including my old friend Hamish from my Gusto days, but I sure wasn't one of them. I hadn't interacted much with Tim, but it was clear that he was one of those people who knew everybody in the digital world worth knowing. Tim had already built and sold a gaming startup while he was an undergraduate at George Washington University in DC.

It was a few days after the Spark debacle. We were in the corner office that I had been enjoying since the Gusto debacle but would soon be moved out of. I was still speaking to Steve and Bill, mostly because I had to. I hadn't formulated a plan B yet. Tim was suggesting that I have lunch with Meg Hourihan. He wasn't speaking hyperbolically about Meg. Meg and her then–business partner Evan Williams (who would go on to found Twitter and Medium) had developed Blogger, the first widely used blogging software, at their startup Pyra Labs.

After a rocky ride that included running out of money and Evan sleeping in their offices, they sold Blogger to Google in 2003—Google's very first acquisition. But Meg had to threaten to sue Williams for her share of the sale proceeds. After the sale, which made both of them independently wealthy before they were thirty-five, Meg's personal blog, *Megnut*, morphed into a food blog.

Of course I wanted to meet her. Meg was one of blogging's original gangsters. We met for lunch at Chinese Mirch, the unfortunately now-shuttered Indo-Chinese restaurant in Manhattan's Little India neighborhood, conveniently located a stone's throw from our office. Mirch's fried okra was a work of culinary genius.

Five minutes into the lunch I knew I had to have Meg join the Serious Eats tribe. Hell, I'd let her be the chief, at least temporarily. Meg was extremely passionate about food, wicked smart, insanely tech savvy, and tough minded in the extreme. Way tougher than me, in fact. Meg could stand up to Bill *and* go toe to toe with David. Meg would not be bullied by anybody. Plus, she had already forgotten more about blogging than Steve and Bill would ever know.

I gave her the Serious Eats elevator pitch. "I want to build an online clubhouse for food lovers, a place they can come to find out where to eat, what to eat, what to cook, be entertained and informed, or just chew the fat with fellow serious eaters. 'Passionate, discerning, inclusive' is the Serious Eats mantra."

I went on: "Come on board as our temporary CEO and consultant. You'll help us launch and *Megnut* can become part of the Serious Eats food blog network. We will sell the advertising inventory on your site." I knew Meg wasn't looking for a permanent full-time job, because she didn't need one. Meg was clearly intrigued, but she wasn't willing to commit on the spot. A few days later she emailed me, "I'm in."

I offered her a monthly retainer that I would begin paying her when my "raise" was completed. She demurred. "If you're paying yourself a salary now, I need to get paid as well." Like I said, Meg was one tough-minded pragmatist.

The great thing about Meg is that once she committed to this arrangement, she was all in. She jumped into the foxhole with both feet because she wanted to, not because she had to.

Hell, at that point she could have funded Serious Eats herself if she chose. I asked her to invest, but she ever-so-politely declined. Meg may have been passionate about food, but she had also seen firsthand just how difficult it is to make a startup work. She had said to me at the outset that she would stay long enough to get Serious Eats on firm footing. That footing would include finding a digitally savvy general manager, who would free me from the financial oversight duties I detested and also function as our product manager.

Meg started to come to all the Serious Eats jam sessions at Park Avenue South—which I, unbelievably, had not closed to Steve and Bill. I just couldn't cut them loose yet. Her blogging and startup chops were immediately apparent to one and all. The resulting clashes were epic, immediate, and not pretty. "These people are so arrogant," she said, referring to the triumvirate of David, Steve, and Bill. *Damn*, she was right. Meg recognized David's indisputable talents as a coder, but she was perplexed by my decision to use a version of David's tumble-blogging as Serious Eats' proprietary content management system (CMS).

Meg was skeptical about David's ability to finish building the platform in a timely fashion. Her skepticism was based on her own experience with Kinja, a proprietary CMS she had been developing with Gawker founder Nick Denton since 2003. Meg was long gone by the time Denton finally rolled out Kinja in 2013. He had poured millions of dollars into the project. So when David kept blowing deadlines, Meg was convinced she had seen this movie before. She was getting more and more annoyed, and she didn't hide her annoyance very well.

Meg and David both had the best of intentions (David was not to blame for the NNN double cross, which had been orchestrated solely by Steve and Bill), but their MOs were completely different. Meg is scarily intense and coiled like a spring. David is seemingly much more laid-back but in the end just as stubborn as Meg. I began to worry about the combustibility of my team.

Having Meg aboard made me realize that I needed more people like her. Meg lived and loved to eat, and then blog about it. Finally, she was very comfortable speaking truth to power, namely the NNN crew. A jazz musician acknowledges another player's prowess with the simple declarative sentence "She (or he) can play." Well, Meg could play, and I needed more bloggers who could play, loved food, shared my values, and could school me about life on the internet. At that moment I realized that I didn't just need a team. I needed a tribe that would blog more and bloviate less.

I had met Adam Kuban, an enigmatic and idiosyncratic pizza lover, in the spring of 2004. I walked into one of my favorite pizzerias in New York City—and the world, for that matter—Totonno's in Coney Island. Totonno's is as plainly and haphazardly decorated as a restaurant (I'm not sure it even qualifies as a restaurant) could be. On its wall you find some old photos of the Brooklyn Dodgers (Totonno's opened in 1928 in Brooklyn); some random photos of the original pie man and owner, Anthony Pero ("Totonno" to his friends); and a bunch of yellowed press clippings, including some written by me.

What about the pizza at Totonno's? It's heavenly. The crust still comes out charred and blistered, with an outer layer of crispness that gives way to tender insides. A Totonno's pizza really does melt in your mouth. If you've never been there and you love pizza, please make your way there ASAP. Start with the white pie, made with fresh mozzarella from the hood, ricotta, grated Romano cheese, and fresh garlic. It is a minimalist masterpiece.

As the founder of the great pizza blog *Slice* (which I had not even discovered yet), Adam was leading a pizza tour of New York that, of course, included Totonno's. When he saw me his bearded face lit up (Adam has one of the all-time great wry smiles). I heard him say sotto voce to his friends, "I can't believe Ed Levine just walked in here." To Adam and his friends, the author of *Pizza: A Slice of Heaven* was a celebrity. Of course, they were probably the only people in the world who regarded me as such.

We sat down and bonded over the two signature pies, the white and the sausage and mushroom (please don't ask for extra cheese on either), and they peppered me with questions about pizza, in New York and elsewhere. I found out that Adam had a day job as the head copy editor at *Martha Stewart Living*. A computer and pizza nerd, he had started his blog as a way to scratch both itches.

It was immediately apparent to me that Adam was extremely smart, a passionate obsessive, and a perfectionist (hence his copyediting gig). We talked about pizza for an hour before Totonno's famously idiosyncratic and sharp-tongued co-owner Louise Ciminieri, aka "Cookie," intervened. There were people waiting for our table. Adam and his crew proceeded on their pizza tour, and we agreed to stay in touch.

I went home that day and started reading *Slice* and Adam's burger blog, *A Hamburger Today* (*AHT*). He wrote enthusiastically and discerningly about pizza and burgers without taking himself or his subject too seriously. His midwestern mannerisms ("Sweet Jesus!" is one of his favorite exclamations) and blessedly square values were on full display in every post he wrote.

I asked Meg about Adam. She nodded affirmatively. "He's pretty chill, and we could use some chill folks at Serious Eats. Too many type A folks in a startup and you're asking for trouble. And I've been reading his stuff for a while. Adam really gets blogging. He can code *and* write." That was the clincher for me.

I arranged to have dinner with Adam at, where else, Celeste, a pizzeria. I got right to the point. "Adam, I raised the money for Serious Eats. Meg Hourihan has agreed to work with me. I want you to come on board as our managing editor. It's gonna be great. And I want to buy *Slice* and *A Hamburger Today.*"

Adam appeared dazed. I think he couldn't quite believe what he was hearing. I was offering him cold, hard cash for his two hobby blogs and a chance to do what he loved for a living. Adam decided to play hard to get. "You really raised the money? I don't know that you can afford *Slice* and *AHT*. They're worth a lot of money. People are saying that each of my blogs is worth $200K."

Actually nobody, not him, not me, knew how much his two blogs were worth. We were both panning for gold in the Wild West days of the blogosphere. A week later we had a deal. I paid him $25,000 each for *Slice* and *AHT*. We were both happy with the outcome. And as it turned out, Adam's two single-subject food blogs were the only ones ever sold. His hobby blogs turned into $50,000 and a great job.

I was becoming Mr. Big Shot. Or actually, the only guy offering to pay cash for single-subject food blogs. Not that I wouldn't do it all over again if I had to. I wanted and needed Adam's undivided attention if I was going to make a go of it with Serious Eats. He knew way more about blogging and the internet than I did, and I probably knew a little more about pizza than he did, at least at the time. Fifty thousand dollars seemed like a small price to pay for Adam's brain, experience, and traffic.

The good Serious Eats tribe, the right Serious Eats tribe, was starting to come together. I realized at that moment that I have always had a knack for spotting talent. I had done it in music, I had done it with chefs, bakers, and purveyors, and now I was doing it with bloggers and technologists. *I got this*, I thought to myself.

Meanwhile things in general were progressing in unexpected ways. One hot August day in 2006, my phone rang. "Is this the Ed Levine who wrote *New York Eats* and who writes for the *Times*?" "Yes," I said. The voice on the other end of the phone went on, "We're from Digitas, American Express's ad agency. We are building a website for Amex cardholders, and we're shooting videos of well-known people in the food world giving cardholders restaurant tips. We'd like to come film you in your office talking about your favorite restaurants." I agreed to this immediately. It was free publicity and I could use the video clip for my reel.

When they came, there must have been ten people. It was a pre–social media video production. Nowadays a savvy ad agency would hire a two-person crew, or maybe a single person who could shoot, write, and edit—"preditors" (short for producer-editors), they're called, in part because they are preying on the entire population of video production professionals.

They taped me blabbing about my favorite places to eat in New York. "Seriously," I said as I looked into the camera. "You have to have the tuna sandwich at Eisenberg's and the burger at Peter Luger's and the spare ribs at Big Wong." I don't think these were the kind of restaurants they had in mind, and a couple of places I recommended didn't take American Express. My bad. Eventually we worked it out.

While they were in our offices I mentioned to them that I had a blog,

Ed Levine Eats, that was going to morph into Serious Eats in November. Serious Eats, I explained, would combine *ELE*, *Slice*, *A Hamburger Today*, *Megnut*, and one other terrific food blog, Adam Roberts's very funny *The Amateur Gourmet* (he's now a television comedy writer), into a single ad-supported network. (I had met Adam at a food bloggers meet-up and we had hit it off.) I suggested that Amex advertising could appear on all of the blogs in the network when we launched Serious Eats. The Digitas folks shockingly responded, "This is interesting. Blogs are something we're just beginning to look at for our clients."

Two days later they called: "We'd like to be Serious Eats' advertising launch partner. We have budgeted $15K for this."

I was in shock. Could the digital advertising game be this easy? Some guys come to your office and ask you to expound on the foods you love, and a month later one of the country's largest advertisers comes aboard as your launch sponsor? Maybe so, maybe so.

We had a hard launch date, December 5, 2006, because of the Amex advertising commitment. So we had twelve weeks to get Serious Eats built and launched. I was desperately trying to stay positive, but it was becoming increasingly difficult to do so. Many all-night jam sessions fueled by Diet Coke ensued. Our progress was halting at best. Finally my anxiety overflowed. "This is my one shot at this," I practically screamed at Meg. "I can't blow it. The content is there, but without a functioning CMS and a finished design and user interface, we are fucked." Meg tried to assuage my fears. "I have seen this movie before. We will get it together. Don't worry."

While Meg was dealing with getting Serious Eats up and running, I was in a full-on sprint to raise the additional funding I knew we would need. Mike had supplied the family side of the friends-and-family funding. The friends side was next. I made a list of the friends who I thought had the wherewithal to invest in such an obviously speculative venture.

One person topped the list. Marc Lasry, a billionaire hedge fund co-founder, had spent twenty years climbing over my back for offensive rebounds in a weekend basketball run at Riverside Park.

I didn't know all that much about his business, but I knew that he had made enough money to live in a house that Michael Jackson had once lived in. The game had fallen apart as we all aged out of it, and I hadn't spoken to Marc in a couple of years, but I felt the bond we had established on the court was strong enough for me to at least get him to meet. He immediately accepted my email invitation for lunch.

Marc was the most down-to-earth billionaire I knew. Actually, he was the only billionaire I knew. We met for lunch in a Greek coffee shop near his house, Soup Burg, where the modest-sized burgers are excellent, especially in comparison with the watery namesake soup. I told Marc about Serious Eats. To my surprise and delight, I got more than advice: "Look, I don't know anything about the food business and, as you know, I don't give a shit about food. But I do know in what esteem you are held in your world"—I had gotten him a table at Per Se once, when he wanted to impress a client—"so I'm going to invest $100K."

As I was putting the last bite of burger in my mouth, Marc said, "So send me the paperwork." As he got up from the counter to leave, he said ever so casually over his shoulder, "And I think I know a couple of other people, way more into food than I am, who might be interested in investing. Give me a couple of days to reach out to them." I couldn't believe what I was hearing. All it took to get $100,000 for Serious Eats was one well-done hamburger at Soup Burg. I left a ten-dollar tip on a fifteen-dollar check.

Two weeks later, I was walking down a quiet Greenwich Village street after finishing off two exemplary slices of New York pizza at Joe's. A plain ol' Joe's slice (not the undersalted fresh-mozzarella version) has a crispy thin crust that bends without breaking, topped with a judicious amount of aged mozzarella and a sauce of pureed canned tomatoes. A Joe's slice was then and still is the quintessential old-school New York slice. I turned a corner and there were Marc and his wife, Cathy, leaving a restaurant with another couple.

Marc saw me and waved me over. He introduced us. "Ed Levine, this is Steve Trost and Beryl Snyder. Steve is one of the guys I was telling you about at Soup Burg." Steve and I started talking about New York bagels, which I had written about for the *Times* three years prior. Apparently Steve was intimately acquainted with my writing. "I think you got it wrong. H&H Bagels are the best bagels in New York." I merely smiled in response, thinking that arguing about bagels was not the best way to secure Steve's money. He was clearly delighted to be talking to me. "I can't believe I am standing on a New York City street talking about bagels with *the* Ed Levine." To Steve Trost I was a celebrity, a celebrity with a business that needed funding.

I didn't know how to broach the subject, but Marc saved the day with an elegant segue. Casually, he told me, "I was just talking about Serious Eats over dinner." Steve Trost was clearly thrilled to talk shop with me; we made a lunch date that night on the street. Two weeks later he sent me a check for $100,000. Friends-and-family funding had become friends-and-friends-of-friends-and-family funding.

The notes Marc and Steve signed were convertible promissory notes with a November 30, 2007, due date. That meant that either or both of them could demand that their loans be repaid on that date if I hadn't raised a million dollars of equity financing for Serious Eats. Otherwise their loans would be converted into equity. I naively thought that would be no problem in 2006, when the world was supposedly awash with available investment money for internet startups.

Meanwhile, back at Serious Eats World HQ, as I'd ironically taken to calling our little office, we were trying to get Serious Eats up and running. The following week, over a lunch of lamb sandwiches and chef Floyd Cardoz's addictive Indian-spiced onion rings (God, those onion rings were good) at the now-defunct Tabla Bread Bar (thankfully you can get them at Cardoz's new restaurant Bombay Bread Bar), even Meg started freaking out. "We can't keep waiting for David. We are now less than three months out and we still don't have a CMS for Serious Eats. That's fucking ridiculous and unacceptable." We had both reached our breaking points. It was obviously time for plan B, which unfortunately didn't exist yet. We weren't sure what to do.

Then, in early October, I went to a party at Meg's house. Meg's husband, Jason Kottke, was another member of the Web 2.0 digerati. His "liberal arts" blog, Kottke.org, was and still is necessary reading. Every day he would search the web looking for interesting stories that he would succinctly comment on and link to. But unlike the *Huffington Post*, Jason made pithy, brief observations about the stories he was linking to. He was not aggregating solely for business purposes.

Meg and Jason were blogging's "it" couple. Their courtship via blog posts had even been chronicled in the *New Yorker* twice, first in 2000 and again in 2006, right before the party.

I went without high expectations for the evening. I thought I was going to be a fish out of water, a food writer surrounded by tech nerds. I couldn't have been more wrong. The geek soiree turned out to be life-changing. It was the equivalent of a Davos blogging confab. Jason and Meg knew everyone in the Web 2.0 world. Gawker founder Nick Denton was there. Future Foursquare founder Dennis Crowley was there. Humanist technology visionary Anil Dash (now the CEO of Glitch) was there. Jonah Peretti, a cofounder of the *Huffington Post* and later *Buzzfeed*, was in the house.

The party was filled with great cheeses, each clearly marked with a tiny identifying flag (computer geeks are precise), and lots of Web 2.0 talk. Everyone I talked to was interested in this cool thing I was trying to do at Serious Eats: bring together some of the most distinctive content creators in the food blogosphere who shared my voice; raise some money; and make it a publishing business built on ad revenues. They were all intrigued, even excited.

Everyone there offered ideas and help. It was the early days of the blogosphere and the Web 2.0 world. Because the idea of blogging as a business was so new, so infinitely expandable, and the air seemed so pregnant with possibility at the time, we were all in it together.

I had inadvertently walked into a room full of true blogging believers. It was like a junkie walking into a party and finding a pound of free cocaine piled up on a table waiting to be snorted. There wasn't a hint of competition or envy in their reactions. Those same conversations even two years later would have been a Darwinian battle.

Meg brought me over to meet Alaina Browne. She was a seminal food blogger (*A Full Belly*) and an early digital businesswoman. As a project manager at the influential digital design firm Mule Design, Alaina was working on *Chowhound*'s redesign. Within five minutes of meeting her I realized Alaina loved food and was crazy smart, down to earth, and digitally savvy. She and her husband, the aforementioned Anil Dash, were living in San Francisco but were thinking about relocating to New York.

Anil at that time was working for Six Apart, a technology company that owned, among other assets, Movable Type, a popular blogging platform/CMS. Meg said, "Alaina, you should come to work at Serious Eats as its GM." Alaina was skeptical. She had been burned by promises of fame and fortune from a couple of internet startups already. "I'll think about it," she said. "You do that," I replied. "Just don't think too long. We're launching in early December."

That was not bravado, merely desperation. When I left Meg and Jason's house I practically skipped home. If my early attempts at blogging felt like I was crossing the digital ocean on a dinghy, all these folks were now equipping me with life preservers, provisions, navigational tools, and an anchor.

After a series of email exchanges, Alaina agreed to be our GM. I was thrilled. She turned out to be unflappable, good with numbers, and always up for a challenge, all crucial character traits for a GM. She was ice to my fire. Most important, Alaina was the kind of person who would just get so much stuff done. And she always did it with a smile. I would share my foxhole with her anytime.

In fact, Meg, Adam, and Alaina were all fearless. And they weren't afraid to challenge either conventional wisdom or me. I had chosen them for the right reasons, not because I was scared.

I wanted to create an environment at Serious Eats built on mutual respect and loyalty to one another. We often jousted about strategies and tactics, but the jousts were all in service of making Serious Eats great, or at least as good as it could be. The very first time Meg, Alaina, Adam, and I got together and started trading fours about the business, I started imagining a Serious Eats without my original team, the digital mercenaries who had stabbed me in the back.

There was one more person at Meg and Jason's party who became an honorary tribesperson. David Jacobs had a web application company called Apperceptive, which would later be acquired by Six Apart. Armed with his computer science degree from Princeton, David and his team were first-rate code writers and problem solvers who could customize the Movable Type CMS to meet the needs of blog owners and digital publishers like me. At the time, he was working on, among other blogs, the *Huffington Post*, which then also ran on Movable Type.

David and I had a long and animated conversation about Keen's farm-house cheddar, one of the cheeses Meg and Jason were serving. *Man*, I thought to myself. *That dude is really into cheese.* My kind of guy. Plus, David seemed to know an awful lot about the technical aspects of blogs.

Worried about our impending launch deadline, Meg suggested we have lunch with David. She was hoping that Apperceptive would have the band-width and the time to develop a customized version of Movable Type for Serious Eats in time for our launch. We gave him the good news and the bad news at lunch. "The good news, David, is you'll get to work on Serious Eats. When you come to our offices, you will find a lot of Keen's cheddar that we will happily share with you. The bad news is that we have two months to get Serious Eats launched." Over yet another burger at Shake Shack, David announced, "I'm in. But you guys have to commit to working with only Apperceptive on Serious Eats, and you have to do so now. And I'm going to hold you to your Keen's cheddar promise." We promised that we would do both, and we did.

But I had another problem. Now I had two developers working on Serious Eats, one more than I needed or could afford to pay even with David's deferred payment agreement. I had to cut David Karp loose. I was running out of time and patience, and his user-generated-content strategy clashed with mine.

David and I parted ways for good on the sidewalk in front of our office building. For this conversation there was no need to take the five-minute walk to Shake Shack. You don't need a conference room perfumed by burgers and fries for an uncomfortable ten-minute chat. "Listen, David," I started haltingly, my voice slightly quivering, "I've been thinking. Tumble-blogging might be right for some blogs, but I really don't think it's right for Serious Eats. I'm going to use some off-the-shelf software with some really cool plug-ins. Plus, I have no idea, and I don't think you do either, of whether your CMS is going to be ready in time for our launch."

David replied matter-of-factly, "I think you're wrong, Ed, but Serious Eats is your company, and if this is what you want to do, you should do it."

I wanted to do the right thing by David, who had worked for hundreds of hours on Serious Eats' behalf before the Spark Capital episode and even after. "I'll pay you for the work you've done when I have completed my raise," I continued. "And maybe we can swap equity in each other's companies. You'll take some shares in Serious Eats and I'll take some shares in Davidville. I do think you're onto something with tumble-blogging. It's just not right for us."

He paused before responding, "That's an interesting idea. Let me think about that." From his tone of voice I wasn't sure just how hard he was going to think about it. We shook hands and gave each other perfunctory man hugs. Unfortunately (for me) the equity-swap deal was never consummated. Davidville and tumble-blogging morphed into Tumblr, which in 2013 was sold to Yahoo! for $1.1 billion. That's "billion" with a *b*. Yup, I left millions of dollars on that sidewalk. But at least David still liked me.

David's slice of the Tumblr pie when all was said and done was reported to be more than $200 million. After that transaction David could buy his own hoodie company and his own Lexus dealership. Two of the chief beneficiaries of that deal: Steve, because he owned a piece of Tumblr; and Spark Capital, the lead venture capital investor in David's company.

But I couldn't dwell on it. Our first order of business at that moment was launching Serious Eats. So every day Meg, Adam, Alaina, and I walked into the offices that would soon no longer be ours, and we just started checking things off the Serious Eats punch list at warp speed.

David Jacobs and his crew at Apperceptive were on speed dial (there was no Slack at the time). I hit "send" on so many emails to David that my fingertips hurt. We were going 24-7. We had no choice. We ate more burgers at Shake Shack than I thought was humanly possible. We encountered so many bugs in the proprietary plug-ins Apperceptive was developing for Serious Eats that I felt like I was on the digital camping trip from hell. Meg would calm me down. "We're good, Ed. Discovering and fixing bugs is part of any software-development process. You want to discover the bugs now before launch so that users don't encounter them when we go live." I had to take her word for it, because I really had no other choice.

And we made it. We killed all those bugs. On December 5, 2006, Serious Eats came into being, complete with American Express ads. If you typed seriouseats.com into your browser and hit "enter," this is what you found:

> We'd like to take this opportunity to welcome all serious eaters by toasting our brand new website. Raise your glass now.
>
> Somehow, you have found your way to Serious Eats, the inclusive, passionate, and discerning website for serious eaters. Here you'll find fellow food lovers, great video, blogs we love, and reliable eating and cooking advice. We hope you'll find that time spent on Serious Eats is satisfying and enjoyable.
>
> We love eating something great and telling everyone we know about it. We love other people telling us about their own food discoveries. We love making great videos and empowering Serious Eats community members to shoot their own pictures and video to share. We love turning people on to great food wherever they are. We love hanging out with and getting to know all our fellow serious eaters.
>
> So we would like to raise a glass to you. May all your burgers be cooked to temperature, your pizza crusts be light, pliant and chewy, and your french fries fresh, not frozen. May all our videos provide a respite from your busy day, may all your food and drink questions be reliably answered here, may you chew the fat with gusto on Serious Eats, may you always feel welcome on our site, and may all your interactions with fellow serious eaters be filled with pleasure and the joy of discovery.
>
> Drink up!

Spiced Onion Clusters with Blackened Ginger-Curry Sauce

J. KENJI LÓPEZ-ALT

"Make me something that's like onion rings but if onion rings were Indian. You know, like Floyd Cardoz's onion rings," is what Ed said to me.

I had never had Floyd Cardoz's onion rings and rather than try to pretend to imagine I can read his mind, instead I'm giving him what I think are Actual Indian Onion Rings (okay, technically not rings, but clusters). Actual Indian Onion Clusters, or onion *bhaji* (*pakora*) are made by dipping little bundles of thinly shaved onion in a batter made with chickpea flour and seasoned with chilies and spices. As they fry the thinly sliced onion caramelizes and gets intense and sweet while the chickpea flour gives the coating a nice flavorful crunch.

For extra lightness and crispness, I cut my gram flour with a bit of cornstarch and use bubbly club soda in my batter as opposed to regular water. This helps the bhaji puff more during frying, adding surface area and creating a crisper end result.

To serve the bhaji, the traditional accompaniment is a simple raita made by stirring Greek yogurt with grated cucumber, chopped cilantro, and a pinch of ground cumin and coriander. To go with that, I like to make a batch of my blackened ginger-curry ketchup, a grown-up version of the sweet curry ketchup you'll find on plates of currywurst (sausage and french fries with curry ketchup) all over Germany. We serve it with double-fried potatoes and grilled Thüringer bratwurst at my restaurant.

Onion Bhaji

TOTAL TIME: 30 minutes   **ACTIVE TIME:** 30 minutes   **YIELD:** About 20 bhaji

2 medium white or red onions, very thinly sliced by hand or on a mandoline

2 quarts peanut or rice bran oil

5 ounces (140 grams) chickpea (gram) flour

½ teaspoon baking powder

¼ teaspoon ground cayenne pepper

½ teaspoon ground hot paprika

½ teaspoon dried ground turmeric

¼ teaspoon ground white pepper

½ teaspoon whole cumin seed, lightly crushed in a mortar and pestle

2 tablespoons onion, grated on a microplane grater

1 serrano or Thai bird chili, very finely minced

½ teaspoon salt

2 tablespoons yogurt

140 milliliters club soda

Recipe continued . . .

1. Soak the onion slices in cold water for 15 minutes. Drain and repeat.

2. Heat the oil in a large wok to 325°F. Maintain the temperature, monitoring carefully with an instant-read thermometer.

3. Combine-chickpea flour, baking powder, cayenne pepper, paprika, turmeric, white pepper, cumin, grated onion, chili, and salt in a small bowl. Whisk until homogenous. Add the yogurt and club soda and whisk rapidly until just barely combined. It's okay if some small streaks or pockets of dry flour remain.

4. Drain the onion slices carefully. Pick up a small handful at a time using your fingertips. Drop them into the batter, then pick them up again, making sure the onions are well coated in batter. Carefully lower the cluster into the hot oil, releasing when your fingertips are as close to the oil as they can reasonably be. Repeat with 6 to 8 bundles. Cook the bhaji, poking and turning them with a wire mesh spider or a pair of chopsticks until they are crisp and golden brown on all sides. Transfer to a wire rack set on a rimmed baking sheet, season with salt on all sides, and store in a 200°F warm oven while you cook the remaining batches.

5. When all batches are cooked, serve with raita (see headnote) or with Blackened Ginger-Curry Ketchup.

Blackened Ginger-Curry Ketchup

TOTAL TIME: 45 minutes   **ACTIVE TIME:** 45 minutes   **YIELD:** About 1½ cups

3 garlic cloves

2-inch knob of ginger, roughly chopped

1 small yellow onion, roughly chopped

Kosher salt

2 tablespoons (30 milliliters) vegetable oil

1½ teaspoons whole cumin seed

1½ teaspoons whole black mustard seeds

1½ teaspoons Madras curry powder

6 tablespoons (3 ounces; 115 grams) tomato paste

6 tablespoons (3 ounces; 75 milliliters) cider vinegar

½ cup (3 ounces; 75 grams) brown sugar

½ cup (4 ounces; 115 grams) canned whole peeled or crushed tomatoes

1 teaspoon (2 grams) freshly ground black pepper

1. Combine the garlic, ginger, onion, and a large pinch of kosher salt in the bowl of a heavy-duty mortar and pestle. Pound until a rough paste is formed, about 2 minutes.

2. Heat the oil in a medium saucepan over medium heat until shimmering. Add the pounded garlic mixture and cook, stirring frequently, until it is dark brown and starting to turn black and sticky in spots, about 12 minutes. Add the cumin and mustard seeds and allow them to crackle a bit, about 30 seconds.

3. Add the curry powder, tomato paste, and cider vinegar, scraping and stirring to deglaze the bottom of the pan. Add the sugar, the canned tomatoes, and the black pepper. Bring to a simmer and let the sauce reduce for about 10 minutes. Season to taste with salt.

4. Working in batches, puree the mixture in a blender adding water with the machine running to thin it to a smooth, ketchup-like consistency. Let the sauce cool and store in the refrigerator for up to a month.

Chapter 12

2007: THE YEAR OF LIVING DELICIOUSLY AND DANGEROUSLY

O h yeah, you started one of those little things, didn't you?" Cal (not his real name), a prominent restaurant critic, said to me and the small group of journalists I was sipping white wine with. Cal was a card-carrying member of the food-writing establishment (the food mafia, I called it) who had always been very supportive of me and my work.

It was a gray December day in 2006, exactly one day after Serious Eats launched, and we were standing around in the reception area of the Kennedy Center in Washington, DC, waiting for the memorial service for R. W. Apple Jr. (Johnny to his friends). Though Johnny had been sick for a while, I still couldn't reconcile the fact that he and I would never again share a table so full of food that Johnny would ask for the adjoining table to hold our spillover.

How Johnny would have loved the fact that his memorial service was at the Kennedy Center. A big, important, showy place for a big, important, showy man. How big was Johnny Apple? One of his eulogizers, journalist Todd Purdum, said he weighed 285 pounds when he died. How important? He had been on *Meet the Press* eighty-one times in his forty-three years at the *Times*.

When Cal joined our conversation, everyone else was congratulating me on what must have seemed to them to be a foolhardy venture, though they were polite enough to say otherwise. "Congratulations on Serious Eats. It's really great," said Frank Bruni, then the *New York Times*'s restaurant critic.

Of course I knew it wasn't really great—nothing only days old is great—but I also knew that if you don't get out of the starting gate, you will never get to great. And I was gratified that Frank Bruni knew that Serious Eats even existed at that moment.

In fact, right after the congratulations came a torrent of questions. "So what exactly is a blog?" "How do you do it?" "Can you make any money from a blog?" But those questions merely revealed the lack of knowledge that established journalists of all stripes had about blogs in December of 2006. A week earlier I had been to a holiday party with my wife. Vicky, ever the supportive spouse, announced to a journalist acquaintance, "Ed started a blog. It's called Serious Eats." "A blog?" the acquaintance responded. "I thought blogs were for freelance journalists who couldn't get any real assignments." Ouch.

Of course, Cal's response was just a more cutting coda to that comment. Just in case I had missed the condescension dripping from his first comment, he followed up with "Aren't you all just talking to the same hundred people?" I managed to keep my cool. "Blogs are really becoming popular," I responded. "You all should think about starting one yourself."

At that moment the lights started blinking, indicating that we should take our seats for the memorial service. Saved by the blinking lights, or should I say saved by the ghost of my friend.

Because there were no more gatekeepers in my life—hallelujah!—I didn't have to pitch the idea of writing about the service to Cal or any other editor. I needed to memorialize Johnny myself. Not just because he had been kind and generous with me but because he represented the bridge between the old and new guards in food writing. He could expound at equal length and enthusiasm about a five-hundred-dollar bottle of Brunello or a half smoke from Ben's Chili Bowl in his beloved home city of Washington, DC. Of all the card-carrying members of the old-guard food mafia I knew,

Johnny was perhaps the only one (*The Atlantic*'s Corby Kummer was in fact another) who would have truly appreciated Serious Eats' voice.

If many of my establishment food writer and journalist friends were skeptical about the very idea of Serious Eats, the tech world was starting to take notice. On the Gawker-owned *Valleywag*, a gossipy blog about the goings-on in Silicon Valley, *Eater* cofounder Lockhart Steele (still moonlighting as Gawker's editorial director at the time) wrote a post on December 19, 2006, titled "Serious Eats Recruits the A-List" a couple of weeks after Johnny's memorial service. In it he said, "You might not have heard of the new food site Serious Eats yet, but at the rate noted food journalist Ed Levine is stockpiling blog talent, you probably will sooner or later."* That it turned out to be sooner rather than later speaks to the speed of digital media.

We may have been on the A-list, but we were being shunted aside at 419 Park Avenue South by NNN. A few days later, the day after Christmas in 2006, we moved out of NNN's offices under cover of darkness. With no one else in the office, we moved all our stuff out, aided by one of those "Man with a Van" dudes. There wasn't much stuff to move, actually. I was using a desk and chair borrowed from Steve, so my stuff consisted of my laptop, a printer, and one box of files. Everything else was stored on my computer. I wasn't going to pay another penny of rent after the shabby treatment I had received from the Next New Networks crew. I actually owed Steve some back rent, but he wasn't hassling me for the money. I just couldn't stand to be there another minute. But I didn't want our departure to create a scene in the office while people were working. Plus, I still held out hope that perhaps the NNN guys would invest in Serious Eats.

We moved into a loft-like space on Twenty-Seventh Street that Alaina and I had found a few days prior, on the campus of the Fashion Institute of Technology. We took it on the spot, and just like that we had an office of our own. It wasn't exactly fancy or even up to date (there was an old-fashioned

---

* Lockhart Steele, "Serious Eats Recruits the A-List," Gawker, December 19, 2006.

six-foot-high men's urinal in the unisex bathroom), but I loved being on that block, surrounded by people who probably knew what a blog was. And it did have the advantage of being four blocks from Pizza Suprema, the slice joint located kitty-corner to Madison Square Garden that serves one of the great slices in New York City. The crust is crisp yet pliant, the sweet sauce offsets the tang of the aged mozzarella, and Suprema's high-traffic location means your slice is almost always taken from a freshly baked pie. We ate so much of its pizza that we used Pizza Suprema boxes as in- and out-boxes on our desks. Only when the boxes threatened to take over our office did we throw them out.

Right after we moved in, on December 29, 2006, to be precise, I got the following email from Jim Cuene, who then headed all of General Mills' digital marketing efforts:

Hi Ed,

I work for General Mills, in Minneapolis. I'd like to get your media kit, please. We have a couple brands that would be a good fit as advertisers on your site.

Thanks!

Damn. General Mills. How could this be? Serious Eats was not even a month old. It was like an athlete being offered a full college scholarship while still playing in Little League.

I called Jim right way. He was so enthusiastic about us. "I love what you're doing at Serious Eats. I've been a fan of Meg Hourihan and Jason Kottke for the longest time. Let's get together after the first of the year. I get to New York frequently, and if you're ever in Minneapolis, let me know. We can have pancakes at Al's." Al's is a tiny breakfast spot in Dinkytown near the U of M campus that serves some of my favorite pancakes in the universe. If Jim Cuene wanted to eat at Al's, he was all right in my book. I ended up sharing some blueberry pancakes with Jim—and many other meals, in fact, in both Minneapolis and New York. No business came directly out of those meals for a couple of years (ah, the seemingly interminable gestation period of making an ad sale), but eventually we saw our fair share of General Mills advertising dollars.

At that moment there was so much love coming in and out of our modest new office. Being a "nice" guy on a mission sometimes served me well, especially at the outset. When I started I vowed that Serious Eats employees would be able to spend 90 percent of their time on the work itself and 10 percent on the other stuff, the office politics and pecking-order issues that I myself found so difficult to navigate, much less adjudicate. And most of the time I made good on that 90/10 vow. How did I do that? I hired the smartest, most passionate young people I could find and afford, and then got out of the way. I was there for support, advice, and access. There was so much work to do, I couldn't let pettiness get in the way.

These were not arbitrary numbers. At most places I had worked before, those numbers were 50/50 or worse. My 20/80 J. Walter Thompson experience was always front and center in my memory. That's why many of the insanely talented people I hired ended up staying a long time at Serious Eats.

Serious Eats' first year was a total adrenaline rush. Adam, Alaina, Meg, and I all loved coming to work. Serious Eats was a cause, not a gig. The energy in the office was palpable. You felt the whoosh of extraordinary young minds (and my old one) focused on one thing: making Serious Eats a success. The air crackled with possibility. We all felt it, Serious Eats readers felt it, and the media felt it.

The office was electric. Everybody wanted in. People of all stripes were lining up just to become interns. Adam had been in touch with Robyn Lee, a blogger and photographer whose blog *The Girl Who Ate Everything* he greatly admired for its innocent but cheeky voice and Robyn's gorgeous photos. Robyn was finishing up her degree in food studies at NYU. She asked Adam if she could intern with us for credit.

We enthusiastically endorsed the idea. She was the perfect Serious Eats intern. Robyn had been blogging since she was fifteen; she was technically savvy; she loved food more than life itself; she had a fully formed writing voice that made her readers fall in love with her; and she didn't take herself too seriously. A typical Robyn Lee post: "This morning I started my day off with a milk chocolate Easter egg from Jacques Torres. Do I normally eat breakfast? Nope. Do I celebrate Easter? Double nope. Am I using Easter as an excuse to eat oversized chocolate sculptures of unhatched chickens? Oh yeah."

Robyn eventually became an invaluable Serious Eats staffer. She started after graduation and stayed for seven years before marrying a Norwegian postman who was a huge fan of *The Girl Who Ate Everything*. It was love at first blog post. In 2018 Robyn joined her husband in the Norwegian Postal Service. She welcomes any and all serious eaters to their cozy home in Bergen, Norway. Dress warmly. It is seriously cold nine months out of the year in Bergen.

Then there was Erin Zimmer. Erin lived in DC and was blogging about food for *Washingtonian* magazine after graduating from Georgetown, where she had started a food column for the school newspaper. In October of 2007 Erin wrote me a fan letter offering to write about DC food for Serious Eats. After she submitted a couple of terrific posts, I offered her the very part-time job (I was paying her twenty-five dollars a post) of being Serious Eats' Washington bureau chief. That title didn't mean much in reality, but I just loved the idea of Serious Eats having a DC bureau chief. Erin's voice and values fit perfectly with ours. There was a bemused smile in every post she wrote. Within six months Erin moved to New York and became a full-time writer and editor at Serious Eats. The tribe was growing, ever so slowly.

Then there were the more unlikely interns. At one point we had a judge and a lawyer as interns, just because they wanted to breathe in the air at Serious Eats World HQ. Why? Because we were on a mission. We may not have had collateral for a loan, but we had a ton of momentum.

We opined about anything we cared about; we took dives into any subject we were intrigued by; we linked to stuff that entertained and interested us and therefore our readers; and we tried to make one another laugh. We posted funny pictures and sound bites from the news; we taste-tested Equal and Splenda; we wrote about every delicious hot dog and slice of pizza we encountered, anywhere in the world.

We had no recipe developers on staff, so I used my contacts to contract with gifted recipe developers who had already been discovered by the blogosphere. There were posts from Dorie Greenspan, whom I had met when she was a guest on *New York Eats*, the regional cable TV show I did with Jeffrey Steingarten and Susie Essman. Dorie has written many wonderful baking books, and she has managed to figure out a way to spend half the year in New York and the other half in Paris. Nice work, Dorie.

When some early food bloggers discovered Dorie's recipes, they started a cook-along blog in 2007 called *Tuesdays with Dorie*. Within one minute of listening to her talk about fruit tarts on our show, I knew Dorie was a serious eater at heart and a very serious baker in practice.

We posted cartoon recipes from the brilliant cartoonist Larry Gonick. From his recipe "Simple Chocolate Sauce": "Continue beating as it cools until your arm gets tired. Then it is done."

Recipes weren't my jam or Serious Eats', and I was convinced after doing a little research that I didn't need them. I did initially investigate various ways of publishing recipes, but I concluded at that point that I would never be able to compete with Epicurious, the leading recipe database at the time. That conclusion was, as my son Will used to say to me all the time when he was five, "wrong, wrong, wrong."

Every day was an editorial improvisation. Though we took our subject matter seriously, we didn't take ourselves too seriously. "It's just food," I would remind everyone every morning. "It is most assuredly not nuclear disarmament or rocket science."

Similarly, we were still experimenting with the format and style that would get us to financial stability. I still hadn't given up the video ghost. In January of 2007 I wrote a memo outlining our video strategy: "We should post at least one new video every day." That, of course, proved to be totally unrealistic cost- or production-wise. Those facts didn't stop us from having daily arguments about the wisdom of video versus texts and photos on blogs. Meg's argument: "Text and photos are cheap and fast to produce, and it's what people expect to see on a blog." My response: "Advertisers are paying far more to run commercials before, during, or after a short-form video."

Meg knew, just as I did, that advertisers buy eyeballs, aka ad impressions, by the thousands. The metric they use is CPM, or cost per thousand. She also knew advertisers were at that moment paying twenty- to forty-dollar CPMs for video impressions, compared to a ten-dollar CPM for a static ad. But Meg, as usual, had the last word: "You can't get enough video views to make it worthwhile to an advertiser to buy. The bottom line is in 2007 people don't come to Serious Eats—or any other blog, for that matter—to watch videos." (My, how times have changed in 2019. These days every advertiser wants video impressions.)

It's important to note that though YouTube had already been bought by Facebook, it had not yet become the behemoth it is today in the realm of online short-form video. Even today, if we post a video on Serious Eats' YouTube channel, YouTube hosts the video on its site but, more important, keeps most of the advertising revenue derived from people watching that video. Great for YouTube, not so great for Serious Eats or any other digital publisher.

Meg and I compromised. As I outlined above, we had a blend of video and static posts on Serious Eats at the outset. We also did a video series, "Tables for Two." It featured two interesting, well-known people breaking bread at a restaurant and chewing the fat about food and life. I recruited—who else?—Jeffrey Steingarten and Susie Essman for the first episode: terrific dumplings at the now-defunct Chinatown Brasserie. (The chef there then was Joe Ng, now the chef and a partner at the two stellar RedFarm locations in Manhattan. He makes the finest dumplings I have ever tasted. Ng's wrappers are tender and paper-thin without falling apart. His fillings are made with superior ingredients and can get creative without being stupid. And yes, they're expensive, but in this case you get what you pay for. I love those six dumplings for a dollar you get at the hole-in-the-wall storefronts in Chinatowns all over America as much as anyone, but they don't compare to Joe Ng's masterpieces.)

"Jeffrey," Susie asked as they perused the menu, "didn't you once write that salad is the silent killer?" Jeffrey's response: "I'm not saying that all vegetables are bad for you, but most of them are."

Jeffrey may have been wrong, but Meg was right. Compared to the traffic our text and photo posts got, the video posts like "Table for Two" were running a distant second. According to Google Analytics, our traffic was increasing by leaps and bounds, which is pretty easy to do if you're starting where we started. Not that the numbers were disappointing. By February 2007, two months after launch, we had received more than 200,000 unique visits and 500,000 page views.

Though the views were rolling in, I quickly realized just how ambitious my plans had been. We had to abandon my video-a-day production and posting plan. It would have exacerbated our burgeoning cash-flow problem. We didn't have enough advertisers, and the big advertisers we did have often didn't pay online publishers for six months. Six months! And there was no way to expedite the payments. The advertisers had all the leverage. Our only recourse would have been to not accept any more advertising from companies like American Express. Talk about cutting off your nose to spite your face.

We weren't *Vogue* or CBS. We needed the big-name advertisers *and* their money to both attract more investment capital and operate the site, i.e., pay ourselves and our vendors. Meg, Alaina, and Mike had all warned me that cash-flow issues sink more startups than anything else does. I would make call after call to both agencies and clients, dialing for dollars. Yup, I was in charge of accounts receivable. Just like my dad was in my uncle's lumber business. Neither of us was cut out for the gig.

In early January I got an email from my old boss Steve. "Just wanted to say Happy New Year, and I miss you." *Really?* I thought to myself. *You miss me after you've screwed me, you son of a bitch.*

The better angels of my nature won out. I—graciously, I thought— emailed him back and suggested we have breakfast. Maybe Steve would invest some of the VC money NNN had raised in Serious Eats. Steve loved breakfast meetings. I think they made him feel important because in his own mind he was having power breakfasts. We met at a nondescript coffee shop–cum–cafe midway between our offices.

We exchanged pleasantries for a minute. He made it clear he wasn't willing to commit any of his company's money to Serious Eats. Then the yelling started. Fine, I admit that I started it. "You all fucked me big time. And you know it." He replied, "I don't know it because I don't think we did. But if you think that, fine. What do you want to do going forward? Just tell me what you want to do."

"I want all of you out of Serious Eats. Now. That's what I want." I have to admit that I shocked myself as well as Steve when I spat those words at him. It was completely out of character for me, and it most assuredly was not part of some grand strategic plan. When I'd made the date, I really was just hoping to come away with some much-needed operating capital.

Steve yelled back, "Fine, Ed, you got it!" I tossed my napkin on the table and walked out. I think I got my point across. And he had to pay the check. I walked back to the office enraged and disappointed by what had just transpired. Steve had not redeemed himself, and he wasn't going to help solve our cash-flow problems. A few days later a mutual friend, an entertainment lawyer we both trusted, negotiated a settlement. If I paid Steve and Bill the consulting fees they claimed I owed them, and paid Steve for all the back rent, they would relinquish their equity in Serious Eats.

For less than $100,000 I was getting back their 15 percent equity interest in Serious Eats, which of course would exacerbate our cash-flow problems. I consulted with Mike before signing the deal. He said, "That's a big chunk of the cash you have on hand, especially considering your cash-flow problems, but I think it's worth it, especially considering how much momentum you and Adam and Alaina and Meg are building. Those three seem to be really smart and know what they're doing." Being smart and knowing what you're doing were the two highest compliments Mike could pay someone.

Mike gave his blessing to this not-so-little financial maneuver with the following kicker: "And I am recommending this as someone who has been telling you to carefully consider every dollar that goes out of the Serious Eats bank account." (Mike would question even the smallest items on our expense ledger, like desk lamps and copy paper. "Can't you use recycled paper for that stuff?") Then Mike issued the clincher: "You probably noticed that I had my issues with those guys at NNN." "Issues" was a Mike euphemism for lack of respect.

In February we had to go out for operating capital again. In fact, I can't remember a moment in Serious Eats history when I wasn't trying to raise money. Our presentation then started with "Serious Eats: Fresh, Hot, Delicious Food Content Served Daily." It went on, "The goal of Serious Eats is to be the home base for eaters on the web." How were we going to do that? With a combination of original video and text and photo content, aggregated and carefully curated links to other great stuff we found on the web, and a passionate, discerning, and welcoming environment.

Our growth pitch paragraph: "To broaden our reach beyond our sites, we've established a content syndication relationship with Yahoo!, which places our original content in front of a larger segment of the web. . . . And this is only the beginning. We are also in negotiations with ABCNews.com, AOL, and the *New York Times* to introduce new audiences to our content." Note the "we are also in negotiations" line.

Those negotiations, which sometimes consisted of a single email exchange or a series of unfruitful meetings, invariably ended in failure or, worse yet, ended in an agreement that generated nothing for Serious Eats. Everybody wanted in at Serious Eats, but nobody wanted to pay an entrance fee. As the late Albert King sang, "Everybody wants to go to heaven, but nobody wants to die."

Yet my pitches always ended with the same optimistic, naive take on the Serious Eats business. "We are seeking to raise $1 million to grow the business over the next eighteen months. At that point we anticipate being cash-flow positive and do not expect to raise further funding." Ah, the lies we tell ourselves.

Going into a constantly evolving business segment like digital publishing with insufficient capital is a recipe for constant agita and probable failure. We were a soufflé ready to fall. When you've never raised money for a business before, you don't understand how much money you need, much less how to raise it. I also didn't understand how fast you burn through capital when something doesn't go according to plan. And I didn't understand that I needed to plan for the plans going awry.

Our pitch for money generated negligible results. One prominent billionaire VC Meg knew kept nodding off during our presentation. His chief lieutenant explained that he'd gotten home very late from a ski trip in Vail the night before. Meg and I flew out to San Francisco to try to tap some of her contacts in the venture community. We came back with nothing but a few worthless pats on the back. "You guys are doing great stuff, but I don't think you're far enough along for us to invest" was the refrain.

In the spring of 2007 friends-and-family money continued to dribble in. Steve Trost's eighty-five-year-old father-in-law, Harold Snyder (now deceased), who'd built a very successful generic drug manufacturing business from the ground up, liked to invest in passion-based startups. After a crudo-filled dinner at the now-defunct Onera with Harold, Beryl, and Steve, I had my first octogenarian investor (he invested $100,000). Eventually Beryl also invested in Serious Eats. The Snyder-Trost family turned out to be incredibly supportive and helpful. Howard, an old college friend whom I'd barely seen since we had both moved to New York after graduation, had become a senior partner at one of the nation's largest investment banks. After much cajoling he reluctantly agreed to invest $100,000. Marc Lasry invested another $150,000.

A tip I learned the hard way: raising money in small increments for a startup is not advisable because it forces you to be in constant money-raising mode. I never went more than a month without having to raise capital. Everybody tells you that it takes the same amount of time and energy to raise $1 million as it does to raise $100,000. I found out that it also takes the same amount of time and energy to be turned down for amounts large and small.

The last bit of money came in that spring from my best and closest friend, Bob Rosen. Bob was incredibly smart but unpretentious, steadfastly loyal, and one of the most generously spirited people you could ever meet. He was also a die-hard Mets fan, just like Steve Trost.

Bob quickly became my most trusted confidant. And he knew my brother Mike and the entire backstory of our relationship, so he was someone I could and did turn to on an almost daily basis for emotional and psychological support *and* business advice. Bob was always up for a food adventure on a moment's notice. He likes food well enough, but mostly he liked and believed in me at all times.

I called him up, feeling incredibly discouraged after another day of unsuccessful dialing for dollars. "Man, raising money is really hard." Bob, who knew the ins and outs of the Serious Eats business as well as or better than me, said, "You know, I've been talking to Marcia [his wife], and we want to invest in Serious Eats. We can put in $50K. It won't get you all the money you need, but it will help."

I was overwhelmed by this show of support because, unlike all the other investors, Bob really didn't have this money to lose. This was money that he had earmarked for their retirement. "I don't know, man," I said. "I would be really upset if I lost your money." He said, "It's all right. I think you have something here, so I think it will turn out to be a profitable investment for us."

I really didn't want to take Bob's money, but I had no choice. Friends and family might get you the cheapest money, with low interest rates and the fewest strings attached. But the strings were attached to my heart.

This dynamic played out many times moving forward. I went to friends and family for money because I had no choice, and every ask was accompanied by two huge side orders of guilt and pressure. Institutional money may be more expensive, but it's not personal. Of course, I'm talking theoretically here. I was never able to raise one dollar of institutional money for Serious Eats.

In the midst of the endless pitches for money, plaudits continued to roll in. One morning when I arrived at the office, Alaina practically shouted at me (an unusual occurrence because Alaina never yelled), "Ed, wait until you see this. We won a 2007 Editors' Award for Online Excellence from the *Morning News!*" At that time, the *Morning News* was one of the most popular and influential aggregator blogs.

And the hits just kept coming. Traffic was going up, and plaudits were coming in left and right. But the money wasn't following. Critical acclaim and love were once again not enough. It was just like after *New York Eats* was published in 1992.

All those great nicknames given to me back then by big-name journalists at the *New York Times*—the "Nabob of Nosh" (Robert Lipsyte); the "Homer of Rugelach" (Florence Fabricant); the "Missionary of the Delicious" (Ruth Reichl)—didn't amount to squat. Fifteen years later, only the names, nicknames, and dates had changed, with the same sorry results. I clearly hadn't learned my lesson. I was being tripped up again by the same things that had tripped me up in my old-media days. Nicknames and plaudits are good for the soul, but not necessarily for the bottom line.

By this time the American Express campaign was long since over. Its agency, Digitas, had, as many digital ad agencies are wont to do, moved on to the new, next "big thing." Our ad sales numbers were running pitifully short of our admittedly rosy projections. With the business hemorrhaging money, I would dread my monthly visit to Mike's to show him the numbers. I would cram for these visits like I was studying for a final in college, to no avail. "If you don't know the numbers, they will kill you. You won't even recognize the problems you have to solve. Eventually you will run out of money, and when you run out of money, you lose control of your business."

I was running out of money. By December of 2007 there was less than $50,000 in the Serious Eats bank account. That was exactly one month's operating capital. The rule of thumb for startups is you're always supposed to have a minimum of three months' operating capital in the bank. I knew from looking at our accounts receivable that the coming winter months would not improve our situation. I started thinking about salary cuts in the new year for everybody else, and a salary furlough for me.

Here was the kicker. Steve Trost's $100,000 promissory note was coming due. I got an email from him alerting me to that fact. If Steve called in his note, that would be the end of Serious Eats. And it would be the end of Bob's money and Mike's money and every other Serious Eats investor's money, for that matter.

With all these disastrous numbers rattling around my brain, I had to pay my monthly visit to my brother to go over the Serious Eats financials. It was the day before Christmas Eve. I hoped he would be in a holiday mood. Alaina had gamely agreed to be our bookkeeper, even though bookkeeping was not in her skill set. She would even occasionally come on these monthly forays to show Mike the numbers, but I decided to spare her the discomfort this time around. Mike was my brother, not hers. Plus, to prepare for this particular meeting, hoping to avoid the usual bloodbath, I had sought the help of an actual accountant. Not enough help, as it turned out. When your numbers suck, your numbers suck, and the best accountant in the world can't save you from that fact.

Mike ripped into me, his usually controlled voice so loud I think the Whole Foods shoppers on the first floor of his building must have covered their ears. We argued about what the numbers showed. It wasn't much of an argument. Mike was winning it from the moment I walked in his door. He lectured, "If you really understood these numbers you're showing me, you'd know just how fucked you are. And because you really don't know them, you won't be able to diagnose your problems, much less solve them. I've been telling you the same thing for months." He was right, of course. Deep down I did know how dire the numbers were. I just couldn't admit it to Mike. But that didn't stop me from leaving enraged. "Happy holidays to you too," I said over my shoulder as I left his apartment. I arrived home in a heap, and Mike, perhaps thinking he had gone too far with his tough-love approach, kept calling to continue the conversation. I didn't call him back until the next day.

In the meantime I emailed Alaina with the subject line "the bludgeoning at my brother's." "Hi Alaina, I thought I might spare you the bloody details of my meeting with my brother until after Christmas, but then I figure you might get annoyed if I didn't tell you. It didn't go well. . . . To get this numbers stuff right I am going to need the AP [accounts payable], Receivables and Cash Position numbers every day. We are going to compute our cash flow numbers weekly. AND IT'S UP TO ME TO DEAL WITH THOSE NUMBERS."

When I did take Mike's phone call, I was still so upset my voice was quivering when I started to speak. Mike, perhaps realizing that he had pushed a little too far, said consolingly, "This shit is hard, Ed. But you will figure it out." *God, I hope he's right,* I said to myself as I hung up the phone.

Chapter 13

MELTDOWNS, TRAITORS, AND TRUTH

S chool was in session. Big time. In a gorgeous duplex apartment in Manhattan's Chelsea neighborhood on a freezing January day in 2008, Professor Michael E. Levine was at his lectern, schooling me on any number of topics.

On Scripps Digital (then owners of the Food Network and all its related properties) selling Serious Eats advertising (Scripps had made a pitch to sell our advertising, which was the first time it offered to sell the advertising inventory of a site it didn't own): "I know you feel really good about this deal because they are the dominant player in the space. But just remember that they also see you as a competitor. And yes, they think they can make money on you now. But don't be surprised if they try to starve you out by not meeting their sales goals and then trying to buy SE when you're in a really compromised position financially. You're a trusting soul, Ed. And you haven't dealt with folks like this. They don't necessarily have your best interests at heart. Maybe they see you as a threat, and they see this as the fastest and easiest way to put you out of business. This may work in the short run, but I don't see this as a long-term solution for your inability to sell your ad inventory."

On the promissory notes being due: "Don't worry about people calling in their loans. Everyone who has listened to your constant pitches for money knows that if they call in their loans, the business is toast. Plus, there's a reason they call this kind of financing 'friends and family.' We are in fact, in varying degrees, your friends and your family. So we all want to see you succeed for your sake and for ours."

On Serious Eats' current precarious financial plight: "I talked it over with Carol. We're going to put another $250K into the business. But that's it. We're not going to invest any more money into Serious Eats. You know how much I believe in you, in the company, in the team you have put together. But at this point it's up to you and your crew to make it work. I will, of course, continue to offer as much counsel and guidance as I can. This investment is not a free pass. I'm still by far the largest single investor in Serious Eats, and I have a right to know how my investment is doing. If anybody asks why I'm not investing any more money, tell them that my investment represents a much greater percentage of my net worth than any of them, that I continue to believe in Serious Eats, and I will be happy to talk to any current or future investor about the business if that would be helpful. But as far as investing any more money, we're done. And there is one more thing I want to say. I hate the strain SE has put on our relationship. I'm sure you do too. I hate it so much that sometimes I wish I hadn't invested. But I did, and so here we are."

I recovered in time to stammer, "I . . . I . . . I, uh, really appreciate your continued financial support and belief in Serious Eats. And I know you are turning off the money spigot as of this moment. I really think we will be self-sustaining by the end of the year, with Scripps's help. Who knows? Maybe Scripps will invest in Serious Eats or even buy us. They seem really excited about the opportunity to work with us."

. I put on my coat, went over to hug Mike, and thanked him five more times. I left his apartment and danced down the hall to the elevator. I was beyond thrilled. It was 2008. Things were tough all over. The economy was in free fall. But my bro had come through again.

Mike was right about my investors. Two weeks earlier I had had dinner with Steve and Beryl at Ouest, then the best restaurant on the Upper West Side (but since closed). I explained where we were as a business, that even though we continued to grow, I hadn't been able to raise the money I'd said I would. Steve understood and said that of course he would not demand the repayment of his $100,000, which would have bankrupted the company. Beryl said to me, "We just want you to be successful. But do keep us informed. We hate surprises when it comes to our investments, and I bet all your investors feel the same way."

With assurances from all my investors that they were willing to be patient and not call in their loans, and with Mike's $250,000, I breathed a sigh of relief. Serious Eats was going to live to fight another day, another month, maybe even another year.

I jumped right back into the fray. When I went to Chicago to introduce Serious Eats to the Scripps sales team, I was blown away by the universally positive reaction they all had to my pitch. After all, Serious Eats' content was worlds apart from the nearly irony- and edge-free universe the Food Network had carefully constructed with the likes of Giada De Laurentiis and Ina Garten (Alton Brown being the notable exception).

"We are going to kick some ass for you, Ed," Sal (not his real name), the head of all of Scripps sales, told me. "Your younger audience is a perfect complement to FoodNetwork.com's. Now I need you to answer an even more important question. Where can I find the best Chicago pizza?"

I don't know if Sal knew that I had gotten in trouble for writing in my 2005 pizza book that "at best Chicago pizza is a good casserole." But there was at that moment one Chicago-style pizzeria that towered above all others.

"Burt's Place," I said without hesitation. Burt Katz's pizza was lighter and airier than his Chicago pizza counterparts. It was like a focaccia with cheese baked into the magically caramelized crust. Katz was a Chicago pizza pioneer. He had perfected his unique pizza style at three different pizzerias in the Windy City, including the very fine Pequod's, which has survived his departure to this day. Katz closed Burt's Place in 2015, but not before the late Tony Bourdain made Burt famous with a visit to his pizzeria in 2009. Katz died in 2016, but two pizza-loving restaurateurs reopened Burt's in its original location in 2017.

I was feeling downright high after my Chicago presentation. The Scripps folks seemed to be interested in becoming members of the Serious Eats tribe.

Scripps started off slowly in the first quarter of 2008, but by the second quarter the strength of its position in the digital marketplace kicked in. By then Scripps had succeeded in getting some big advertisers on the site, like Häagen-Dazs, Visa, and Walmart. In June of 2008 alone Scripps sold $100,000 worth of Serious Eats advertising, so our split entitled us to $60,000—more than the $50,000 we needed to break even every month. I was thrilled to tell Mike about Scripps's success, but he had an immediate counter: "Celebrate your first month of profitability. That is a milestone your whole team should savor. But it's a long race, Ed."

He was right. As the year went on—maybe because it was 2008 or maybe because Mike's other, less-charitable interpretations of the facts were correct—Scripps sold about half of what they had thought they were going to sell. And since Scripps was the exclusive seller of our advertising inventory, there was nothing we could do to improve our sales picture. We were handcuffed by the exclusive ad representation deal we had signed.

Serious Eats did get an infusion of capital on June 1, 2008. An employee of Marc Lasry's had introduced me to Chandler Bocklage and Sol Kumin, two young hedge funders who were multimillionaires before they were thirty. As traders, they were used to being gamblers. And because they had both won a majority of their million-dollar bets on behalf of their hedge fund employer, they had some dollars to spare to take a flyer on what was then the latest, hottest thing in media, a blog. Over a terrific dry-aged steak and burger dinner at the Minetta Tavern (finance folks love their red meat), they agreed to invest $75,000 between them in Serious Eats again as convertible promissory notes. It may have been 2008, but to some young hedge funders it was, as Prince sang, 1999. Their money wasn't the million dollars I was desperately searching for and in need of, but it was something. I couldn't believe how many friends and family I had found to invest—and how generous they had been. I'm a pretty popular guy, but even my Rolodex was beginning to be strained. Friends-and-family-and-friends-of-friends financing is not meant to go on forever.

In the meantime, traffic continued to skyrocket. It went from 549,033 page views in July of 2007 to 2,456,357 page views in July of 2008. The unique visitors numbers told the same story: in the same time period we went from 187,237 monthly unique visitors to 898,937. By year's end we had crossed the magical one million unique visitors mark. That was the threshold everyone in the know told me you needed to exceed to get business from the large, mass-market advertisers like Coke and Budweiser. Of course, as the internet grew, so did that number. It went from one million to three million to five million to ten million to twenty-five million. Every time the number grew, I felt the way Charlie Brown did when Lucy moved the football when he was about to kick it.

Even so, the media world continued to take notice. *Time* magazine named us one of the fifty best websites of 2008. PBS's website, *MediaShift*, wrote, "Serious Eats represents the next generation of food media."

In spite of Scripps's Serious Eats sales difficulties and the challenging macroeconomic climate, I got an encouraging email on April 8, 2008, from Sameer Deen, then the head of business development at Scripps Interactive. He wanted to set up a meeting later that week to discuss a potential Scripps investment. *This can only lead to good things*, I thought to myself. Maybe Mike was wrong.

I didn't realize this kind of talk is beyond cheap. It's free. Sameer and I met on and off for a few months and seemed to be making progress. Until we weren't. Scripps's business development team dropped off the face of the earth. I emailed Sameer to find out what was happening. No answer. I called my other contacts at Scripps. "Change of strategy," I was told.

A few days after I sent that email, I saw *Apartment Therapy* and *The Kitchn* cofounders Maxwell Gillingham-Ryan and his wife, Sara Kate, at a book party at Per Se. "Hi, Max, hi, Sara. How are you guys doing?" Both of them looked like they were in a daze. They replied, "We had a deal to sell our sites to Scripps. We had been negotiating for months with Deanna [Scripps

Digital president Deanna Brown] and her team [I knew Deanna from her days running Yahoo!'s lifestyle content business]. We had a deal. We signed the paperwork. They didn't sign it right away. Deanna told us not to worry. A week later we got a phone call from Deanna saying the Scripps board wouldn't approve the acquisition. They said they didn't know where the bottom was in the downturn." This didn't bode well for my own discussions with Scripps.

By October, the first month of the crucial fourth quarter, it was clear that Scripps was going to fall way short of projections. They had told us they expected to sell $1 million worth of advertising on Serious Eats in 2008, but they now thought they would come in closer to $600,000. That was a huge loss that I couldn't survive unless I cut costs.

I cut Alaina's and Adam's salaries by 25 percent and promised to restore them when we were on sounder financial footing.

I didn't pay myself for a month.

Vicky was understanding, up to a point. "The whole point of Serious Eats was to make us more financially secure. This is not my idea of security. But do what you have to do. I know you're going to make this work." I nodded, but frankly I didn't have the slightest idea how.

I was dealing with other personnel decisions as well. We had hired a designer/developer at the end of 2007. Randy (not his real name) was smart, talented, and totally connected; he helped develop many of the software plug-ins that kept us ahead of the curve. He was also moody and difficult. More important, he was into snark in a big way; he thought that we had to be more like Gawker and *Eater*. And he didn't mind wading through some questionable legal waters; if a chef said something provocative on a talk show, he would figure out a way to steal and post the clip, even if the network it had originally appeared on wouldn't allow it. I didn't have much interest in snark or copyright theft.

When we had to reduce overhead, I cut Randy to three days a week in October of 2008. He was not happy. At almost the exact same moment, a new competitor appeared out of nowhere, *Eat Me Daily*. The food blogosphere was abuzz with it because its owners and creators were anonymous. Here's its mission statement, which you can still find on the web.

> *Eat Me Daily* is a critical (and cynical) take on food, media, and culture, comprised of:
>
> • Commentary and criticism—not mean-spirited, but with teeth;
>
> • Aggregation of links deemed important, irreverent, redeeming, absurd, or plainly awesome;
>
> And occasional features of the grown-up, long-format kind.

Sounds familiar, doesn't it? Take out the snark and the cynicism, and *Eat Me Daily* sounded suspiciously like Serious Eats.

The new year rolled around and things were pretty dire. An email Alaina, ever the clear-eyed pragmatist, sent me on January 14, 2009, summed it up nicely. "Looking at the numbers again, it seems like the real choices are: raise more money, or find a buyer. I don't see a clear plan for making it to the other side outside of these scenarios, but maybe you can come up with one. We've got to decide which path we're taking and act accordingly."

Time for the first Serious Eats layoff; time was up for Randy. We would just depend on our outside developers more and use freelancers for our design needs. Again he seemed to take it well, and I was happy not to walk into the office every day only to see Randy's often-angry face. Afterward I said to Adam, "It's going to be tough around here without Randy. In some ways he was a great Serious Eater." Adam gave me his Cheshire cat smile: "You do know that Randy is one of the founders of *Eat Me Daily*, don't you?" I replied, "I most certainly didn't know that. That motherfucker. Why didn't you tell me?" "I thought you knew," Adam replied.

That turncoat Randy had started a competitor while I was paying him a salary and benefits. Mike's words came back to me. "You're a trusting soul,

Ed." *Yeah*, I thought to myself, *being a trusting soul and an undercapitalized entrepreneur do not mix well at all.*

We did get a temporary reprieve in October 2008 when a bank miraculously granted Serious Eats a $100,000 credit line. Our then-accountant was tight with a senior loan officer there. I made a presentation to the bank that laid out our plans for expansion. When they presented me with the paperwork, the loan officer kept stressing one thing: "This money is to be used for new initiatives. Don't use it for operating expenses. Remember, we can call back this money anytime." I barely heard him, and I should have. His words would come back to haunt me over and over again.

It was a lifeline, but with strings attached. I had to personally guarantee the loan with our own assets. That meant I had to get Vicky's signature. She was not thrilled. "What happens if we don't have the money to pay them back. Will they take our apartment? The apartment we raised our son in?" My response? "They don't want our apartment. They're not in the real estate business. I asked Mike about this and he said they would just work out a repayment plan with us." That was true, but as Mike had explained to me, the repayment plan would still put us in a world of hurt. He explained that the bank would garnish any of our future wages.

With the strategic investment talks on hold with Sameer and Scripps, I reached out to them in January of 2009 to see if they'd give us a $50,000 guarantee a month no matter how much advertising they sold on Serious Eats. Jeff, Scripps's head of digital advertising, seemed amenable. "I get where you're coming from. It's really rough out there. And it's a totally reasonable ask. We've just never given anyone an advance. But let me talk to my boss." His boss was Sal, the food enthusiast who had seemed so excited about Serious Eats in Chicago. Surely he would see the wisdom in giving us an advance. Surely Scripps would come to our rescue.

Being a little smarter and a little wiser, I had started talks in the fall of 2008 with Federated Media, one of the leading online ad networks. FM signed up lots of blogs that were not big enough to have their own sales team and used its very large sales organization to sell the aggregated ad impressions. They had been after me for months to leave Scripps and go with them.

We would be a trophy blog for them to parade around to other blogs they were trying to sign up. I told them over and over again, "If you want my business, I need a guarantee of at least $50,000 a month."

For me it would be a way to smooth out my cash flow. It would become FM's responsibility to collect from the ad agencies. Although FM had never offered anyone a guarantee either (and we were still in the middle of the financial crisis), they agreed; I guess they really wanted us. But I wasn't going to tell Scripps until every *i* was dotted and every *t* was crossed on the proposed contract. True to form, when the FM guys were in sell mode, they were genial and flattering to excess. But when it came time to actually negotiate the contract, they turned me over to their pit bull business affairs dude. Every time I thought we had a deal, the pit bull would send my lawyer and me a slightly different version of the contract than both parties had verbally agreed to. Finally they sent us a contract we could live with.

I still hadn't heard from Scripps on their willingness to give us an advance. I hadn't told them that I was negotiating with someone else seeking the same deal. I had been schooled enough by Mike to know that this was how the game was played. Finally Jeff called. "I couldn't get my boss Sal's okay. We can increase your share of every ad sale we make for you, but I'm afraid that's as far as we can go."

A few days later I read numerous press reports about a new blog Scripps was starting called *Food2*, which, according to a statement from Deanna Brown, "goes beyond recipes creating a conversation that takes a fresh look at all things food in a new and interactive way."*

WTF! Scripps was creating its own version of Serious Eats! I thought of a business truism that my old boss and former partner Steve was fond of saying: "You can always tell the pioneers. They're the ones with the arrows in their back." I called my point of contact to complain. He soothingly said, "Don't worry. We're not trying to screw you. I promise."

I called Deanna, who had originally approached me about Scripps

* "Scripps Networks Serves Up Food2, New Multimedia Website at the Intersection of Food, Drink and Pop Culture," *Business Wire*, May 1, 2009.

selling our advertising. "Calm down, Ed," Deanna told me. "You're getting upset over nothing. *Food2* is not meant to compete with Serious Eats. We're targeting a younger demo with it, twenty-one-to-thirty-four-year-olds." "A younger demo?" I said incredulously. "The median age of a serious eater is twenty-five. If the demos for *Food2* are any younger, you can kiss off 90 percent of the advertisers you call on. This is complete bullshit and you know it." Mike was right. Scripps was trying to put Serious Eats out of business. They knew our business inside and out, and they were gunning for us.

When I calmed down, I took Federated Media's offer. I got about five "Welcome to the family" emails from various FM executives. I desperately wanted to believe them, but I was starting to see that Mike was right. Who the hell can you trust when you're starting a business? *Nobody,* I thought to myself. Certainly not Scripps and, after my Randy experience, not even all the Serious Eaters.

Serious Eats was, as Mike would say repeatedly, "still in the game." Only the game was getting harder, with new, sometimes better-financed competitors seemingly cropping up every day. We were getting better too— I was proud every time I refreshed my browser. But were we getting better quickly enough?

Chapter 14

THE GREAT, SLOW PIVOT
TO RECIPES

E ven as I was fighting tooth and nail to win advertisers to keep the lights on, I was being questioned about our content strategy, what we focused on, namely where to eat and what was going on in the food culture. A crucial suggestion came early on from the most unlikely source, a man who rarely set foot in a kitchen.

"I've heard about you. You're too nice." Gawker founder Nick Denton and I were having breakfast at Nick's regular table at Balthazar, Silicon Alley's power breakfast spot, on a late winter's day in March of 2007. As power breakfast spots go in New York, it's a fine place to have a morning meal while discussing business. The Balthazar cochefs at the time, Riad Nasr and Lee Hanson (now the chef-owners of the extraordinary restaurant Frenchette), along with its wonderful baker, Paula Oland, developed a most excellent breakfast menu that remains largely intact to this day.

Then, as now, you couldn't go wrong with the breakfast bread basket, the brioche French toast, or the "Eggs En Cocotte"—eggs, cream, and thyme baked in a ramekin and served with "soldiers" (thin strips of toast perfect for dipping).

That morning I wasn't there just to eat. I was there to soak up as much wisdom as I could from one of the blogosphere's most successful entrepreneurs. Nick Denton had, as I have previously noted, invented the group-blog business model with sites like Gawker, *Gizmodo*, and *Lifehacker*. Meg Hourihan had asked Nick if he would have breakfast with me. "Nick's a fierce competitor, and he is all business, so don't buy his bemused half smile," she said. "But since he doesn't have a food blog as part of his stable and he could care less about food, he's willing to talk to you."

Nick said, "I've looked at your site. It looks good. But why is there no chef gossip on the site?" He paused before answering his own question—I was "too nice." I explained, "Guilty as charged. But that's because I just don't care about who's having sex with whom in the walk-in at a restaurant. I'd much rather tell people where to get the best pizza in the city, or the whole country for that matter."

Nick chuckled in response (he could give a rat's ass about the best pizza anywhere) before asking another penetrating question: "What about recipes?" I hastily responded, "I don't think the world needs another recipe database, Nick. Do you? There's Epicurious, Allrecipes, AOL, Yahoo! . . ." I added with false confidence, "Recipes have become a commodity on the web. Plus, recipes aren't my jam."

Nick, being all business, gave me a quizzical look (as if to say, *Who cares what your jam is?*), before posing an essential question: "How many recipe searches are there a month on the web right now?" "I don't know. I must admit that I've never thought about that question before." Nick shook his head in disbelief before pulling out his phone and Googling the recipe search question. He handed me the phone so I could see the answer for myself. "Thirty million. Holy shit!" He paused to laugh at me before delivering the coup de grâce of the breakfast. "If I were you, I'd figure out a way to do recipes, Serious Eats style." And with that I paid the seventy-five-dollar check. It was the best and cheapest advice I ever got from anyone. I ignored the gossip advice. Not my jam.

The suggestion to do recipes, Serious Eats style, was obviously great advice. There was just one little problem. I had never developed a recipe in my life. Actually, that's not true. In *New York Eats* I had helped the owner of Eisenberg's write his tuna salad recipe.

Here it is:

Eisenberg's Tuna Salad

1 can Bumble Bee solid white tuna

Hellman's mayonnaise

Mash the tuna and the mayonnaise with a big spoon. If you use a fork, it won't turn out right. All the tuna salad must be eaten the day you make it.

Eat your heart out, René Redzepi, Thomas Keller, and Ferran Adrià.

The rest of the Serious Eats crew as it was configured then was not much help either. Alaina, Adam, Robyn, and Meg were curious home cooks, but they were certainly no recipe developers. Erin had worked in the kitchen at 1789, a very good restaurant in DC, when she was a student at Georgetown. But she had no experience in developing recipes either.

I had investigated buying recipe databases and talked to cookbook editors but quickly discovered that I didn't have the money or the time to negotiate with big publishing houses or really successful cookbook authors who had retained their intellectual property rights.

So what did I do? As mentioned earlier, I convinced a couple of established recipe developers I knew who were getting some traction on the internet, like my friend Dorie Greenspan, to write for us. And I took a page out of old media's book by aping what the newspapers and food glossies were doing on a regular basis. I got permission to publish a few recipes we would adapt from a newly published cookbook on Serious Eats in exchange for writing multiple posts about the book. And we would also do a book giveaway. The publishers were thrilled about this promotional exchange and the accompanying publicity. I named the column "Cook the Book."

All of these posts did all right, traffic-wise, but I certainly hadn't come up with a way, in Nick Denton's words, to do recipes Serious Eats style. I really needed someone and something to break through the recipe internet clutter, a column that was Serious Eats native and couldn't be read anywhere else. It ended up taking me two years to come up with that someone and something.

In 2008 Adam Kuban had hired a *Cook's Illustrated* editor and writer named Kenji López-Alt to do some burger reviews for our burger blog, *A Hamburger Today*. *Cook's Illustrated* founding editor and publisher Chris Kimball allowed Kenji to freelance for us only because he was writing about things *Cook's Illustrated* would never write about. Kenji's burger posts showed an insatiably curious scientific mind, major cooking chops, and an encyclopedic knowledge of pop culture. He was unabashedly geeky, a fine writer, and a great storyteller. Kenji was as serious an eater and writer as I was, if not more, even though our backgrounds and work experiences were completely different. Plus, he shared my love of everyday foods from many different food cultures around the world. Burgers, check. Hot dogs, check. Pizza, check. Ramen, check. Tacos, double check.

The very first post Kenji wrote for us, on May 12, 2008, put all his insanely prodigious talents on display. It was about what he dubbed the Blumenburger, the difficult and time-consuming burger recipe developed by the famous, scientifically oriented British chef Heston Blumenthal. It begins:

> England's **Heston Blumenthal** follows in the footsteps of Spain's legendary **Ferran Adrià**, in that he attempts to create a cuisine that places a high value on innovation and stimulation of the senses beyond taste. So **what happens when one of the most highfalutin' chefs in the world tries to tackle the hamburger,** one of the most well-loved yet humble foods in the world? . . .
>
> So in the name of science, research, and saturated-fat intake, I followed Blumenthal's recipe for the ground beef sandwich nonpareil. All 12 pages of it. Here's what I found:

> **Interesting Figures**
>
> - Number of ingredients to make a cheeseburger:
>   3 (meat, cheese, bun)

- Number of ingredients to make a Blumenburger: 32

- Cost of average homemade half-pound cheeseburger: $3

- Cost of Blumenburger: $9

- Time required to make average cheeseburger: 7 minutes
  (3 minutes of prep, 4 minutes cooking time)

- Time required to make Blumenburger: 30 hours, 4 minutes
  (30 hours of prep, 4 minutes cooking time)

You didn't have to be a food science geek to recognize a major talent on display in this post. It was hilarious, revealing, and indisputably true.

Kenji was no stranger to the blogosphere. He and a friend had created GoodEater.org, which Kenji described to me in an email as "a website and blog that merges conversations on food quality, enjoyment, sourcing, and sustainability." It was actually really good but hadn't gotten much traction in the blogosphere. They were still maintaining it when I met Kenji. Unlike Serious Eats, it was never meant to be a business.

Kenji was also no stranger to recipe development. His years at *Cook's Illustrated* had given him a deep understanding of how to develop a recipe. Those years had been preceded by many years spent cooking for some of Boston's best, most thoughtful chefs, folks like Barbara Lynch (No. 9 Park), Ken Oringer (Clio, Uni), and fellow geek chef Tony Maws (Craigie on Main).

Kenji, Robyn Lee, and I agreed to meet for lunch at Trailer Park Lounge, a kitschy spot four blocks from our offices on West Twenty-Seventh Street. I ordered. A lot. In fact, we ordered just about every item on the menu: cheeseburger, turkey burger, grilled cheese, Philly cheesesteak, sloppy joe, chili mac and cheese, nachos, sweet potato fries, and tater tots. I would have ordered more, but there were only three of us.

I said to Kenji right after my prodigious ordering, "I love your burger reviews, but I was wondering if you would be interested in writing a food science column for us. You would have complete freedom to write about whatever you want, in your voice, which I love. You could write about burgers, fried chicken, pizza, anything. I'm thinking it would have both recipes and technique content. I think that given your background [Kenji is an MIT grad whose father is a professor at Harvard Medical School], your passion for both science and cooking techniques, and your strong storytelling abilities, this column would be something you could get excited about."

Kenji's face lit up. "I can't believe you're asking me to write a food science column. I've always wanted to do that." "Great," I replied. "We could call it 'The Burger Lab' when you're writing about burgers and 'The Food Lab' when you're writing about other stuff, because you would be digging deep into the science of cooking."

Over the course of the next few days, Kenji came up with a couple of different ways to structure the column. The one that appealed to both me and him was what he called the *MythBusters* approach. Kenji would examine the conventional wisdom on any given food-related subject and see if it held up to his extremely close scrutiny. Given his take on the Blumenburger, Kenji had clearly been thinking about this subject for a very long time.

Before Kenji, food science was primarily the province of two other food writers, Harold McGee and Shirley Corriher. McGee's 1984 *On Food and Cooking* was groundbreaking, the definitive word on the subject, but he took a scholarly approach (no surprise, as McGee got his PhD in Romantic poetry at Yale, where he studied under Harold Bloom). Corriher's 1997 book *Cook-Wise* was a little more down-to-earth, and her voice was friendlier and more conversational. But neither of their voices was particularly contemporary.

On TV, the Food Network's Alton Brown had taken the food science mantle from Corriher and McGee with *Good Eats*. Kenji and I both love Alton. But Alton's voice is completely different from Kenji's (a little more acerbic, less pop culture oriented, and a lot more theatrical), and he has a very different style of visual storytelling. Plus, Alton's voice is first and foremost a television voice, though he has also written many books and even developed a stage show that he's successfully taken on the road.

We agreed that I would pay Kenji thirty dollars a column to start. Before you start laughing, that was five dollars more than we were paying everybody else—not because I was taking all the money we were (not) making and spending it on helicopter rides to the Hamptons, but because that was all we could afford. And sadly, it was double what a lot of other food blogs were paying for posts.

The first Food Lab post, "How to Boil an Egg," appeared on Serious Eats on October 9, 2009. It was an immediate viral sensation that became the most popular column on Serious Eats at the time. It was quintessentially Kenji. First he busted the three myths that egg boilers have had foisted upon them for years. It turns out that the age of the eggs, the pH of the water, and whether your pot is lidded or not make no difference when you're trying to optimally boil an egg. And he tested a host of other variables that really did matter.

That post was pure genius and pure Kenji. I loved everything about Kenji's Food Lab posts: his "Harold McGee meets the Simpsons," perfectly pitched, pop culture–drenched writing voice (Kenji claimed that two of his major influences were Mr. Wizard and the old TV show *MacGyver*); the way he framed his narratives by taking his readers on a journey; his obsessive rigor; and his methodology, which readily admitted his failed attempts along the way to perfection. I ate a thousand slices of pizza when I wrote my pizza book in search of the perfect slice. Kenji probably ate a hundred hard-boiled eggs in his search for the perfect hard-boiled egg recipe. Same obsessiveness and passion, different subjects. The Serious Eats community agreed with me about Kenji's talent. Within three months his "How to Boil an Egg" post had gotten 144,000 page views, ten times what any recipe post had gotten on Serious Eats at the time.

A few days later Robyn Lee, now editing our burger blog, *A Hamburger Today*, emailed Kenji to see if he was interested in being our burger recipe tester. Which he was.

One of Kenji's first Burger Lab posts was about his attempt to re-create Shake Shack's burger, our favorite fast-food burger.

There's nothing special about the burger—**regular squishy bun,
a ¼-pound patty of griddled meat, lettuce, tomato, and sauce**—
but like all good burger experiences, the sandwich is far more than
a sum of its parts. To recreate the experience at home, I had to eat it,
dissect it, deconstruct it, research it, eat it some more, rebuild it,
break it down again, reconfigure it, taste it, eat it one more time,
and finally reconstruct it again. Here are the results of my labor,
from the ground up.

I was at his apartment when he was trying to replicate the Shake Shack burger, and after about a dozen tries, boy, did he nail it. One bite, and he sent me hurtling back to the line in Madison Square Park. More Kenji brilliance. Taking something seemingly mundane and making it sublime. Kenji was put on this earth to become the Serious Eats recipe czar. Plus, it seemed only right that Kenji idealized the Shake Shack burger, given its prominence in the history and evolution of Serious Eats. The Shake Shack burger is still a pretty damn good one to this day, even though there are now hundreds of Shake Shacks around the world, and Shake Shack is a publicly traded company.

A recipe strategy that would satisfy Nick Denton was forming before my very eyes, thanks to one extraordinary find. Kenji's voice and storytelling style were the essence of Serious Eats. Successful blogs like Serious Eats created a world unto themselves that readers wanted to live in. Successful magazines do the same thing. I realized at that moment that something was either right for Serious Eats or it wasn't. I recognized Kenji on an almost cellular level not only as somebody whose creative output fit perfectly within the Serious Eats ethos but also as someone who could push our mission of serious deliciousness forward.

I asked in a follow-up email if Kenji wanted to take charge of all of our recipe development content. "We could call you our recipe czar." Kenji responded in an email: "Recipe czar sounds fun and interesting, and I'm a free agent as far as Chris [Kimball] is concerned. [I had asked if his recipe czar duties would conflict with his *Cook's Illustrated* relationship.] What would the details be in terms of turnaround, number of recipes, and compensation? And finally . . . I was asking if we'd be able to start at $30 from the beginning (which is what I was getting for my AHT stuff), with the possibility of getting a per-piece raise if it proves to be worthwhile for you in the future."

I couldn't believe our good fortune. I had my recipe czar, as we quickly worked out a contract for those duties that was both fair to Serious Eats and helpful to Kenji in his quest to generate regular income as a freelancer.

There was one small problem. I had no one on staff to edit Kenji's recipe posts. Those duties fell to Erin and the newest member of the tribe, Carey Jones. Carey had interned for us in the summer of 2006, when she was still in college. Carey is a terrific, prolific writer with a passion for cocktails, and a very precise line editor. However, neither had a lot of recipe editing experience. But Carey and Erin, always up for a challenge, threw themselves into editing Kenji's recipe posts. Some heated moments ensued, but mutual respect allowed them to work out most of their differences.

The Serious Eats community embraced Kenji immediately. And so did everyone else at Serious Eats headquarters, including Carey and Erin. Kenji was headstrong and opinionated but a good and funny colleague. The tribe was coming together rather nicely.

Kenji turned out to be ridiculously prolific. He immediately started turning out multiple posts a week for Serious Eats in addition to all the other freelance gigs he had to take to earn a semblance of a New York living. "Do you ever sleep?" I asked him one day when he was at the office. "Four hours a night," he replied with a chuckle. His wife, Adri, has since confirmed that he was not kidding.

Being married to a literary agent and having written a couple of books myself, I had a pretty good sense of what goes into a book worth writing and publishing. I immediately saw a Food Lab book in my head. In December of 2009 Kenji and I went out for another burger lunch at a now-defunct branch of Bill's Bar & Burger in New York's then-newly-fashionable Meatpacking District.

We sat down for lunch. Kenji knew the drill. I ordered for both of us: a modest four burgers, sweet potato and regular fries, Bill's excellent onion rings, and a couple of malts. "See," I told Kenji, "I can show some restraint when ordering if need be."

I quickly turned the conversation to the matter at hand. "Kenji, you need to write a book, dude, a Food Lab book. My wife is a terrific agent and a big fan of your posts. You should talk to her and see what she thinks. If you like her, she can be your agent. And if you don't like her, talk to other agents. You don't have to go with her on my account." Somehow I didn't think paying him thirty dollars a post allowed me to dictate his choice of agent.

Vicky and Kenji got along famously. Kenji worked really hard on his book proposal for *The Food Lab: Better Home Cooking Through Science*—"the book that [geeky British celebrity chef] Heston Blumenthal would have written if instead of a multimillion dollar research lab and an infinite source of high-end ingredients, all he had was a home kitchen and a supermarket like the rest of us."

He and I made a deal. I would license him the name "The Food Lab" for free for two books. And I would also grant him a gratis license to use some of the Food Lab's content in his book. Serious Eats and I would not participate in any way financially in his book. Again, at thirty dollars a post I didn't think it would be fair to do that, though my experience in a similar situation had been that old media would ask for either a licensing fee or equity participation in the book.

To me this was a win-win negotiation for all concerned. Kenji was growing my business exponentially in terms of audience for the princely sum of thirty dollars a post. As long as he continued to do that, he should be able to reap the full benefits of writing a book. It turned out to be the best deal either of us ever made, given what's happened to both Kenji's career and Serious Eats.

While Vicky was shopping the book to publishers, Kenji continued to write his posts for us as a freelancer and oversaw all our recipe posts as our recipe czar. Even all of that plus private-chef and catering gigs did not add up to a New York living. Adri, an equally brilliant fellow MIT grad, was in graduate school at NYU getting her doctorate in computer science, so it's fair to say that money was really tight in the López-Alt household.

By the spring of 2010 Vicky was getting a lot of interest from cookbook editors all over town. They were all reading Serious Eats religiously by that time. It certainly looked like a smart and forward-thinking publisher would be making an offer for the Food Lab book.

One lovely late March morning Kenji emailed me and asked me to meet for coffee. I sat down. Kenji looked concerned. "Listen, Ed, somehow Chris Kimball got wind of my book proposal. He offered to pay me what he said was a fair advance and publish my book under the *Cook's Illustrated* umbrella. Not only that, he also said he would put my name on the cover as the author. Chris said it would be the first time a name other than his would appear on the front cover of a *Cook's Illustrated* book. Finally, he said he would publish any other books I wanted to write. But—and I know this is a big 'but' for both of us—he said that I could never write for Serious Eats again."

Damn. Kenji had quickly become our most popular writer on Serious Eats, far eclipsing the rest of us. We really couldn't afford to lose him, but then again I didn't have the money to offer Kenji the full-time job with benefits he really needed. So I was in no position to make any other counter-offer than the promise of a bright future at Serious Eats once I did have the money to put him on staff.

I didn't have any right to, but I took Chris's completely legal and legitimate offer personally, as an attack on Serious Eats itself. I didn't know Chris well, but we had spoken on a number of occasions. In fact, in one phone call he had professed to be a fan of Serious Eats.

I tried to smile as Kenji was telling me about Chris's offer, but I'm sure he could see from my now-ashen face that I was crestfallen. I managed to quickly recover. "Look, Kenji, I understand why you're thinking about taking Chris's offer. Your wife's in graduate school, you're writing for me for thirty dollars a post plus your modest monthly stipend for being our recipe czar. Frankly, I don't even know how you're making ends meet at the moment. I wish I could offer you a full-time job right now, but I just don't have the money to do that. I think I'll have it within six months, but there's no guarantee of that. I do think that in the end you'll end up having a more fulfilling and remunerative career at Serious Eats, with the freedom to write whatever you want in your own voice. But I also know that it's self-serving for me to think that. So if you decide to take Chris's offer, I'll totally understand."

Kenji was clearly conflicted. "I understand what you're saying, Ed. Let me think about this over the weekend and talk it over with Adri. I'll let you know on Monday where I'm at."

The weekend seemed endless. I went into catastrophe mode, trying to imagine Serious Eats without Kenji. Things would definitely be harder, but I consoled myself by telling myself that we had been growing and getting better without Kenji, and somehow we would figure out a way to keep doing both. I kept going over the numbers to see if I had the money to hire Kenji, but it just wasn't there. And I kept trying to put myself in Kenji's shoes. Chris had made him an incredibly compelling offer.

By the time I walked into my meeting at Ferrara with Kenji on Monday, I was prepared for the worst, convinced that Kenji was going to be leaving. Even before ordering, we got down to business. "Adri and I talked a lot about Chris's offer, and though Adri, who's in charge of money in our household, was certainly tempted by it, in the end we both decided that staying at Serious Eats is the best thing for me to do. I have a lot of faith in you and Vicky."

Wow, wow, wow. I couldn't believe my ears. I was blown away. I almost started to cry, but I caught myself just in time, dabbing my eyes for an imaginary speck of dust. "Obviously I am thrilled with your decision. We are going to kill it together. I'm going to try to find the money to hire you ASAP."

I left the coffee shop still feeling stunned and jubilant. For Kenji to make that decision at that moment was not just courageous. It showed that he had enough faith in both Serious Eats and me to turn down what was clearly on its face a better offer. I also felt the added weight, the responsibility, of justifying Kenji's confidence in me by delivering what I promised. I added Kenji and Adri to the growing list of people I had made promises to: Mike, Vicky, Bob, all the other investors. I couldn't bear to think that I might let them all down in the end.

Later that spring Vicky secured an excellent offer from a legendary, now-retired cookbook editor, Maria Guarnaschelli, at W. W. Norton, one of the most prestigious publishing houses on the planet. More important for both Kenji and me, that offer was healthy enough to take a lot of the financial pressure off Kenji and Adri.

In August of 2010 I made good on my promise, which had been more of a wish and a prayer at the time. I hired Kenji full time. He went on to stay seven years as our recipe czar and culinary director. He wrote an email to everyone in the office when he was about to start: "Hey guys—just wanted to write to let you know how excited I am to be coming on board at Serious Eats. I told myself when I finished at Cook's that I'd never work for 'the man' again. Somehow even after taking this job, I don't feel like I've broken that promise (though to be honest, I'll miss the vacation days that freelancing offers). I couldn't wish for a brighter, smarter, more passionate hardworking, or downright fun group of people to work with. I'm really looking forward to it. See you in the office in September, and at my place for pizza on Sunday, 2 p.m." Little by little, the Serious Eats tribe was growing in all the right ways.

With the guidance of Vicky and Maria, Kenji's *The Food Lab: Better Home Cooking Through Science* became a runaway *New York Times* bestseller when it was published in 2015. Unsurprising, even though in typical Kenji fashion it ended up as a fifty-dollar, 910-page book. *The Food Lab* won both a James Beard Book Award and the IACP Cookbook of the Year Award in 2016.

When I brought Kenji on full time, I still hadn't solved the riddle of how to make Serious Eats a self-sustaining, profitable business. But hiring Kenji and focusing on recipes brought me and Serious Eats into a business realm that could more easily scale without raising a lot more money. Or so I thought at the time. The success of Kenji and the Food Lab also bought me an even more valuable commodity: time. Why? Because potential investors saw original, innovative recipes that generated exponentially more traffic as a valuable commodity. Serious Eats and I could take a moment to breathe.

Chapter 15

SOME DREAMS DIE HARD

You know, I didn't invest in Serious Eats to become a big-time concert promoter," Mike said to me over a brilliant lunch at one of his
favorite restaurants, Gotham Bar and Grill, in May of 2009.

I immediately replied, "I understand that. It's just that we
need more sources of revenue. Ad sales are a lot harder to come by than I
had projected. Events can help make up the shortfall." Mike's response:
"They can also bring the whole damn company down."

Mike was more right than he knew. We didn't lose the company over an
event, but we came damn close. And I came dangerously close to something
even more frightening—a very real threat to my psychological equilibrium
and well-being. What Mike couldn't have known was how this event would
bring me face to face with demons that I thought I had long ago exorcised.

Since college, I've been a live-events guy. As I wrote earlier, I was the
concerts chairman at Grinnell and then made a living producing shows for
the NYC Department of Cultural Affairs and then a concert production
company called New Audiences.

I still loved the thrill of putting on live events. Somehow the decades
had blunted the lessons I had learned about how high risk and low reward
the concerts were. So when it came to Serious Eats putting on events, even
with my family responsibilities, I was all in. Risk be damned. Our first event
was a sold-out Hot Dog Hootenanny in May of 2010 at a small venue,

beloved New York city wine shop Astor Wines & Spirits. I love hot dogs. Who doesn't?

Two hundred people came to sample the best hot dogs in the New York area: Katz's, Papaya King, bulgogi dogs (topped with shards of Korean-spiced beef), deep-fried hot dogs inspired by Rutt's Hut in New Jersey (try the well-done Ripper, so named because putting a hot dog in a deep fryer long enough rips a gash running the length of the dog), and two midwestern imports, Usinger's (a famous sausage purveyor in Milwaukee) beef and pork hot dog and a Vienna beef hot dog enlivened by celery salt and neon-green sport-pepper relish, by way of Chicago.

Each purveyor set up a table to serve from. The hot dogs were cut in thirds so that everyone could sample each one. We had hot dog symposiums in the adjoining teaching classroom equipped with a full kitchen. I didn't get the same charge out of watching people eat great hogs that I had gotten out of putting on a Ray Charles and Staple Singers concert, but it was still pretty great. And it fed my addiction to events.

Mike came and had a great time, though he grumbled all the way. We sold out despite the cold and rainy day. I was intoxicated by the seemingly easy success we achieved without spending one bit on advertising. We only made a couple thousand bucks after all the expenses were accounted for, but I felt sure that my proof of concept had been achieved. We made plans to do a whole series at Astor Wines & Spirits: an ice cream social, a hot chocolate hoedown, and a holiday cookie swap, an event with the Pioneer Woman, and a dinner with the legendary Chicago hot dog auteur Hot Doug.

We were definitely ahead of the food events curve, but all that meant was that we made mistakes first so the others who followed didn't have to. I was thinking now that we had one successful event under our belts, we could leverage that success and find sponsors for the series. Sponsorship dollars are the way all event producers offset their otherwise substantial risk. When you see something called the Budweiser Concert Series, know that Budweiser is paying so much for the naming privilege that the promoter's risk is substantially reduced.

But there was a megasized event that had been lurking in the background for months. It started with a phone call I had received the previous October. The guy who succeeded me at New Audiences had gone on to become a very successful talent agent booking big-name rock and folk acts. Stu (not his real name) called one perfect fall day and said, "You know that giant food and music festival you and I tried to get off the ground fifteen years ago?"—I certainly did remember that aborted debacle, which ended when some music exec stole the idea and failed miserably when he tried to put it on himself—"Well, Marty, another agent, has been out selling a very similar idea. Maybe we should team up; he said he'll bankroll the whole thing." I was so happy to hear this that I didn't stop to think how or why this third partner was able and willing to do this—or to consider what would make anyone take the completely unreasonable risk of being the sole source of festival funding.

One fine lunch later, the Great American Food and Music Festival was born. The positioning line I came up with for the event: "The Best Food in America in One Place." I imagined a series of booths serving iconic American foods that I had gathered; a couple of demo stages to showcase Food Network personalities and local chefs; and a main concert/demo stage with seating for five thousand people.

Marty found a venue, the Shoreline Amphitheatre in Mountain View, California, right across the street from Google headquarters. The venue was famous for the many Grateful Dead shows it had put on. It was booked and managed by mega–concert promotion and facilities management company Live Nation. I would book the food purveyors and my partners would book the music. We decided to charge thirty-five dollars, which would include the first plate of food.

I was elated. This was going to be my long-awaited dream come true. I had lunch with Mike to tell him about it. That's when he doubled down on the dire warnings he had issued before the hot dog event. "I'm not kidding, Ed. This kind of event could really tank the whole business. Even if you're not putting up any money, you are putting up your brand as collateral in lieu of capital, and that's the most valuable thing you have at the moment."

Mike hesitated for a second before continuing. He couldn't help himself. "Okay, I am going to give you one piece of advice. Don't call it the Serious Eats Festival or Serious Eats Live. That way if things go south, the site's name won't be sullied as badly." *That is true,* I thought to myself. Of course, that would limit the event's upside for Serious Eats, but I conceded Mike's valid point.

I went about securing the food purveyors. Barney Greengrass's grandson Gary was going to fly out from New York and serve smoked salmon and cream cheese on a bagel. Katz's chef and general manager, the late Kenny Cohen, had talked to Katz's owners, and they had agreed to come to the festival to serve that wondrous hundred-year-old institution's pastrami sandwiches (hand-carved deli sandwich serious deliciousness). Pink's (my hot dog of choice my senior year of high school in Los Angeles) was going to serve chili dogs. The Bracewell family, who owned one of my favorite barbecue joints in Elgin, Texas, Southside Market, agreed to drive their mobile smoker 1,500 miles to serve their brisket and sausage. Cincinnati-based Graeter's Ice Cream (whose black raspberry chocolate chip is one of the great ice cream flavors on the planet) was going to scoop their ice cream. Philadelphia icon Tony Luke would provide roast pork sandwiches and cheesesteaks. My friends from Zingerman's, the great deli and food mail-order catalog based in Ann Arbor, Michigan, were going to make BLTs with Tennessean Allan Benton's great bacon, along with peanut butter and jelly sandwiches made with Oakland-based June Taylor's celestial plum jam and Koeze peanut butter from Kalamazoo, Michigan. It was going to be a menu for the ages. How could it not be an event for the ages?

My dream was coming true. We added some local Bay Area foods, like Charles Chocolates and It's-It ice cream sandwiches, to round out the menu. And we guaranteed each purveyor a certain amount of money so at the very least they wouldn't lose money doing the event. And if the event made money, they would share in the profits.

We augmented the food offerings with celebrity chef cooking demos by Guy Fieri, Bobby Flay, Anne Burrell, and a host of local chef talent, like Boulevard's Nancy Oakes and her sausage king and meat cookbook author husband, Bruce Aidells. Some of the Food Network chefs cost as much as

$100,000 to book, but we felt that they would be a sufficient draw to be worth it. Thinking back on it, conceptually the whole thing made total sense. It was the execution that tripped us up. And that, my friends, is an understatement.

The other partners booked the music. We had a decent-sized music budget, but it turned out to be not enough to attract the kinds of bands we thought would be a serious draw. We ended up with Little Feat, Big Bad Voodoo Daddy, and Marshall Crenshaw as our music headliners.

We made deals with local media to be our marketing partners. We advertised on the radio. We hired a PR firm with extensive music business experience. Vicky's cousin Lisa Knox went around Palo Alto putting up posters.

We massaged the numbers for the festival a million times over. We would break even at five thousand paid attendees, if we succeeded in getting at least $200,000 in sponsorship money. Which we didn't. The problem with securing sponsorship money was that big brands want to see proof of concept before they write big checks, and the only way to prove a concept is to execute it. So inaugural events rarely attract major sponsorship money. We tried. God knows we tried. We met with senior Food Network executives, and though they were enthusiastic, their involvement was at best minimal. But we (actually it was Marty's call as he was putting up all the money) decided that we would be okay with losing money at Mountain View. Why? Because our thinking was that once we proved the concept, we could turn the festival into a twelve-city tour. Talk about delusions of grandeur.

We put the tickets on sale eight weeks out. Sales were really slow at the start, mostly because people didn't know what to expect at a first-time event, so they didn't want to commit to buying tickets until they learned more about what they would find when they got there. Our ads just listed the foods, the bands, and the chefs. I think people found it confusing. We were selling a hundred tickets a week or even fewer.

Things were looking dire: slow ticket sales and nonexistent sponsorship dollars were a recipe for complete disaster. We had endless conference calls to figure out whether we should cut our losses and cancel. But we had all convinced ourselves that we were creating the next big thing in events. We believed that there might never be another (or better) opportunity to realize our dream. Our collective passion overwhelmed everything else, including reason. So we pressed on, ignoring the many red, flashing warning lights that even a blind person could have seen.

Once the press release went out, the publicists and I reached out to the food section editors at the *San Francisco Chronicle*. I suggested to the publicist that I fly out a few weeks before the event with some of the foods we were going to serve at the event. The *Chronicle* food editors loved the idea of building a story out of those foods and my obsession. So, armed with two coolers packed full of pastrami, smoked salmon, bagels, and brisket and sausage from Southside Market, I went straight from the airport to the *Chronicle* offices downtown.

I was in full pied-piper mode, and the *Chronicle* food staff enjoyed the tune I was playing. Not only did they urge readers to go to "The United States of Yum" in an article published on Wednesday, but they added another huge spread about the festival in Thursday's Weekend Calendar section, calling the event "The Super Bowl of Regional Food."

After the *Chronicle* story appeared, ticket sales took off like a Tesla going from zero to sixty. By the time we opened the doors, we had sold eight thousand tickets. By 11:00 a.m. the day of the event, there must have been a line a half mile long to get in.

I had flown out two days beforehand. I got thrown off the first plane I was on because I didn't turn off my cell phone in time. The flight attendants decided to make an example of me. After the doors were closed and we were about to push away from the gate, two air marshals appeared out of nowhere. "Get your bags. We're taking you off this flight. They asked you three times to get off your cell phone, and you didn't get off."

I couldn't believe it. I stammered, "But this is ridiculous. I'm off the phone now. I was just calling my ride from the airport in San Francisco to tell her that, after a two-hour delay, we're about to take off." "This plane is taking off, all right," said one of the air marshals sternly, "but unfortunately you're not going to be on it." I refused to get my bags. The air marshals took them down for me.

They escorted me off the plane. Every passenger was looking at me with daggers. It was an aeronautical perp walk. I demanded to see a JetBlue rep to plead my case. Nothing doing. He told me, "You violated the rule. Now you're paying the price." It was the last JetBlue flight to San Francisco going out that night, so they booked me on the first flight the next morning. "Next time we'll have to arrest you," they told me. I couldn't believe this was actually happening. I felt like I was watching myself in a far-fetched scene from a movie. I called Vicky, went home to sleep, and caught the flight the next day.

Carey Jones, a Palo Alto native, picked me up at the San Francisco airport the following day. She had flown out the day before to make some last-minute preparations. Carey saw that I was shaken from being thrown off the airplane. As was her wont (Carey never, never loses her cool), she succeeded in calming me down. After a brief stop at In-N-Out near the airport for a Double-Double burger and fries (a quasi-religious, must-stop experience for an East Coast burger lover ordinarily deprived of In-N-Out), we headed over to the venue.

My partners were freaking out big time. We had contracted to use a futuristic (at the time) cashless payment system to make transactions easier and the lines move faster. Everyone who had a ticket would get a wristband loaded with the amount of money they had elected to spend on food and drink. When they wanted to add money, they could reload the wristbands at kiosks around the venue. The cashless system would make it easy for festival-goers to buy stuff and easy for the producers to keep track of the money.

Unfortunately, it didn't work. We spent all night trying to get it to work—and it did, for a while, but then it would go down again. We called every tech whiz we knew—including those at Google, whose offices were right across the street. Shockingly, Larry Page and Sergey Brin didn't return our calls. By midnight Friday, we thought we had it fixed once and for all. Of course, we convinced ourselves of that, because we had no plan B.

The first sign of trouble came when we opened the doors at eleven on Saturday. There were two lines, one for people who already had tickets, the other, a thousand people long, for those wanting to buy tickets at the door. The venue had never done a food festival before, so it only had a few people selling and taking tickets. When I asked the GM of the facility why there was only one person taking tickets, he blithely said, "When we do music events, nobody shows up when the doors open." I shook my head and explained, "This is a food festival and it's approaching lunchtime. These people are hungry." The lines got longer and longer. Our paying customers were not happy. "Let us in" chants started.

Still, it was a typically beautiful northern California late-spring day—sunnier than not, sixty degrees, and low humidity—so we stayed optimistic. The venue was perfect too, with wide walkways to allow for easy transportation of food and drink, lots of shade, plenty of tables, and gorgeous landscaping.

My nieces Anna and Sara toasted Serious Eats' good fortune with Will and Vicky and me. "To many more days like this," I said as we raised our glasses.

Shortly after the toast, I started walking the grounds. A guy with his wife pushing a stroller came up to me. "Are you in charge here?" he angrily asked. "Yes, I'm one of the producers. How can I help you?" I asked solicitously. He poked his index finger into my chest, practically leaving a mark, and shouted, "How can you help me? How can you fucking help me? I'll tell you how you can help me. My wife and I paid three hundred and fifty dollars apiece for two VIP tickets. When we went to get our child a bottle of water, they asked me for five dollars. Do you mean to tell me that three hundred and fifty dollars doesn't include the water?" VIP tickets were standard operating procedure for food events. They allow buyers early admission and usually other perks, like more-comfortable seating areas and all the beverages you can consume. Even more important, for event producers in general, VIP tickets are tremendous revenue generators because of their incredible margins.

"Oh, shit," I said to myself. The venue's management had kept the rights to sell soft drinks and beer because that's what they always did for concerts, and though we grudgingly accepted that fact, we had not made a side deal to accommodate the VIP ticket holders. "You're absolutely right, sir," I replied soothingly. "Let me go get your whole family bottles of water."

As I was walking to the producers' trailer to deal with the water problem, Katz's Kenny Cohen tracked me down. "Ed, we don't have any power yet at our station. I can't heat my pastrami." If Kenny couldn't heat his pastrami, that meant that all the other vendors serving hot food were in similar straits. More important, the festival-goers, expecting to eat as soon as they got in, were going to find that many of the dishes they had bought tickets to try were not available immediately.

Shoreline, we have a problem. Many problems, in fact. I went to the producers' trailer to try to find out what was going on with the power and the bottled water for the VIP ticket holders. There I discovered more bad news. The cashless payment system was down for good. People had no way to pay for their food unless they had brought cash. We didn't even have a way to take credit cards. At the time, there was no Square, no easy mobile cashless pay system. We scrambled to find change for all the vendors and brought in a couple of cash machines. It was not ideal, but we thought we were making the best of a bad situation.

We were not. The cashless payment system going down had created hysteria and chaos, inflaming irritation at the long lines—both to get in and then for food—and the power problem was making a bad situation worse. People were pissed. Really pissed. Thousands of people were demanding refunds, tweeting things like: "This is the worst day of my life. I have been waiting on line for two hours for a Katz's pastrami sandwich."

Alaina texted me, "If this is the worst day of someone's life, I'd like to be that person." True, but I didn't feel any better. We had failed to make good on our promises to the attendees. We learned something the hard way that restaurateurs have known from time immemorial. People expect perfect service, and when even a relatively small thing goes wrong, they get pissed and they want their problems solved immediately. We completely whiffed on this part of the event equation. In online parlance, we blew the user experience part of the festival. Even inhabitants of the United States of Yum expect good service when they are in line to buy chili dogs, and rightfully so.

What I thought was going to be one of the best days of my life was becoming one of the worst. One person tweeted something to the effect of "If I were Ed Levine, I'd be very careful about walking outside after this." That's right; people were threatening me over a pastrami sandwich. We managed to keep the festival open all day, and by the late afternoon, things seemed to have calmed down. But the damage had been done. Most of the people attending were demanding refunds.

I couldn't sleep that night. The nightmare that was the day kept me awake. I'm no psychiatrist, but it felt like I was having, in older psychological lingo, a mini–nervous breakdown. Mountain View felt like much more than a mere business setback. I felt like I had let the Serious Eats community down; they were all angry at me; they would all forsake me and Serious Eats. My missionary zeal had led thousands of people astray. I became convinced that Serious Eats was going to die right then, and that meant I was as good as dead.

The next day I huddled with my partners. We did a thorough postmortem. Our inadequate planning and lack of experience were the principal causes of the event's problems. We didn't educate the venue operators at all, we didn't adequately provide for our VIP ticket holders, we depended on the cashless payment system to work even though it was clear there were bugs galore, and we didn't provide power to the purveyors in a timely manner. I couldn't stop beating myself up over all of our mistakes. My partners were more businesslike. They were discussing the mechanics of refunds while at the same time mapping out future events. I didn't want to hear anything about more big events. I was a puddle. My chest was pounding the whole time. I was sweating profusely even though it was fifty-five degrees when we gathered by the pool to figure out what to do next. We concluded that we had to give a refund to anyone who asked for one. Mountain View was a complete debacle, and it shook me to my core. A big dream had been shattered. Marty was out a lot of money. I thought it might be the end of Serious Eats.

The flight home with Vicky and Will was the longest five and a half hours of my life, trapped in a too-small-by-half coach seat with my very dark thoughts. Vicky was a rock, as always—albeit a rock who would occasionally question what had gone wrong, who was responsible for the problems, and why I'd needed to do this event in the first place.

All three partners thought we knew how to throw an event like this. We didn't. It was simply too big a project, with too many moving parts to tackle. I did use the five-hour flight to compose a sincerely apologetic post for Serious Eats, which went up the following day.

The comments on the post were so vituperative we took them down. There were some positive, supportive ones too, but every negative comment felt like a knife twisting into my psyche.

The next night I went over to the apartment of a psychiatrist friend, Eric Marcus, desperately needing to talk. When my friend answered the door, he immediately saw what kind of shape I was in and hugged me. I stayed for two hours, well past both our bedtimes. Eric showed more empathy and compassion than I knew existed in the world.

It felt to me like someone, maybe the beloved and respected Ed, had died. The angry, hostile reaction on Serious Eats to my apology and to our day-of-the-festival post yanked my heart and soul right out of my guts.

I couldn't keep it together, even at the office. Dr. Lawrence Sandberg, an extraordinary psychiatrist whom Eric recommended, did over the course of the next few months play a major role in saving me and convincing me that Serious Eats did not need saving.

He helped me see that in my zeal to be my missionary self, to turn people on to great food and music, I had failed to heed the many warning signs that were revealing themselves to me about Mountain View. Dr. Sandberg helped me connect the Mountain View experience to the other real losses I had felt, of my parents and my home, to name two. Crucially, Dr. Sandberg pointed out that the festival was not even remotely in the same league as those earlier losses, catastrophe-wise.

He also helped me see that my feet had left the ground pursuing this dream. I had convinced myself that my invincibility, the ability to survive and rebound from trauma that I had developed to keep me moving forward as a teenager, would keep me afloat. Only in this case I had crashed to the ground hard.

Most important, Dr. Sandberg allowed me to forgive myself. I felt that I had let down Vicky, Mike, and all of my investors and employees. With many therapy sessions my depression lifted over the course of a few months. I realize now that I am one of the fortunate souls who have managed to overcome a serious bout of depression. My brief experience with it left me with a lot of respect for that monster.

Also, in my self-flagellating haste I completely forgot that it was in part the comments on my Mountain View post that I was reacting to. Memories are generally very short on the internet. People had spoken their piece and then moved on. But it took me a while to do the same.

The therapy helped (tremendously). But it wasn't until we'd put on another successful event—one that I truly felt represented Serious Eats and everything we stood for—that I really felt I'd put Mountain View in my rearview mirror.

Chicago hot dog auteur Doug Sohn, of Hot Doug's fame, had always been the one that got away for me. I'd tried to get him for Mountain View, but he'd said he couldn't handle the scale of the event. (He obviously knew something I didn't.)

Before his "retirement" in 2014 (miraculously, you can still find him at the Chicago Cubs' Wrigley Field during day games slinging his haute dogs), Doug had become the hot dog crown prince of Chicago, no mean feat in a city full of hot dog royalty. (I would say Gene and Jude's, where they put wonderful, salty french fries on the dogs, and Superdawg also belong in the royal family.)

Doug was the hot dog philosopher king. The experience of eating at his restaurant was like no other. People would start to wait in line at 9:00 a.m. By the time they made their way to the front, they were pretty pally with their line-mates. Once they arrived at the counter, there would be smiling, bespectacled Doug to take their order. They could certainly get a fine classic

Chicago hot dog at Hot Doug's. But that's not what they were there for. They were there for his haute dogs made with foie gras, and on weekends for his duck-fat fries. And they were there for the welcome, the experience, and of course the food itself.

Doug Sohn was everything we loved—he was an independent and idiosyncratic operator who'd become a success on his own terms by perfecting and innovating his passion. Who better to help us fly our flag than someone who'd elevated the quintessential street food into something three-star chefs would wait in line for?

We put the tickets for Doug's hundred-person-capacity event in New York on sale two months after Mountain View. They sold out in minutes. Doug was the hot dog version of the Stones or U2. We tried to approximate the Hot Doug's experience at the event. Each table would, when called upon, go up to a counter and order from Doug himself. Of course, it wasn't quite the same because we served only three things: a classic Chicago hot dog, a foie gras dog, and duck-fat fries.

Everyone who was there had a great time. I didn't hear a single complaint. It was the antidote to Mountain View and proof that we could do events our way, Serious Eats style—events where people felt well taken care of, well fed, and happy to be among fellow serious eaters. It was the Hot Dog Hootenanny Redux.

The Serious Eats tribe forgave me my trespasses. My two partners in the Mountain View event, Stu and Marty, went on to fine careers in the music business, though it did take a little while for Marty to dig out of the considerable financial hole we had all collectively dug for him. In due time, every vendor got paid.

Nobody on the staff or in our community abandoned me. Serious Eats didn't come crashing down. In fact, our traffic continued its dramatic rise, and so did our revenues. I even convinced a new writer to come on board: Maggie Hoffman, who started a Drinks blog for us. Maggie was a college friend of Carey's who had been writing a beer column for us since 2009. Maggie is another prolific writer; she wrote more than 1,400 posts for

Serious Eats during her six-year tenure at the site. By the time she left, Maggie had risen to managing editor. Maggie was put on this earth to make things run on time.

Even more exciting to me, I started writing again. The festival had consumed so much of my energy that I had stopped posting anything except festival updates. Readers and other serious eaters noticed.

I wrote a guide to fancy-pants hot dogs a few days later and felt like things were getting back to normal. We had survived my folly.

Not all big dreams should be pursued or realized, in business or in life, and crossbreeding them can be particularly dangerous. Serious Eats by itself was a big enough dream for me.

Chapter 16

THE DRAMAMINE YEARS

We really enjoyed meeting/seeing again the SE staff. And it was very heartening to see how much they care about SE and especially how much affection and admiration they have for you. Love, Mike."

Mike and a couple of other Serious Eats investors had attended the party we had thrown ourselves for winning two James Beard Awards. The awards were important to me. The James Beards are like the Oscars or the Emmys of the food world, and I'd become known as their Susan Lucci. I had been nominated at least half a dozen times but I'd never won. Serious Eats had been nominated twice before too, only to watch those awards go to other blogs. This year, 2010, Serious Eats had taken not one but two awards, for best food blog and best web video. The web video award was especially satisfying because it was for a video sponsored by Kraft about a day in the life of a greenmarket, and sponsored content is not usually considered Beard-worthy.

The Beard Awards meant my peers were recognizing the work I had been doing for almost twenty years. Even my old friend Cal came up to me afterward, gave me a hard fist bump, and said, "Serious Eats is so great. It's amazing what it's become." I thought that maybe advertisers would start to pay a little more attention to Serious Eats when our reps called the Beard

Awards to their attention. We weren't just any old food blog anymore. We were the food blog that had won two Beard Awards in one night.

We threw the Beard Award celebration at Motorino, a fine Neapolitan pizzeria in Williamsburg. We designed the menu in consultation with Motorino owner Mathieu Palombino, and what a menu it was. There was a beet salad with soft-boiled eggs, anchovy, and olives; addictive fire-roasted chicken wings with chili, mint, lemon, and sea salt; and seemingly endless quantities of every pizza on the menu, including Palombino's butter-basted take on clam pizza and the celestial brussels sprout pizza. (Don't miss it if you go, and if you haven't gone, do.) For the few with room for dessert, there were miniature bombolini with vanilla cream and preserved strawberries.

I gave a speech at the party thanking everyone who had contributed to Serious Eats: my wife, investors, editors, freelancers, and family. I of course got very emotional, because, well, these were my people. Serious Eats had already become much bigger than just me. Mike was right. I felt the love of everyone at the party that night.

It was a little like a victory party held by an underdog political candidate who came out of nowhere to topple a firmly entrenched incumbent. Everyone there was a true believer in me, Serious Eats, and what we were doing. And just like the folks at a victory party, we really felt we were on a mission: to change and democratize the food culture through food media without dumbing it down or pandering.

Maybe art and commerce could coexist peacefully. Maybe they could even complement each other. Maybe my belief that creating good content could and would lead to financial success wasn't as ridiculous as the money guys seemed to think.

Indeed, that dream seemed to be borne out. Or on the cusp of becoming borne out. Our high profile in the media and the James Beard Awards seemed to make us a hot business property. Never mind that we weren't profitable. Big media companies were convinced that digital media was something to reckon with, even something to fear. Their huge bank accounts might not be enough to vanquish us feisty upstarts. But they were willing to use that money to buy their way into the blog party.

Shortly before the Beard Awards, I got an email from Tom Middleton, an old business school friend, who had become an investment banker at Blackstone. He had a friend, Suzanne Grimes, who was then the CEO of *Reader's Digest*. Suzanne had written the following email to Tom: "Hey Tom, Asked one of my guys to take a look at serious eats for me. Do you know what his ambition is? Does he want scale to monetize with advertising, or does he have another idea?"

Three weeks later I met Suzanne for lunch at Maialino, where chef Nick Anderer's porchetta pasta is revelatory. *Reader's Digest* was coming out of bankruptcy, and she knew that she needed to have media assets that appealed to younger audiences to assure the magazine's future. At lunch, between bites, she seemed very excited about the idea of buying Serious Eats. I was so excited by her interest that I never thought the whole thing through. *RD* and SE? Talk about a culture clash. *Reader's Digest* was beyond old school. Its audience was and still is almost entirely folks fifty and older. It represented the distant past in the media biz. We were cutting-edge (or so we thought), web native, with a primarily millennial audience, and represented media's future. But then I realized that Suzanne Grimes had a serious case of FOMO, so her interest made perfect sense. And I sure was flattered. When it comes to relieving my Serious Eats–related stress and anxiety by investing in or buying us, flattery will get you everywhere.

During my conversations with Suzanne, I realized that I was drowning in my own ignorance. I couldn't answer 90 percent of the financial questions she was asking me. I didn't even have a bookkeeper at that moment, and Suzanne had an army of number crunchers to back her up. What I needed was an investment banker. Even Mike had no investment banking experience, except for some meetings when he was in the airline business. Hell, I barely knew what investment bankers did. It was time to put on my big-boy pants and take the numbers seriously, the way Mike did and the way he was always imploring me to. In other words, at least pretend I was a real CEO. It dawned on me that if I didn't take the numbers seriously, I couldn't expect potential acquirers to take me as a CEO or my company seriously.

I asked Tom if he could recommend an investment banker. Simultaneously I asked my neighbor Paul (not his real name), who happened to be a media investment banker and a very nice guy, if his boutique firm would be interested in taking me on as a client. I met with his firm. I thought his boss, whom I had had some negative dealings with before, was not someone I wanted to do business with. He acted like he would be doing me a favor by taking me on as a client. My neighbor quoted a percentage that his firm would take. The firm also demanded a hefty retainer of $75,000, due to them whether or not they sold Serious Eats. That number was a nonstarter for me. It was more money than we usually had in the bank.

Shockingly, Tom called and said Blackstone's media banker and his colleague Peter Cohen would be interested in talking to me. I was surprised to say the least. Big old Blackstone would take me and Serious Eats on as a client? Really? Peter Cohen is a legendary media investment banker, the dude who sold the Dodgers for more than $2 billion. We met in a fancy conference room at the Blackstone offices on Park Avenue. It had an incredible view and was furnished with expensive leather chairs and a beautiful, huge, dark wooden conference table. The whole place smelled and looked like Money and Business with capital letters. It was a place I had never seen before and couldn't imagine working in. Peter said, "I've looked at Serious Eats; it intrigues me. I am very interested in digital publishing, and I'd love to represent you. I can introduce you to some of the clients I deal with every day. I think we could help you in a lot of ways." Sold, right then and there.

Peter sent me an agreement. There was no retainer involved, just a sliding percentage scale based on how much Serious Eats sold for. I don't know if I got a friends-and-family discount (a lot of people told me I did), but I was sure appreciative.

I signed on the dotted line. Right before Tom reached out to me on behalf of Suzanne Grimes and *Reader's Digest*, my old friend Sameer from Scripps reappeared. I had been having encouraging conversations with Bob Madden, one of Sameer's colleagues, who was Scripps's head of digital content. They were interested in reengaging. Rather than engaging with him directly, I responded by telling him to talk to my new investment banker.

Sameer called me the next day: "Blackstone is representing you? Very impressive. It seems to me that you're bringing a nuclear warhead to a border skirmish. How'd you pull that off?" I didn't answer, but I knew from his question that I now had sufficient finance firepower to negotiate with Scripps, or anyone else for that matter. I had put myself on equal footing with any company that approached me the moment that I signed the Blackstone agreement.

I still felt I was in over my head. I had a hard time accepting the fact that all this was happening to Serious Eats so fast. I checked in with Mike often. Both sides of my head, the business side and the creative side, were ready to explode. I found it very hard to slalom between the two. The creative side was sheer joy. The business side not so much.

In the meantime Peter and company were doing their thing. They became the finance staff of Serious Eats, my CFO, controller, and bookkeeper all rolled into one. Blackstone's team was Peter, his young and hungry associate Jordan, and their even younger and just as hungry twenty-four year-old MBA Anthony, who crunched numbers twenty-four hours a day for his salary, which almost certainly exceeded mine.

They were armed with pretty compelling evidence that Serious Eats' star was ascendant. *Time* magazine named us one of the top fifty websites in the world for the second time in 2010. Traffic had doubled in that same year, up to two million unique visitors a month. We sold almost $2 million worth of advertising in 2010. It would have been $2.5 million if a major financial services company hadn't pulled their $500,000 buy one day after sending us a signed contract. You might remember that episode from the prologue.

The Blackstone crew built an insanely granular business model that had us scaling big time by 2012. I learned very early that if you couldn't show prospective buyers that your business could become huge with or without their assistance and money, nobody would be interested. According to Blackstone's model, our traffic would go from 2,057,393 unique visitors in 2011 to 6,554,299 in 2015 (we actually bettered that particular number). Total revenue would go from $1,668,371 to $14,179,762 in the same period (we didn't come close on that one). Earnings before interest, taxes, and amortization (EBITA) would go from a loss of $591,837 to a gain of $6.718 million. We were business pole vaulters, at least according to the model.

Peter was reaching out to his contacts. By the end of the year he had meetings set up with Time Inc., Discovery, *Reader's Digest*, and Scripps. I got a call from Peter relating a message from my old friend Sameer: "Tell Ed not to come to our meeting with some bullshit hockey stick numbers." Peter and I shared a couple of chuckles over that. Why? Hockey stick numbers are financial projections that are relatively flat for a year or two and then immediately go up exponentially. On a graph they would be shaped like a hockey stick. Here's the great irony about startups and hockey stick numbers. If your numbers and charts show steady incremental growth represented by a gradual diagonal line, potential acquirers will question your ability to scale in a timely fashion. And if you show them hockey stick numbers, those same acquirers will tell you that those numbers are not realistic. So you can't win.

Back at the office, Serious Eats continued to flourish. On the site we declared January 8, 2011, International Serious Eats Day. There was no significance to that day, so we figured we could imbue it with meaning. Serious Eats devotees met in seventy-three cities all over the world. Readers gathered everywhere from New York to Los Angeles to Jakarta to meet, eat, and drink with their fellow serious eaters. *A Hamburger Today* contributor and television producer Damon Gambuto actually deigned to eat Korean food at the Prince in Los Angeles, instead of his usual medium-rare cheeseburger. In Toronto the serious eater with the screen name "Salanth" and company ate gefilte fish and brisket and pickles at legendary deli Caplansky's. Serious eater Mizbee brought her baby, Denver, to Milagro Modern Mexican in St. Louis. Babies Lev and Malcolm were among the huge crowd that gathered in New York at Radegast Hall and Biergarten in Williamsburg (and they weren't even carded). We did the same thing the following year, and cities like Mexico City, Singapore, Jerusalem, Nantes, and Stuttgart participated. Serious Eats was starting an international movement.

On the way to the Scripps meeting at the Blackstone offices in January 2011, I bought a miniature hockey stick at the sporting goods store Gerry Cosby near Madison Square Garden. The first thing I did when we walked into the conference room at Blackstone was give—or should I say shove—the hockey stick (ever so gently, of course) in Sameer's face. He laughed. Lunch was from the great Cambodian sandwich shop Num Pang. Those folks make a mean pork belly sandwich. We gave what I thought was a kick-ass presentation. Nevertheless, Scripps dropped out.

The process was dizzying, and Peter warned me that it could be a huge distraction. When you're engaged in a startup, a wise woman once told me, "you will experience the highest of highs and the lowest of lows, often in the same day." And she was right. Some days were alternately thrilling and terrifying. But we were still on the upswing, in terms of both traffic and revenue. Peter repeatedly warned me to focus on my business instead of fantasizing about all the acquisition talk. "It ain't over," Peter said to me more than once, "until the check clears."

Then I got perhaps the weirdest inquiry ever. An investment banker from a boutique firm inquired in an email whether or not we were for sale. Said banker told me his Latin American client, who had just moved to Miami, was looking to acquire digital media properties as soon as possible. We set up a meeting. Over sandwiches from the Midtown East branch of the 2nd Ave Deli (young Latin American bankers apparently love pastrami too). The young, impossibly handsome banker said he had been forced to leave his country, capital in tow, and had started acquiring properties. I Googled him and discovered that Interpol was very interested in finding this person. In short order he disappeared. Sometimes I still wonder what happened to him.

It wasn't just Latin American bankers on the lam who were calling. At the request of Michael Wolf (not the *Fire and Fury* Trump chronicler of a similar name but rather a big-time media consultant doing a lot of work for Condé Nast who was really enamored of Serious Eats), I met with Condé Nast's then-CEO, Bob Sauerberg, who ultimately stepped down in 2018.

I was going to bring my laptop up to Condé Nast's gleaming Times

Square headquarters, meet him in the huge wood-paneled conference room right down the hall from his office, give him the pitch, show him Serious Eats. I fantasized that he would be so taken with Serious Eats that he would at the very least make a strategic investment in us and relieve us of our constant cash-flow crunch. Or maybe he would even buy us. My rescue fantasies always came into very clear focus in these interactions.

I was instructed by his assistant to go to said conference room and meet the IT guy, who would hook my computer up a big screen so that Sauerberg could see Serious Eats in all its glory. The only problem: the poor IT guy could not get my laptop connected to Condé's intranet. That was his only gig. At Serious Eats everyone except me could fulfill that function. Sauerberg would periodically wander into the conference room wearing his custom-made Armani suit that cost three times more than my laptop, see that we hadn't gotten connected, curse a few times, and walk out. Finally, after three or four trips to the conference room, he said, "Fuck it. Just come into my office, sit at my chair, and pull SE up on my desktop." The whole episode was an apt metaphor for the uneasy relationship between old media and the blogosphere.

I went into his office and immediately noticed that the furniture and the artwork on his walls were probably worth more than my whole company at that moment. I pulled up Serious Eats and showed it to him. "This is great," he announced, much to my surprise and delight. "But we need ten of these." Sauerberg was a finance guy. He didn't understand that laser-focused, high-quality blogs were not widgets coming off an assembly line. When Michael Wolf suggested in a subsequent conversation that he buy or invest in Serious Eats, Bob said, "Sure, when he gets his EBITA up, we might do that." Spoken like the former CFO that he was. And of course we never did get our EBITA up high enough for him to be interested.

Back at Serious Eats World HQ some of our posts were going viral. Kenji chronicled in words and pictures the "In-N-Out Burger Survival Guide," in which he ate every single item on its twenty-eight-item secret menu. That one post attracted 3.5 million unique visitors in the first year it was up.

Kenji wrote another clever post that fit in perfectly with the food zeitgeist at that moment, "Ramen Hacks: 30 Easy Ways to Upgrade Your Instant Noodles." Spurred on by a suggestion from one of our ambitious interns, Grace Kang, Erin Zimmer made sushi out of marshmallow Peeps for another post that went viral. Carey Jones and her boyfriend tried all 127 flavors that a new, high-tech Coke machine dispensed. What a wacky food lover's joy ride we were on.

We had what I thought were great meetings with *Time*, *Reader's Digest*, and Discovery. Peter and his crew dealt with the zillion follow-up questions. We even set up what they call a data room to serve as a repository for all of our financial information. Data rooms cost three thousand dollars a month to rent, more than a studio apartment in a fashionable New York neighborhood like Williamsburg, Brooklyn.

The data room allowed potential acquirers with a password to access Serious Eats numbers 24-7. *Reader's Digest* made a nonbinding offer of a range from $6 million to $8 million. Discovery made a nonbinding offer of a range between $8 million and $10 million. The range became a specific number only if one of the two companies made a binding offer. I couldn't believe it. Mike and Vicky were going to be so proud and happy. Mike was going to make a solid return on his investment, and Vicky was going to have her faith in me justified. Was this really happening? Maybe it was. I conveniently forgot about the nonbinding aspect of the offers. Peter often emphasized this point in our conversations, but I believe even he thought one of these offers would become concrete.

I went out to dinner with Beryl and Steve at a very expensive Italian restaurant, Italian überchef Michael White's Ai Fiori. We ordered black truffle pasta (the white truffle season had passed) and drank to our impending good fortune. I did mention that these were nonbinding offers. Not to worry, Steve and Beryl said. They too felt confident that at least one of the offers would become a reality. And since they invested in many startups, mostly biotech companies, I thought they must be right.

We made our second presentations to both companies. Everyone seemed to be nodding appreciatively. I'm a damn good, compelling presenter when I'm presenting my ideas. Everyone laughed at my jokes. I even incorporated a hockey stick joke into my spiel.

Both *Reader's Digest* and Discovery passed. I learned that companies often make nonbinding offers just to see more cards, to get more information about your company. It was a not-so-subtle but completely legal form of industrial espionage. It turned out that in the end neither Discovery nor *Reader's Digest* bought any food blog; maybe they learned that they shouldn't as a result of our presentations.

For me, though, this was a doubly difficult result of the "process" to digest. Why is the only way to learn this stuff the hard way, through often-bitter experience? Well, if you're reading this book, maybe you can learn a different way to navigate this minefield.

My reporting chops kicked in. I needed to find out more about why these companies had ultimately passed. I met with the Discovery deal guy, Jorge (not his real name), for a tuna sandwich at Eisenberg's in March. Jorge and I had really hit it off at the presentations, and I had learned that we shared a passion for those perfectly constructed sandwiches. Pro tip: have it on rye toast with lettuce, and skip the out-of-season tomatoes. The tuna sandwiches were glorious, and the conversation was edifying to say the least. "Ed, you have built a great company. Serious Eats is a great site. Blackstone did a great job with the financial model. Your presentations were spot on. But after your second presentation, my team and I discussed Serious Eats. We realized that we were going to have to put in at least $5 million in order for it to grow and maybe become relevant scale-wise in the Discovery Communications world. We are not a small company, so every company we buy has to have a big upside. We just decided it wasn't worth it to us. We only get to go to our board a few times a year on behalf of companies we want to buy, and I decided we couldn't waste one of those opportunities on Serious Eats. Now you might come to us a year or two from now with better numbers to show us, and we'd be happy to pay a much higher price than the one we offered in our letter of intent. Why? Because then my team's sales job becomes that much easier to our board."

I bought the tuna sandwiches, as what I had learned at that lunch was worth ten tasting-menu lunches at Le Bernardin. The blog- and website-buying craze that resulted from big media companies' FOMO was coming to an end. Blogs, schmogs, Jorge was saying. Building a successful, profitable, and therefore self-sustaining company with the potential for growth was going to become our only path to selling Serious Eats for a decent price.

These experiences should have put my rescue fantasies to rest for good, but unfortunately they didn't. I had just been having those fantasies for too long. And all the business news stories at that moment about unprofitable companies being bought for astronomical sums just fed into them. Mike had been trying to disabuse me of these fantasies ever since we launched Serious Eats. His mantra to me: "Nobody's going to rescue your company except you."

I was pretty down, but my resilience kicked in. Then our offices were broken into, apparently, the police said, by some people who lived nearby in a massive apartment complex. They had traced some of our equipment to one of the buildings in the complex, but by the time they went to investigate, the laptops had been successfully fenced. I just saw this as a further test of my resolve. By this time I knew full well I was likely in the early stages of a marathon. We replaced the thick glass front door to our office, but that didn't deter thieves from breaking in a second time a week later.

The third time we were broken into, I was in Rome with Vicky and Will on vacation, enjoying Gabriele Bonci's astonishingly delicious newfangled (for Rome, at least) focaccia-like pizza at Pizzarium, and Giolitti's extraordinarily intense gelato. The nocciola (hazelnut) and the Sicilian pistachio flavors there are so vividly flavored they taste like you're eating a fistful of freshly roasted nuts. My cell phone rang at Giolitti and it was the police in New York. "We want to tell you about what was taken from your office from the break-in." I replied exasperatedly, "We've already had this discussion. I know exactly what was taken." Pause. "No, Mr. Levine, we are talking about last night's break-in." I couldn't believe it.

Using Skype, which Vicky had to teach her tech startup founder husband how to use, I managed to secure a new space I had been looking at before we left for Rome. It was a funky loft space in New York's Little Italy that had previously housed the legendary Italian bakery Ferrara wholesale cannoli operation. Even the backstory was perfect for Serious Eats, though most cannoli are not to my taste. There wasn't much natural light in the space, and there was no kitchen for Kenji to cook in, but I figured that somehow we would make it work.

And we did. We moved into the new offices the day before I got back from Rome.

When I returned, I had lunch with Mike at DBGB, Daniel Boulud's now-defunct attempt at a scene-y downtown restaurant. I thought it was just going to be a check-in lunch that would feature descriptions of my eating exploits in Rome. I wasn't looking for comfort or rescue or even advice. I thought it was just going to be lunch with my brother.

I hadn't even told Mike about the third break-in or the amazing pizza bianco at Antico Forno in Campo de' Fiori when he blurted out the unthinkable. "I've taken a close look at the numbers. I think you're in more trouble than you realize. You had to take most of the money out of your line of credit just for payroll, and I don't have to tell you that the bank will come down on you hard if you don't put the money back in right away. And because you personally guaranteed the loan, the bank will come up with a plan for you to repay them with personal funds if you can't pay them back out of your business account."

Then came the crusher: "I don't believe in Serious Eats anymore. I still believe in you, but I think you bit off more than you could chew with the business. I know you don't want to hear this. I just don't see how you're going to make it work. If I were you, I would just sell it and get whatever you can for it. I know I'm going to lose just about all the money I put in, but so be it. Live and learn."

I couldn't believe what I was hearing. "But Mike, there's so much good stuff happening. Traffic is going through the roof. Ad sales are picking up. Kraft, General Mills, General Motors, American Express, and Visa are all repeat advertisers on our sites. And there's still lots of interest in buying the site. We're going to make it."

Mike wasn't buying it. "Look, I can't force you to do anything, and even if I could, I wouldn't. It's your call, but I would really think long and hard about selling now. I know it will hurt if this is the way Serious Eats ends, but I can also see how much the business side of SE is causing you pain and angst every day."

I walked around the city for hours trying to process what Mike had said. He was certainly right about the angst and pain the business aspects of Serious Eats were causing, but in his attempt to paint an accurate portrayal of the big picture, he was missing how much progress we were making as a business and the change we were effecting in the food culture. We were changing the way people cooked and ate. We taught people to think critically about received wisdom in food science and to appreciate and glorify even the cheapest and most common foods, like pizza and hot dogs and burgers. We popularized sous vide cooking. I also don't think he understood how proud I was of the team I had built—and am still building to this day. Perhaps most important, he didn't understand that at that moment I so identified with Serious Eats that if Serious Eats died the kind of ignominious death Mike was describing, I would die too.

And maybe I had to tell myself this to keep going, but I really did think business success was imminent. I didn't know if I could get through this. I just told myself that Mike didn't know the business as well as I did (though he did know a lot of things), and I resolved to keep going. He would never force me to sell, nor could he. He didn't own a majority of the business. And he wouldn't marshal all of the other investors against me. That would be a serious betrayal, one neither of us was willing to risk. By my second lap walking around the island of Manhattan, I resolved never to sell Serious Eats like that. There would be no fire sale. At least not then.

When I finally arrived home, Vicky took one look at me and realized that I was hurting big time. She asked me what happened. I told her in the most dispassionate way I could (which was not all that dispassionate) about my lunch with Mike. "Maybe he's right. He is a really good businessman, but he didn't need to ambush you like that. And maybe he's not right. Sleep on it. That's what I do in my business. It's so much easier to make decisions

in the morning. My guess is you'll figure out what you should do by then."
Vicky must have said those very same words to me a hundred times. And
while she was, of course, right, sometimes sleep was hard to come by. I did
manage to sleep that night, and when I woke up I knew that I could never do
what Mike had suggested.

Mike on some level realized he had gone too far in his effort to "tell it
like it is." I didn't return his many calls or emails over the course of the next
few days. Finally I responded, defrosting the chill on our relationship but
making it clear that I didn't want a repeat ambush.

Mike wrote back, "It's clear (and not a novel thought) that mixing business with intense personal bonds is a potentially explosive combination.
Family relationships have broken up over this sort of thing and I think neither of us wants to take that risk. Finally, since it won't be a business event,
I'll buy the next lunch, which I hope will be soon. Love, Mike."

Love, Mike? The weird thing about these kinds of back-and-forths between us is that Mike really thought he was exhibiting his love for me by
leveling with me. He didn't realize that his leveling with me was going to in
fact level me unless I could find the strength not to listen to him.

I was still holding out hope for a savior. I hadn't told Mike about another interested party, Bonnaroo's parent company, Superfly Productions.
A wine store owner in Berkeley who had helped me with the Mountain View
debacle had written to me the year before and asked if he could digitally
introduce me to two of the Bonnaroo founders. When we met, it turned
out that Kerry Black and Jonathan Mayers loved food and music as much
as I did.

We had dinner at Balaboosta, one of my favorite restaurants in New
York, in June of 2011. The cauliflower with currants and capers should not
be missed. Flush with cash from Bonnaroo, Jonathan and his partners
wanted to either buy Serious Eats and install me as the CEO of the Superfly
food events division or at the very least make a significant strategic investment in us. Their thinking, according to Jonathan: "You've developed an
amazing audience, a passionate audience, and a very big audience quickly.

Food is the next big thing in events. We want to go into the media business. If we buy you, your audience could be the foundation of many food events."

Bonnaroo made the event we'd thrown in Mountain View seem like a picnic. More than a hundred thousand believers gather every year on a farm outside Nashville for three days of eating, drinking, listening to music, and doing what young people do everywhere they gather in large numbers.

Unfortunately, the deal Superfly was proposing wasn't a slam dunk. Though Bonnaroo was very profitable, our deal was predicated on their raising a lot of money from some Baltimore-based bankers so that they could (a) buy out their original money partner and (b) buy us. So their way of buying Serious Eats was like a bank shot in basketball or a shot off two rails in billiards.

That bank shot was even more improbable than it seemed. Though Bonnaroo was insanely profitable, Superfly's attempts to scale its business by creating other festivals hadn't really worked (other than the Outside Lands festival in San Francisco, which does have a more built-out food and wine and beer component), so potential investors were scared off by that. Then there were the *huge* potential legal liabilities created whenever a hundred thousand young people get together and get high on an often-muddy, shade-free farm in central Tennessee. Any countercultural historian can tell you that people do occasionally take unnecessary risks and die at big music festivals.

Finally, Superfly's original backer and money partner was Coran Capshaw, a music business legend. As a result of managing the Dave Matthews Band, owning a hugely successful rock and roll merchandising company (think millions of logoed T-shirts at venues all over the country), the dude was hedge fund wealthy. Oh yeah, for a little added flavor, Capshaw also owned many Five Guys franchises. Not the best fast-casual burger mini-chain (that honor goes to Shake Shack), but not the worst either. So Capshaw's motivation to sell was basically zero unless they came to him with the proverbial offer he couldn't refuse.

Nonetheless Superfly persisted, plying Alaina and me with VIP tickets to Bonnaroo (twice, actually), which is a thoroughly enjoyable, downright anthropological experience. Alaina and I were shuttled around in a golf cart. We were put up in a nice new hotel right outside the entrance to the festival. And we did see a lot of great music. Stevie Wonder and Jay-Z were performing the first year, Arcade Fire, Eminem, and Dr. John the next. *These people really know how to run a huge festival*, I thought to myself. Bonnaroo and other festivals like it are marvels of organization and structure.

The food offerings both years were pretty meager, a collection of not particularly inspired food trucks, which included a decent wood-burning pizza oven on wheels. But the musical and comedy offerings were smartly booked and beautifully curated, and I could see that there was an opportunity to match those choices with some amazing food.

I smoked pot at Bonnaroo for the first time in years and got incredibly stoned (though I had heard that growers had gotten much more sophisticated and were producing ever-more-powerful cannabis, I hadn't experienced their handiwork firsthand), and then one of the Superfly partners invited me to go backstage and listen to the Black Keys play. I said okay, but on one condition: "You must always be by my side. I don't want to be on that stage stoned out of my mind staring out at a hundred thousand people with no one to lean on for moral and emotional support." "Sure, Ed, no problem. We won't leave you hanging." Which of course is just what they did, as they turned out to have business to attend to. I became insanely paranoid. The minutes we were separated seemed like hours. But it was also fun in that scary, adolescent, "I'm not quite in control but I'm having a great time" way.

Bonnaroo was a pure adrenaline rush, until one of the Baltimore bankers, hitching a ride with me on the Bonnaroo CFO's golf cart, casually mentioned that he'd heard someone had died overnight. I think after that moment the enamored bankers became much less enamored. The blinking lights of liability couldn't be looked away from. The bankers dropped out. And so did we, shortly thereafter. The Bonnaroo boys had a lot less money to throw our way.

In the end, two months after my fateful lunch with Mike, the Bonnaroo guys made me an offer I could refuse. They sent us a preliminary deal that basically repaid my debts and gave us a tiny bit of money up front, with the rest to be paid out depending on the performance of the company (an "earn-out" in mergers and acquisitions parlance). And, oh yeah, we would all get to keep our jobs. It was an easy deal to pass up.

I said to Jonathan, "All I'd get out of this deal is a job and out from under my debts and a minority interest in your food and wine division." He said, "What's wrong with that?" *Everything*, I thought to myself. *Everything*. I hadn't started Serious Eats to get a job that *might* turn out to be a good one. I learned some valuable lessons in this negotiation that really came in handy in the madness of the ensuing years.

Jonathan then came to me with a different proposition: curate the food at a huge food and music festival they were planning for Prospect Park in Brooklyn in exchange for an annual fee of less than a hundred grand and a small piece of equity in any festivals we did together. You would think my Mountain View experience would have had me swearing off events like this. But I figured that the Bonnaroo guys would know how to do this.

I verbally agreed to do it and started introducing them around to chefs who loved music, like Andrew Carmellini, a James Beard Award winner who is even more of a music freak than I am. Soon the project was taking up all my time. The young Serious Eats staff, never ones to hold back their true feelings on any subject (that's in part why I hired them), rebelled: "You're never here! We need you here. We have a business already." And here was the kicker: "This thing is going to be a shit show, and you're putting us right in the middle of it." Those young whippersnappers had seen the debacle in Mountain View and learned a lesson; meanwhile, their much more experienced boss continued his journey into fantasyland.

I wasn't too far gone to hear reason. After the young Serious Eaters made their case, I reconsidered, called Jonathan, and told him we were not going to be involved. He was really pissed—in fact, he hasn't spoken to me since. But the young Serious Eaters were right. The Great GoogaMooga, as the Superfly guys called it, was a total shit show, full of unhappy attendees and purveyors. There were long lines and rainy weather and a very unhappy

NYC Parks Department, which did not take kindly to Prospect Park getting stomped on and turned into a muddy lake. The festival lasted two years before they pulled the plug.

The Bonnaroo folks were supposed to be the big festival Jedi masters, and even they couldn't pull off a big food and music festival. I owed the Serious Eaters a debt of gratitude for yanking me out of the line of fire—thank God the Great GoogaMooga wasn't our disaster.

Jonathan, Kerry, and their CFO, Avi Kent, ended up making just about everyone who was involved in GoogaMooga whole. Eventually Superfly sold Bonnaroo to Live Nation, and though the terms of the deal were not disclosed, I am sure Jonathan, Kerry, and Coran did very well. They deserved every penny they got. They had built something on a very large scale that was extremely profitable, and had provided pleasure to hundreds of thousands of people while doing so.

With the Bonnaroo deal dead, I went back into survival mode. I moved Serious Eats to another ad rep firm, Federated Media's archrival, Say Media. Say offered us almost double the guarantee. We made more than $100,000 a month most months, though it was based on some convoluted formula that to this day I still don't fully understand. Stayin' alive.

I was in fact focused exclusively on making Serious Eats self-sustaining when the phone rang one morning in July of 2011. It was Peter Cohen from Blackstone. "Believe it or not, Ed, I got a call from the CFO at Amex Publishing this morning. They said they were interested in buying Serious Eats. I told them that I would not even call you unless they were dead serious. And I quoted them $10 million as a starting point in any valuation discussions. They said they were serious. They want to set up a conference call with you, me, and two of their senior guys who are vacationing in Italy at the moment."

They must be serious, I thought to myself. Peter set up the conference call. One of the execs started the conference call this way: "Look, we're blown away by what you've been able to build at Serious Eats. We want you to spread your special sauce not only to FoodandWine.com but to all our other magazines as well, *Travel + Leisure* and *Departures*. You know how to build an audience online and produce great content cost-effectively. That's exactly what we need to do. We don't know how to do that. We need you to guide us into the future. We've talked to the higher-ups at Amex, and they have told us to pursue this."

Two weeks later we found ourselves in a very large conference room at American Express Publishing. There must have been twenty-five people from that company present. It was standing room only. Then–company president Ed Kelly had a great seat, and so did a couple of senior American Express corporate executives. There must have been ten bean counters present too, their HP 12c financial calculators at the ready. We gave our pitch. They were all nodding their heads in unison at the appropriate moments, even the bean counters.

Two days later Peter called me. "They want to make an offer. I really think they're not fucking around. Amex corporate has given them the go-ahead. They're going to throw out a few dates for Amex's chief marketing officer to make us an official binding offer." *This is crazy,* I thought to myself. After everything, we were finally going to get a real offer from a real company. I called Mike with the news. Even he was excited. "Wow, it sounds like these folks are serious."

A week passed with no date set up for the official offer phone call. Peter called his counterpart at Amex Publishing.

"Everything is still a go. We just have to take it a few more places up the food chain at corporate, and then we'll make a date to present the offer." A few days later they called again. "So sorry for the delay. It will be just a couple of more days. Hang tight."

A week later the CFO called Peter, very embarrassed. "Corporate just decided they won't sign off on any acquisitions for Amex Publishing. As far as corporate is concerned, American Express is a financial institution, not a publishing company."

I was speechless. I got a bunch of chagrined emails from the Amex Publishing team, apologizing more ways than a cheating spouse. I had to admit, this one really hurt. I mean really, really, hurt. But what could I do? Go back to work and try to make Serious Eats consistently profitable.

Here's a quick tally of all the failed acquisitions from 2010 and 2011:

Scripps, *Reader's Digest,* Discovery, Condé Nast, Bonnaroo, and American Express Publishing, not to mention an on-the-lam South American banker wanted by Interpol. And there were five more that I haven't even bothered to mention. What a ride.

The day-to-day was exhausting, a never-ending financial crisis. But Serious Eats was still intact. So was my relationship with my brother, and with Vicky. That ever-escalating, personally guaranteed line of credit for Serious Eats did almost prove disastrous to my marriage, my relationship with my brother, my business, and many longtime friendships. But it was also life support—the oxygen that enabled us to stay alive for the next four years. And so, in spite of all the ups and downs, the air really still seemed pregnant with possibility at Serious Eats. That was all I could ask for. I am either an incurable optimist or a fool.

Chapter 17

ONLY THE STRONG SURVIVE

s there one person here who has any interest in putting any more money into Serious Eats? It seems like a losing proposition to me. I don't think Ed could get a million bucks for it at this moment. What about you, Mike? You're his brother!"

Stephen McDonnell, my most recent investor, was sitting at the white Ikea Serious Eats conference table with many of his fellow Serious Eats investors on a warm May evening. While clearly not thinking straight, I had come up with the disastrous idea of convening a meeting of all of my investors in our practically air-free offices to convince them to put more money into the company. McDonnell was holding forth on Serious Eats, a topic that was obviously near and dear to his heart. Steve knew how to hold forth, all right. He is the intense, super-smart, hyperfocused founder of the organic meat company Applegate Farms, sold three years after this meeting for $775 million.

McDonnell had invested $400,000 in February of 2012 because, as he said to me countless times, "I just fell in love with you and Serious Eats. And love makes you do foolish things."

Right before the meeting I had asked him for more money at a breakfast at Maialino, a hotel restaurant–turned–power breakfast spot for hip entrepreneurs. McDonnell was furious. He started yelling at me, loud enough for the entire dining room to hear. "You're coming to me out of the blue and asking me for more money less than a year after I wrote you my first check. And what about the periodic financials I asked you for that you have not sent to me once?" Guilty as charged, I'm afraid. I was almost uniformly terrible about keeping my investors informed. The occasional, almost always naively optimistic newsletter didn't cut it. When I recounted my breakfast to Vicky, I told her, "I had a 'powerless' breakfast with Stephen McDonnell." I barely touched the lemon ricotta pancakes, which rank up there with the city's best.

I had spent days preparing a PowerPoint presentation that made the case that, yet again, Serious Eats was poised at the precipice of a great business breakthrough. We had gotten a $550,000 campaign from Wendy's the previous October that I used as exhibit A to show that we were finally winning the ad sales game.

I had attempted to ply the investors with food—platters of mozzarella and prosciutto from Di Palo's Dairy and Middle Eastern platters overflowing with falafel, hummus, and baba ghanoush from Taïm. Nobody was eating a thing, which was a telling sign of the mood even before Steve McDonnell had commandeered the meeting with his opening diatribe.

Mike explained, "I am already the largest shareholder and the largest investor in the company. I just don't feel comfortable putting in any more money, though I think Ed's plan is a sound one." McDonnell said, "Okay, if Ed's brother isn't willing to put in any more money, I don't see why we should."

The only other person who voiced support for my plan was my friend Bob, who was there exclusively for moral support, as he was tapped out as far as further investment in Serious Eats was concerned. "I have looked at these numbers closely and spent a lot of time with Ed going over everything. I think Serious Eats is ready to take off ad sales–wise." Mike weakly echoed Bob's point: "I am in regular consultation with Ed on the business, and the numbers are trending in the right direction." *Not exactly a ringing endorsement*, I thought to myself.

The conversation went on from there. By the time everybody was ready to leave, it was clear that I wasn't getting a dime from this obviously ill-conceived effort. Looking back, this meeting never should have taken place. Mike had even warned me, foreseeing what would happen when he was forced to admit that he wasn't going to invest further. Plus, the fact of the matter was that McDonnell was right. Stephen McDonnell did nothing but help keep Serious Eats alive with his money and advice, his comments at this meeting notwithstanding. Any experienced investor would have responded the same way. Maybe Serious Eats' sell-by date had come and gone. I just refused to admit it to myself. I just could not do that. I not only wanted to win, which everyone does; I absolutely refused to lose.

Everybody filed out. Bob and Mike stayed behind, Bob to help me clean up physically and emotionally, Mike to offer moral support. "Besides Bob, I was the only one at the table who was defending you. I supported you and your Serious Eats plan as well as I could," he said. "Are you kidding?" I yelled. "You sold me out with your half-assed show of support."

Bob stepped between us. He knew more about the history of my relationship with Mike than anyone else on the planet. At that point he had been a witness to that relationship for more than forty years. Bob and I both knew that nothing good was going to come out of this already-freighted confrontation. We all calmed down, Mike left, and Bob and I cleaned up in silence. I called Peter Cohen with the news. "It was worth a shot," he said matter-of-factly.

The all-hands investor meeting was merely the latest in a string of setbacks. In May of 2013, right after the disastrous investors' meeting, Alaina asked me to have coffee with her at our de facto conference room, Ferrara. Ferrara is a century-old iconic bakery in New York's Little Italy. "Iconic" doesn't always mean good. The coffee is terrible there, but any kind of cheesecake is more than okay. A member of the Ferrara family was our landlord. We spent so much time there in spite of the subpar coffee (as there was no privacy in the office) that they used to give me gift certificates for Christmas.

Alaina started right in before we ordered: "I've gotta get off the roller coaster, Ed. I don't know how you stand it. But I need to get off. I've been doing this with you for too long." It felt like a punch in the stomach, but I wasn't all that surprised. Alaina had taken a year off after her adorable son, Malcolm, was born. When she came back, she seemed to more easily tire of the endless drama, the constant search for money, and the limits placed on the business by our lack of funds.

It was impossible for me to contemplate life without Alaina. She had shared every foxhole with me since the very beginning in 2006. Still, I didn't try to talk her out of it. I was pretty sick of the drama myself.

In April of that same year our wonderful co-managing editor Erin Zimmer asked me to meet her for coffee at Ferrara. She explained, "I've been offered a job with this startup Good Eggs." Good Eggs is a farm-to-table grocery delivery service started by a couple of Google millionaires. Erin continued, "I think I need to take it. Serious Eats just doesn't feel all that secure at this moment. Plus, I don't know if there's much more for me to learn here or room to grow."

My first reaction was to look down at my feet, simply because I couldn't bear to watch Erin utter those words. The Serious Eats family was my tribe. I offered to match and even beat Good Eggs' salary offer, but it wasn't enough to keep the band together. Erin's last day was two weeks after the coffee.

A week later, her co-managing editor, Carey Jones, asked me to meet her for coffee at Ferrara. I was starting to hate the sight of the place. "I hate to do this to you now, Ed, but I'm leaving as well. I need to go freelance. It's time for me to leave the Serious Eats womb." Every time somebody left, I felt abandoned, and at this moment I felt the tribe fraying, big time.

I asked Kenji to meet me at Ferrara the next morning. We strategized a reorg. Kenji began, "Max and Maggie are ready to move up. They know how we think and how we like to do things." I nodded in agreement. Max Falkow-itz had started at Serious Eats shortly after graduating from the University of Chicago in 2010. A few months before he graduated, Max had sent me the best job-seeking email I have ever gotten. He wrote in part, "I'm crazy about food. I'm usually making it, eating it, thinking about it or reading about it. I equally adore haute cuisine and deep-fried Oreos. I'm a proud native of Queens, the most ethnically diverse community on Earth, and have grown up drinking in Jackson Heights' aromas, playing Guess That Smell in Flushing."

Within weeks of his joining the staff in 2012, it was clear that Max was a talented and serious Eater. He could write, think, and edit like someone who'd been doing all those things in the food world for decades. Maggie, our drinks guru and editor of Slice and our Drinks blog, was similarly thorough and skillful, and devoted to the site.

Kenji reassured me, saying, "We'll be all right, Ed. It will be good for us to get some new people in here. I think we've all gotten a little stale. Max will give us all a jolt of energy, and Maggie will make sure the trains run on time as managing editor."

I hated to admit it, but Kenji was right. I had mistakenly thought that if I could keep everyone happy in their work, staleness would never be an issue. Change can be disruptive, but I was coming to learn that a little turnover isn't always a bad thing. New people bring new ideas, new interests, new approaches.

We had in fact started working with this extraordinary Kentucky-based pastry writer and recipe developer, Stella Parks, in August of 2011. Kenji had discovered her entertaining, informative, and incredibly smart pastry blog, *BraveTart*, in July of that year. They actually met on Twitter. Stella is a pastry wizard, a brilliant writer, and a myth-busting recipe developer who shared Kenji's penchant for pop-culture references and writing resonant prose that connects with readers in a visceral way. Like Kenji, she is an obsessive, testing any recipe she publishes a minimum of a dozen times. Stella came on staff as our resident pastry wizard in January of 2016. BraveTart won my heart when she once spent an hour on the subway to deliver a piece of perfect cherry pie to our house at ten o'clock at night. The crust was oh so flaky, and the filling was bursting with whole cherries and very little syrupy cherry goop.

But all the fresh editorial ideas in the world weren't going to solve our cash-flow problems. Even when the Wendy's money started coming in, we would still be short. And all the Q4 ad dollars would only get us through May 1—and that was assuming Wendy's paid on time!

I had started to engage another company in talks to acquire Serious Eats, but even in the extremely unlikely event that this one came off, I had no idea how long it would take.

Vice had started as an avant-punk magazine in Canada. After twenty years of ups and downs, it had ended up as a hip media company, beloved by old- and new-media types alike.

The Vice guys were flush with hundreds of millions of dollars of private equity and old-media investment capital, and they were on the prowl for acquisitions.

In the meantime, to tide us over, I had to find new sources of financing, fast. I asked one of my oldest chef friends, Tom Douglas, if he would lend Serious Eats $100,000. Tom was the biggest and most successful chef-restaurateur in Seattle. I had selected him to be one of the members of the Northwest Airlines consulting chefs team I had put together twenty years earlier. He was also one of my favorite dining companions of all time—he routinely orders the entire menu (for R&D, he always says) even if we are the only two people eating. Amazingly enough, Tom has the capacity to do this at two or three restaurants in a night. He always calls me a wuss when I beg off after one meal of this magnitude.

As the founding father of the Seattle food scene, he had more than a dozen restaurants (he now has nineteen), from a pizzeria (Serious Pie) to his flagship fine-dining restaurant the Dahlia Lounge to the incredible Dahlia Bakery, home of the finest coconut cream pie you will ever eat. (Don't take my word for it; ask President Barack Obama, who ate it at a fund-raiser, then asked if he could take a couple of slices to go when he left.)

Tom is one of the most generous-spirited people I know. He just said yes to my request on the spot, when we were sharing a drink and some snacks at the bar at Del Posto. The next day he sent me a simple, two-page agreement along with a check. He did say one thing that haunted me for a couple of years: "You know, I've lent money to a lot of friends for their businesses, and not one has paid me back—on time, at least." I told him that I would be the first one to do so. The on-time aspect of my boastful guarantee certainly gave me pause.

It was a good thing that Tom wrote the check right away, because the Vice talks were taking forever. They were hard guys to pin down. Meetings were always being postponed, and phone calls and emails often went unanswered for weeks if not months.

We went through Tom's money in a couple of months, and I was forced into money-raising mode once again. A former colleague from my marketing days, Louisa Baur (Lou to her friends), was married to a partner at the very successful hedge fund Greenlight Capital, Nelson Heumann. The four of us had become close friends because Nelson and Lou and their three children rented a house every August right near ours on Martha's Vineyard. I had been talking to Nelson for months about all the acquisition interest in Serious Eats, just to get his perspective on it.

I also told him about our constant cash-flow problems, as well as my worries about how those cash-flow problems would appear to prospective acquirers. Nelson offered to help by lending $125,000 to Serious Eats. The interest rate was reasonable, as was another term, namely that there would be a cash kicker if and when Serious Eats was sold. It was a fair offer, and it was the only offer I had at the time. It allowed me to get some relatively inexpensive money for Serious Eats that I desperately needed, so it was only fair that Nelson benefit in some meaningful way beyond interest if and when Serious Eats was sold. I had convinced both myself and Nelson that the sale was imminent.

When I received the check, I realized that this was the last friends-and-family check I was going to receive; I had run out of friends and family who could afford to invest in such a speculative venture. In retrospect I can't believe how many did in fact take a flyer with me and Serious Eats. Which it most assuredly was, no matter how much I said to the contrary—in fact, Serious Eats in 2013 might have been an even more speculative venture, seven years in, than it was at the outset.

Our talks with Vice continued. They finally made us an offer heavy on earn-outs and very light on cash. The offer gave Vice control of Serious Eats at the outset, which meant that the earn-outs were going to be based on their accounting. My lawyer, Andy Beame, wasn't sure about this. I'd been working with Andy since 2007 and found that he was invariably skeptical and almost always right. "I have been involved in a lot of deals involving earn-outs, and most are either never realized or end up in court." That barely mattered to me; I was sick to death of the roller coaster.

I called Bob and laid out the specifics of the offer. He suggested I call our college friend Michael Kahn, a senior executive at the financial services company TIAA (formerly TIAA-CREF). Seemingly laid-back, Michael is a soft-spoken business Jedi. He possesses one of the best financial and business minds I know.

I left the apartment after dinner one night in July, telling Vicky I was going to the grocery store, and called Michael on my cell phone from the sidewalk right across the street from Fairway's loading dock. I don't keep secrets from my wife, but I couldn't bear the idea of her hearing my pained, quivering voice explaining how dire the situation was.

I told Michael what was happening, every sorry detail. He responded in his characteristic low-key way, "I know it's hard right now for you to see things clearly. I can hear in your voice how discouraged and stressed out you are. My guess is you want to take this offer to relieve the stress, if nothing else. I really understand that. But, Ed, if you take Vice's offer, you will regret it the rest of your life. They will make your life miserable. This is not a good deal and this is not a good fit for your company. You've worked too hard on Serious Eats, and you've built something great that you shouldn't give away." Michael was right. He talked me off the ledge, at least temporarily.

The next day I did my usual half-hour swimming regimen at the health club in the Holiday Inn Crowne Plaza in Times Square. As I was walking through the lobby to leave the hotel, my cell phone rang. It was Jim Bankoff, the CEO of Vox, a relatively new digital media company with deep pockets and a hunger to be in the food space. Alaina's husband, Anil Dash, had introduced me to Jim a few years prior to see if there was anything we could do together. At that point Jim said it was too early for him to get involved with Serious Eats, but we should keep in touch. We hadn't, which made his call all the more surprising. "Hi, Ed. It's Jim Bankoff. I think it's time for us to reengage with Serious Eats. You've done a great job building your brand." I said, "Your timing couldn't be better. We're in serious negotiations with another company right now, but no term sheet has been signed. I'll put you in touch with our banker, Peter Cohen of Blackstone." "Great," he replied, "I'll look forward to hearing from him." Almost giddy with anticipation, I sat at one of the tables in the hotel lobby and e-introduced them on the spot.

Weeks went by, and Peter heard nothing from Jim. I emailed him, asking if he was still interested in talking to Peter. He immediately emailed me back, saying he most certainly was and apologizing for the delay. They did have one brief conversation, promising to exchange numbers.

That never happened. Why? Because when I opened the *New York Times* on Monday, November 11, I saw the following headline: "Vox Media Buying Curbed.com Network of Sites." The Curbed network included—what else?—*Eater*. What the hell? I surmised that when Jim had reached out to me, his negotiation with Lockhart Steele had hit a roadblock. Serious Eats was merely his plan B. Some people really do have plan B's. I just didn't get the memo.

I was pissed, but I knew that a gracious email was the appropriate way to communicate with Jim. I wrote, "I know those guys. They're good people and good at what they do. I hope this doesn't mean that we will stop talking. Let me know. Ed." We didn't resume our conversation for two years.

Peter and I went out to Vice's HQ to try to negotiate better terms. Its headquarters then were in a huge minimalist reconfigured factory. It was a loft-like space. Just about everyone scurrying around the Vice offices was heavily tattooed and pierced, or maybe it just felt that way to a fifty-plus digital media entrepreneur. We walked past a wall filled with framed *Vice* magazine covers that mostly featured what appeared to be stoned models in various stages of undress.

This was, of course, years before the shit hit the fan regarding the toxic, sexist culture that pervaded the company back then, but the news didn't surprise me in the least. Everyone in the meeting from the Vice side, senior executives all, either was actually hung over or had gone to hair and makeup to get the look. One of them was lying down on a sofa exposing his sockless ankles. Directly above the sofa was a stuffed moose head. "Peter," I said under my breath, "we're not at Blackstone anymore."

I started the ball rolling: "I have talked to my investors, and they have unanimously voted to reject your offer." Of course, I hadn't spoken to any of my investors. But they didn't know that.

"Why?" then–vice president Andrew Creighton asked. Peter, ever the smooth, unemotional customer, responded, "Because it's all based on earn-outs, and since you will be acquiring 75 percent of SE right away, you're going to control the accounting."

Andrew put his arms around me and Peter. "Okay," he said," I'm sure we'll be able to work this out. We want to own food online, and as far as I'm concerned, we can't do that without Serious Eats. We'll get back to you with a sweetened offer. Stay tuned." And with that, he walked us out to a waiting Town Car.

We never heard from them again.

I went right back to the Serious Eats hustle. For years I had been pitching the Food Network on the idea of a Serious Eats show. I thought it would be great to do a magazine-format show following four Serious Eats stories in each episode: think *60 Minutes* for food, served up with a side order of humor and self-deprecation. We had a series of meetings with a programming executive from the Cooking Channel (the Food Network's little-watched sibling network), who seemed really excited to be in business with us. The most senior Cooking Channel executive said, "I don't know if a magazine show is a way to go, as they're pretty passé now in TV, other than *60 Minutes*. But with a couple of brainstorming sessions I bet we'll come up with a great idea for a pilot."

The executive recommended we use Joe (not his real name), a television agent at William Morris Endeavor. We met for dinner at Marea, Joe in the agent's uniform of expensive suit with no tie. I liked Joe. He was smart, articulate, experienced, and as smooth as the best chocolate pudding. Joe even seemed to enjoy the amazing sea urchin pasta there; I thought that was a good omen. We made a deal to have Joe represent Serious Eats for our deal with the Cooking Channel.

The Cooking Channel show was being developed at the same time the contract was being negotiated—and neither was going well. Young Cooking Channel executives started coming to our office, along with some folks from the production company the Cooking Channel wanted to produce the show. The questions and comments we heard from these folks were not promising. "Oh, wow, you have interns here. This show could be like the Kardashians." "If you were an Avenger, which one would you be?" And finally the kicker: "Who doesn't get along with Ed? We need tension in the show." They didn't want the *60 Minutes* of food; they wanted a docu-soap, as they were calling it in the trade at the time.

The contract negotiation wasn't going any more smoothly. The Cooking Channel wanted to license the Serious Eats name for the show title for free. It also wanted complete creative control and wanted us to promote the show so heavily on Serious Eats that I worried that our audience would be turned off—especially since we didn't have creative control. And all this for a lousy $2,500 an episode.

I thought these were ridiculous terms. Joe disagreed: "Ed, I know it's not a lot of money, and I'll try to get you more if the show does in fact become a series. But if I were you, I'd do the show for free. If your show is a hit, it's going to cause your brand to explode and exponentially increase the value of your company." Even though I knew in my heart of hearts that this was not true, that in fact the show could make a mockery of our brand, I signed the deal. That's how desperate I was.

Over the course of the next six months, the executive championing our cause at the Cooking Channel left; the producer attached to the show quit because Scripps had screwed him on another show; and no matter how many meetings we had, we couldn't agree on a format. Then, out of nowhere, when it seemed that we were actually going to shoot the pilot before the end of the year, I got a phone call from the Cooking Channel executive who was now in charge of our show: "Ed, I went into a programming meeting this morning to tell everybody we had a strong concept for the Serious Eats pilot and that we were going to shoot it in early November. My boss told me that the SE show had been in development for too long; they're canceling the pilot." I'm sure it's not a television first, but the Serious Eats television show was canceled *before the pilot even got made.*

I called Joe to tell him the news, but he didn't seem all that upset; agents get this kind of news every day and are trained to not take "no" personally. We got $2,500 for six months of agita and total frustration.

Many media business analysts talk about how great it is for creative people now that all the cable and broadcast networks have so much competition from the likes of Netflix and Hulu. While that is true, as one friend of mine put it, "it also means there are more places to say no to you."

I was running out of options and resolve. The losing streak had gone on too long. It would take drastic measures to keep Serious Eats alive, and so I went to Vicky, hat in hand, begging her to sign on to raising the line of credit to $650,000. It had been only a year since she agreed to raise it to $400,000, and at that point she had rightfully expressed extreme misgivings. But I had no choice. I was a desperate and determined man, so desperate and determined I had to engage Vicky one more time in this extremely difficult discussion.

Vicky is as strong-willed and resilient as I am, maybe moreso. Almost twenty years before I started Serious Eats, right after Will was born, she started the first successful business in the family, the Vicky Bijur Literary Agency. She grew that business single-handedly over the next decade. Books by authors she represents end up on movie screens all over the world, from *Still Alice* to *Drive* to *The Man Who Knew Infinity* to *Every Secret Thing.*

We encouraged each other's risk taking in our respective careers. When Vicky was thinking about starting her own literary agency, I said go for it. When I was thinking about starting Serious Eats, it was Vicky who encouraged me to do it. But even with all those mutually supportive experiences, we weren't prepared to deal with the sacrifices involved in keeping Serious Eats alive.

So there we were, two strong-willed people who loved each other madly, trying to hash out a really difficult situation. Our love, which has actually gathered strength over the years, was put to the test. We were both faced with the same conundrum: could we figure out a way to make each other happy while being true to ourselves? Staring at the documents to increase the line of credit, these seemed like irreconcilable goals, and the tension created incredible pain. After all, when you fall in love, nobody asks you about your comparative risk tolerance.

In the end Vicky made the decision that enabled Serious Eats to stay alive: she signed the paper, making it very clear that this was the last increase she would sign. I think it was because, even with all her misgivings, Vicky still believed in Serious Eats, even when almost no one else did. It was an act of courage that I will be forever grateful for—a complicated and complex act of love on her part.

For me, the stakes were higher than ever.

Classic Cherry Pie

STELLA PARKS

Cherry pie is the first dessert I ever made for Ed, who ate a slice out of hand while standing in the old Grand Street kitchen. I think he said something to the effect of "Holy shit, this is fuckin' good!" Is it bragging if I agree? The crust is buttery and crisp along the top and bottom, encasing a gooey cherry filling that's equal parts sour and sweet.

YIELD: One 9-inch pie

1 Old-Fashioned, All-Butter Pastry Crust, prepared as directed (see the next page)

For the Filling:

2 pounds whole, unpitted cherries, preferably a mix of yellow and red (6 heaping cups)

1 ounce fresh lemon juice (about 2 tablespoons)

7 ounces white sugar (about 1 cup)

¾ teaspoon Diamond Crystal kosher salt

1½ ounces tapioca flour or tapioca starch, not pearls or instant tapioca (about ⅓ cup plus 1 teaspoon)

For the Egg Wash:

1 large egg

1 large egg yolk

½ ounce heavy cream (about 1 tablespoon)

⅛ teaspoon Diamond Crystal kosher salt

1. Wash and pit the cherries, then measure 28 ounces (5 heaping cups) fruit into a medium bowl; add the lemon juice, sugar, salt, and tapioca starch, tossing with a flexible spatula to combine. Scrape into the prepared pie shell and refrigerate.

2. With a ruler and pastry wheel, cut the chilled sheet of dough into even strips, and arrange as desired over the fruit-filled pie. When covered, trim the excess dough flush to the edge of the pie plate, and refrigerate until firm and cold, at least 30 minutes. Meanwhile, adjust the oven racks to the middle and topmost positions and preheat to 400°F.

3. In a small bowl, whisk the egg, yolk, cream, and salt together until smooth; brush over chilled pie. Bake on a parchment-lined aluminum baking sheet until golden brown, with juices starting to bubble through the center, about 75 minutes or 213°F on a digital thermometer. Halfway through, you may want to slide an empty baking sheet onto the top rack to act as a shield and prevent excess browning.

4. Cool the pie until no warmer than 85°F, and cut with a chef's knife to serve.

Old-Fashioned, All-Butter Pastry Crust

8 ounces low-protein all-purpose flour, such as Gold Medal blue label (about 1¾ cups, plus 1 tablespoon)

1 tablespoon white sugar

1½ teaspoons Diamond Crystal kosher salt

8 ounces cold, unsalted American butter, cut into cubes no smaller than ½ inch

4 ounces cool water, around 60°F (about ½ cup)

1. Whisk the flour, sugar, and salt together in a medium bowl, then add the cubes of butter. Toss to break up the pieces, then smash each cube flat between your fingers. Do not work the butter any more than this at all; the pieces should be chunky and large. With a flexible spatula, stir in the water and knead until the dough comes together in a ball. Do not add more water, just keep kneading until it comes together. Transfer to a generously floured work space, sprinkle with more flour, and roll until about 10 by 15 inches, sprinkling with more flour as needed along the way.

2. Fold each 10-inch side toward the middle, then close the packet like a book. Fold once more to make a thick block. Divide the dough in half, aiming to make one piece slightly larger than the other. On a well-floured work surface, roll the larger piece into a 10-by-15-inch rectangle; transfer to a baking sheet, cover with plastic wrap, and refrigerate.

3. Roll the smaller, roughly 9-ounce portion into a 13-inch round, and transfer to a 9-inch glass pie plate. Fold the excess dough over itself to form a tall border that sits atop the rim of the pie plate. Cover with plastic wrap and refrigerate at least 2 hours, or until needed.

4. Troubleshooting: when room temperature rises substantially over 70°F, equipment and pantry staples may act as a heat source to the butter, causing it to soften and melt. To avoid problems with a sticky dough, chill the mixing bowl, flour, and rolling pin to just 70°F, and use bags of ice water to cool the countertops before rolling. The idea is to mimic cooler, but not frozen, conditions, so don't go crazy.

Chapter 18

THE JIG IS UP

By 2014 it felt like I was out of options. Increasing the line of credit (LOC) to $650,000 didn't turn out to be any kind of panacea for Serious Eats. We were still scrambling for ad dollars. My ad sales director, Sam (not his real name), had pulled rabbits out of his hat in Q4 of 2013 and sold a million dollars' worth of advertising, but there were no rabbits in sight in 2014.

I still didn't have any money to expand our video program, which was something we desperately needed to do. I couldn't afford to hire a social media manager, and we were already late to the social media party. Our Facebook and YouTube and Instagram presence was markedly smaller than some of our competitors.

I also hadn't replaced Alaina with another general manager, and I felt her absence more keenly every day. Alaina knew everyone and everything when it came to digital media. I had faced every roadblock we encountered at Serious Eats with Alaina alongside me. She came to presentations at the Blackstone offices when she was eight and a half months pregnant. When she left, I didn't just lose a general manager; I lost my running partner. And all the decisions that had to be made fell to me.

Everyone had lots of ideas on what to do with the site. But every idea required resources that I didn't have. Not wanting to disappoint people by just saying no, I would say, "Let me think about it." And then I would never get back to them.

Kenji came to me one day. "Morale is really low, Ed. People see you looking unhappy and defeated, and they become unhappy and feel defeated. We come to you looking for answers, and you never give us any. You have to do something. You have to replace Alaina, for one thing. And you have to rally the troops."

I went to Sam to see how ad sales were looking. "It's early, and Q1 is always slow. But let me give my guys a little booster shot. And I know a kick-ass salesman in Chicago who might be willing to work for us part time." At that point we had a team of five in the ad sales department.

In the meantime I hired Sally (not her real name), a friend of ours (really an old, old friend of Vicky's) who was a high-end management consultant, to interview everybody at the company and take their temperature. I had previously done a similar exercise with Therese Steiner, another old friend, and it had proved useful. Sally and I met for two days, in eight-hour sessions, to discuss her findings.

Sally didn't pull any punches. "You're in danger of losing a lot of people. They think the company is in serious trouble, and even though they can see with their own eyes how unhappy and stressed you seem, you don't tell them what's going on. They just see you leaving the office looking really discouraged to make cell phone calls. Your inability to make decisions leaves them high and dry. The first thing you have to do is hire a GM. If you don't do that, a lot of folks are going to walk out the door."

Serious Eats was in danger of imploding. Wanting to leave our two-day marathon session on a lighter and more positive note, Sally shook my hand, chuckled, and said, "The one thing all your employees could agree on is how much you love your wife."

For the GM position I ended up hiring Chris Mohney, an experienced digital media executive and very smart guy. Chris could be impolitic in his dealings with me, but he was a friend of Sam's and he quickly gained the trust of everyone at the company. So I let my reservations about him slide.

Chris and I met with Sam every week; the news went from bad to worse.

We tried to up the pressure on Sam, but we really had no leverage; we needed him to both manage the sales team and sell advertising himself. And we couldn't afford to fire Sam, because getting his replacement up to speed would be costly and time-consuming, and time and money were two things we didn't have.

My mood darkened even further. I would come home and immediately go into Will's old room, shut the door, and turn on the TV, trying to drown out the stress and anxiety that had taken over every fiber of my being. To say I was defeated would be an understatement. Once a week I would call Bob and say, "I just don't see a way out. I don't see us lasting more than a couple of months." As an investor, Bob was privy to the numbers, and he was much more experienced in these matters, and he would say, "I don't think you're in such bad shape. You'll figure it out. You always do."

Trying to shut Vicky out by turning on the TV was not a good idea. She would come in and say, "What's wrong? You look like you lost your best friend. Talk to me." I did look like that, but I couldn't share my worries. If Serious Eats went under, I didn't know how I could ever explain it to her. We had a lot on the line.

Chris and I kept putting pressure on Sam, which made him lash out at us. "What do you want me to do? If you want to fire me, fire me. Don't leave me hanging like this. Everyone on my team is working their asses off. It's just super hard out there right now. There's way more supply than demand for digital ad impressions right now, so prices are coming down and there are a million desperate sites, willing to do anything to get an advertiser on board."

Ad sales had always been the biggest problem at Serious Eats. I had the lingo down: "We are not sufficiently monetizing our traffic." Every potential acquirer would mention that the monetization issue was the first problem they would try to tackle if they bought Serious Eats.

Here's the biggest problem I had with ad sales professionals. They are by definition mercenary, and mercenaries don't necessarily get on well with missionaries. So I didn't understand anything about them, how they thought, how they acted. Everything they did was foreign to me.

But the biggest problem with Serious Eats' ad sales from the outset wasn't the people I hired. Maybe they weren't the greatest salespeople who ever lived, but I think for any entrepreneur, hiring *the* salesperson who will lead you to the promised land of profitability and growth is pure fantasy.

No, the biggest problem was the evolution of the digital ad sales marketplace. It wasn't just the glut of available inventory, though that was a serious problem. The humongous problems were Facebook and Google, the two five-hundred-pound gorillas in the digital ad space. When I started Serious Eats in 2006, Facebook had been selling advertising for only two years. The first year it sold advertising, 2004, it sold a mere $382,000. By 2007, the first full year of Serious Eats' existence, that number had become $153 million. In 2014, when our ad sales had started to tank and I was forced to go to Vicky for the last time, Facebook sold $12.466 billion in advertising.*

You could have hired the LeBron James or the Serena Williams of digital ad sales in 2014 and it wouldn't have made a damn bit of difference. If Facebook was big, Google was even bigger. Its ad sales took two forms, the ads that companies bought at auction to advertise in Google's search results, and the advertising that YouTube sold on its billions of videos. By 2014 Facebook and Google were getting somewhere between seventy-five and eighty cents of every new digital marketing dollar spent. Together they controlled more than 50 percent of the digital ad sales market worldwide.

Nevertheless, even in September 2014 we were still holding out hope. Sam would update the sales forecast every week in a spreadsheet he would send to Chris and me. In the first week of September we had our weekly meeting with Sam. He said, "Look, I want to give you a heads-up. We're not going to book the million dollars I thought we would in the fourth quarter."

Knowing full well that the future of the company depended on his answer, I asked, "So how much do you think we're going to do?"

---

* HubSpot, "The History of Facebook Advertising" (slide show), September 19, 2013, www .slideshare.net/HubSpot/hs-facebook-slidesharev05.

Sam took a deep breath and replied, "About four hundred thousand."

It was over. As soon as I heard that number, I knew we were doomed. We had no way to cover a $600,000 shortfall without an immediate cash infusion, and I'd knocked on every door too many times. The situation was really dire.

I made one more Hail Mary pass. My billionaire basketball buddy, Marc Lasry, was in the process of buying the Milwaukee Bucks. During one of my periodic Sunday-night visits to Marc at his home, I dropped a hint. "Marc, Serious Eats is in a pretty deep hole right now. Ad sales are looking really soft. We are bleeding cash." Marc replied in his ever-encouraging tone, "You've been here before, and my guess is you'll figure out a way to get to the other side. But I can't help you this time. I don't feel comfortable putting any more money into Serious Eats."

I left his house not at all angry at Marc, just deeply deflated. I was going to have to work my way out of this hole myself.

And I had to tell Vicky.

Vicky once told an old friend, "I married Ed because I knew we would lead an interesting life." By 2014 we had been married more than thirty years. But I had never put any of our money or assets at risk in my business dealings before Serious Eats.

It was a hard conversation.

I promised Vicky that if things hadn't turned around by the end of the year, I would put the site up for sale. And if and when I did sell Serious Eats, I assured her, at the very least we would get enough money to repay the bank loan.

I believed what I was saying, but of course it wasn't a sure thing—and nobody knew that better than Vicky, who had also experienced every near miss, every nonbinding agreement, every "almost" sale.

The hole I'd dug for us was pretty deep, and both of us lay awake at night wondering how we'd haul ourselves out of it.

Vicky was one thing; the investors were another. A sale at this moment, given the shape we were in, was most likely going to leave them with pocket change—at best. I didn't say that to Mike, in so many words, but I'm sure he could smell my desperation and extrapolate what that desperation would mean for him and the other investors.

I investigated taking money out of my retirement account prematurely. The 25 percent penalty put an end to that thought. Actually, Vicky put an end to it. "You can't do that," she said. "We need that money for our retirement."

A few days later Vicky proposed a different solution. "We can borrow the money you need using our IBM stock as collateral. I talked to our financial adviser and he assured me that this is the cheapest money we can find." Vicky had been given that stock by her grandfather when she was born. That stock meant a lot to Vicky—emotionally as well as financially.

So that's what we did. I was the one in our household with an MBA, and yet it was Vicky who figured out how best to navigate the financial depths we were in. Her savvy business thinking was grounded in reality; mine was still in la-la land.

Nobody—not Vicky, not me—was happy with the rescue mission. The day we signed the papers, Vicky turned to me and said very clearly, "We're not doing this anymore. I am done, and you need to be done too. We can't live like this anymore."

Even I knew she was right: my marriage and my business were hanging by the same thread.

The 2014 holiday season was not one of good cheer in the Bijur-Levine household. I had no more chips to put into the pot. It was time to fold.

Chapter 19

WAITING TO EXHALE

Peter, the time has come for me and Serious Eats, my friend. I'm gonna sell the business. The stress has taken years off my life, the business has strained my marriage almost to the breaking point, and if I can't at least get my investors most of their money back in the transaction, I will have let my brother and many of my friends down, big time." Peter Cohen and I were picking at our medium-rare cheeseburgers, made with dry-aged short rib and brisket, at the newly restored Monkey Bar, a New York institution that has risen phoenix-like many times. I was even picking at the great fries that came with our cheeseburgers. I pick at great fries only in moments of real stress.

It was a frigid, snowy winter's day in early 2015. Meeting with Peter was the first concrete step I had to take in selling Serious Eats.

"Are you sure you're ready to do this?" he asked. He could have been a doctor asking me if I was prepared to take a loved one off life support. Peter knew how much Serious Eats meant to me. "I'm sure," I replied. "It is time. I've been dragging this boulder up the hill like Sisyphus for eight years now, and I just can't do it anymore. Telling myself that it's going to be great just isn't doing it for me anymore. Every time I check our bank balance I see the same flashing red lights over and over again."

Peter didn't know the half of it. I hadn't had a full night's sleep in a year, and my use of sleeping pills had increased dramatically. Vicky wasn't sleeping either. Every time my phone rang I flinched, dreading the bad news on the end of the line. My relationship with my brother was strained to the point where I was dodging his calls. Even if the company did sell, I was likely to disappoint the people closest to me; I was convinced that some of my closest friends were going to become former friends. Even food, usually a source of joy and comfort, was literally leaving a bad taste in my mouth.

I continued, sounding quite resigned to my fate, "I've made a list of the companies that might be interested." Peter replied, "I'm happy to talk to the clients I have that have previously expressed interest in Serious Eats." I stopped him. "I appreciate that, but I don't think those kinds of companies are going to be interested. We're no longer the next big new thing. We've become just another digital media company struggling to monetize our audience."

It was true. In the digital media business the rate of change is so fast that a company's moment can come and go in an instant. MySpace was hot before it wasn't. So were AOL and CompuServe and Prodigy. Hell, I had worked for Prodigy and AOL. I knew how fast a company went from hot to cold, profitable to fading, growing to stagnant. The digital economy waits for no one. Its swift currents can take you so far off course that you have no idea where you've ended up or how you got there.

I picked at another fry before continuing, "I have no idea how much I'll get for Serious Eats. But I figure at the very least I can get out from under all the debt, including the $650K that we still owe on the line of credit."

Peter was surprised. After hearing me talk about Serious Eats in such passionate terms for so long, I think he had a hard time believing that I was a man resigned to this fate. "Can you really do this?" he asked. I answered, "I can, and I will. The time is now."

Peter saw that I was serious. He didn't try to talk me out of it. He responded supportively, "By all means, man, go for it. Let's see what happens."

Peter had become a trusted friend and adviser, but he worked for an investment banking firm that of course expected to get paid if Blackstone sold Serious Eats. In that case, as our investment banker Peter and Blackstone were entitled to what was for us a hefty commission. I had signed an engagement letter to that effect when we first started working together in 2009.

Wanting to assuage his fears, I said, "In all likelihood I'm going to find the buyer at this moment, not you, since I know the smaller players that are likely to be interested. But don't worry; you'll still get your commission. It's the least I can do after everything you've done for Serious Eats all these years."

I meant it, even though Blackstone's commission for the Serious Eats sale would likely be hundreds of thousands of dollars. They deserved that, and more. Peter and his colleagues Jordan and Anthony had spent thousands of hours on Serious Eats' behalf so far, with absolutely no compensation. It was way past time for them to receive some, no matter how meager that compensation was going to be for investment bankers.

What came out of Peter's mouth next almost caused me to faint. "You know what, Ed? You're probably not going to get that much for Serious Eats, our fees will be much more meaningful to you and your investors than to my bosses, and let's face it: for whatever reason I have not been able to sell your company, and that's what you were paying us to do. Plus, our engagement letter has expired. You won't owe us a cent if you sell Serious Eats to a company I haven't found."

"Whoa, whoa, whoa," I replied. "I'm gonna need you if and when I do start negotiating with somebody in earnest. You can't abandon me now." He interrupted, "Ed, listen. You and I have been working side by side on Serious Eats for six years now. You know every one of my moves. You can do this on your own. You've got your brother for backup. And if you do need me, just call my cell anytime, and I will help you any way I can, no charge."

No charge? What kind of investment banker offers to advise a now-former client for free? A mensch (Yiddish for stand-up person), someone with a generosity of spirit you don't often find in an investment banker—especially not an investment banker who had recently sold the Dodgers for reportedly more than $2 billion.

I left the restaurant in a bit of a state of shock. I was sure I would need Peter at some point in the process, and I couldn't quite believe that I'd had the good fortune of engaging an investment banker with a heart and a soul. I had felt a kinship with Peter the first time we met. Every tribe needs at least one person who can rock a navy-blue suit and command respect from other similarly attired humans. Stop the presses! Investment bankers are human too.

On the other hand, I was not as confident as Peter was in my ability to function as my own investment banker. I may have picked up all his moves as far as what to say, but I had no clue how to create financial models that would be enticing to potential acquirers.

By the time I met Peter for lunch, I had spent the holiday season fruitlessly trying to find a buyer willing to pay what I thought was a fair price for Serious Eats. I hadn't included Peter in these pursuits because, frankly, I felt guilty about the amount of work he and his team had done on behalf of Serious Eats without getting paid a cent.

Just launching Serious Eats and hanging around for eight years had put me in contact with many of the players I thought were possibilities. First I dallied with another food site, Tasting Table, owned by media mogul and sometime visionary (MTV, Daily Candy) Bob Pittman's venture arm, Pilot. I knew one of the principals, Mayo Stuntz, from my MTV consulting days.

I had gotten to know Tasting Table's CEO, Geoff Bartakovics, in a series of breakfasts. Bartakovics came from the banking world and was financially savvy. He is also a very good salesperson who monetizes his relatively small audience really effectively. Geoff did seem to have trouble holding on to employees. A former Tasting Table employee once told me that Geoff even told prospective hires that their tenure at the company was probably going to be short. Unlike me, he did not feel the need to be loved by everyone working at his company. I quickly discerned that this marriage would be a terrible cultural fit. But without many other options, I pursued it anyway. By this time I was desperate to dispense with the boulder of stress that was weighing down every step I took.

Tasting Table was basically an email newsletter business at a time when those were out of fashion. Why? Because it was becoming more and more expensive to acquire and keep subscribers, and the number of subscribers was the basis of a newsletter's appeal to advertisers. So Geoff and company were trying to reposition Tasting Table as a media company generating revenue from multiple sources (website, events, targeted email blasts) in order to facilitate a sale. Bundling Serious Eats with Tasting Table would go a long way toward demonstrating their desired repositioning.

After weeks of much posturing by both sides, we finally had a serious sit-down on December 17, 2014. Geoff and his partners proposed a deal that had us assuming more risk and losing control of Serious Eats, a merger/ stock swap in which we would end up owning 25 percent of the merged entity. They calculated that the entire entity would be worth $32 million, so we would end up with $8 million if in fact it could be sold.

This wasn't just a bank shot. It was a three-rail bank shot. First we would combine the companies. Then Tasting Table's sales team would go out and sell our collective inventory. If it was successful doing that, Geoff and Mayo would then take the merged entity out to the market and fetch $32 million. As we were leaving, Geoff said, "I don't think you're going to find a better deal. It's rough out there." He wasn't bullshitting. They had been trying to sell Tasting Table for a couple of years without finding a buyer willing to meet their price.

Even billiards professionals have a hard time making three-rail bank shots. Plus, I would be giving up all the control I had worked so hard to maintain, with no guaranteed outcome. The only appealing aspect of the deal—and it was mighty appealing—was that the merged entity would assume all our lines of credit, which would take Vicky and me out of the line of financial fire. So at least the first offer we received would make good on my promise to Vicky that whatever happened with my efforts to sell Serious Eats, we would get out from under our crushing personal debt.

In the end, when I consulted with Mike and Peter, we all concluded that the overall deal was so bad I had to turn it down. I called Geoff. "At this point I think we're going to pass. If we change our mind, I'll let you know." Four years later Tasting Table is still in limbo, searching for a buyer. I hope they do find a graceful and profitable exit, because knowing how hard that is to do, I now root for anyone who starts a business to succeed, whether it's a dry cleaner, a newsstand, or a website. They're all hard to bring across the finish line. Every time I pass an empty storefront I think to myself, *Oh, there goes someone else's hopes and dreams.*

I took a break for Christmas (it wasn't all that merry) and then began reaching out to other likely candidates. My first call after New Year's Day was to *Eater* cofounder Lockhart Steele, who was now Vox's editorial director. Why Lock and Vox? Well, I knew and liked and respected many of the people who worked there, from Lock to Jim Bankoff to *Eater* editor-in-chief Amanda Kludt. Bankoff had also raised another $47.5 million in the capital marketplace at the end of 2014, so Vox had plenty of cash on hand. Combining *Eater*, with its restaurant news and gossip focus, with Serious Eats' reviews, recipes, and technique content seemed to make perfect sense.

Over breakfast at Baz, a decent bagel place a few doors down from the Serious Eats office, I gave Lock my rap, which I must have rehearsed a hundred times on the subway. I'm sure my fellow subway riders thought I was more than a bit strange. "Lock, over the holidays I decided that Serious Eats needed to be part of a larger company to realize its full potential. You and Vox were the first people I thought of. Combined, *Eater* and Serious Eats could take on sites like FoodNetwork.com and Allrecipes.com and beat them."

Lock seemed to love the idea. "This could be really great, Ed. Let me talk to Jim. I'm going to see him later today."

After our breakfast Lock emailed to say that he had filled Bankoff in on our breakfast, and that Bankoff was intrigued.

The next day I heard from the man himself: "Am flattered that you would think of us and would be happy to discuss." Five days later we met in Vox's dingy temporary offices kitty-corner to Bryant Park. Mike and Peter had always told me, "Ed, never throw out the first number when you start a negotiation. Always force the other guy to do so. That way you're not bidding against yourself or showing your hand too early."

But after so many unsatisfying negotiations with the other side throwing out the first number, I decided to play it another way. "Have you thought about a number that would satisfy you?" Jim asked. I replied, "I would need $8 million at a minimum. That's a little more than three times revenue." There was a lot of conflicting conventional wisdom swirling around digital-publishing valuations, but that was certainly a plausible valuation metric that Peter and I had tossed out to many other potential acquirers over the years.

"That sounds reasonable, Ed. I think we can figure out a way to get there." By this time I knew enough not to be overly encouraged by that kind of ambiguous language. The devil is always in the details. The structure of the deal, not the number either party throws out, is the key element. How much of the purchase price is in cash, how much is earn-out based on future profits, how much is in stock, what kind of stock it is—those were the words and the numbers that really mattered. The permutations of acquisition terms are endless, but suffice to say the sheer number of permutations renders the gross dollar amount thrown around in conversation meaningless.

The next day Bankoff copied me on a note he wrote to the *Eater* crew: "Lock, Lauren and Josh, Ed (copied here) and I had a really great conversation today. I'll brief the three of you on Monday, but I'd like for you to follow up with him to see if we can work out a way to acquire Serious Eats. First step, Lauren, can you get him a mutual NDA? I think we already have an expired one."

While all this was going on, I had a site to run and a team to manage. I felt certain that by now Kenji was being deluged with job offers. Why not? He was the food blogging equivalent of a bankable star. Most of the job offers were quickly dismissed, but on a cold February day in 2015 he asked me to go out to Ferrara for coffee. "Ed, I have an old friend from high school who works at Vox. They have offered me a big job starting a food section at Vox.com." Vox.com was the new political site former *Washington Post* columnist and policy wonk Ezra Klein had launched with Bankoff.

This freaked me out. It would be virtually impossible to sell Serious Eats without Kenji on board. Not even asking how much money Vox had offered him, or if it had even gotten that far, I started negotiating with Kenji to give him a more lucrative compensation package. We arrived at a mutually satisfactory package pretty quickly. Kenji used his MIT buddies who had gone into finance as his advisers. I used Mike.

In the meantime Vox sent me an NDA to sign. Conspicuously absent from it was a standard mutual nonsolicitation clause, which merely states that while the two sides are talking, each company's employees can't be recruited or hired by the other. Makes perfect sense. In a publishing business, many of the most valuable assets go up and down the elevator, or in our case the stairs, every day. I signed it after adding a nonsolicitation clause. The response from the Vox lawyer: "We cannot sign it just yet, as we do not have sign-off on the inclusion of the non-solicitation clause. It is outside the norm for us, so I need to run it up the food chain."

Later that day I got another email: "OK, so as I suspected we are getting pushback on the non-solicitation obligation as part of an NDA. While we don't have any designs on hiring your folks (especially for Eater), we just can't promise that no one in the company will take an interest in any of your folks. And we don't expect you to make that promise either."

I was furious. The "especially for Eater" parenthetical was especially galling because they were talking to Kenji about a job at Vox.com, not *Eater*. I called Bankoff on his cell phone and left a message: "Jim, it's Ed Levine. Please call me back ASAP. There is something important I need to talk to you about." Less than an hour later, Jim returned the call. After barely acknowledging it was him with a "Hi, Jim," I said, "We're haggling over including a nonsolicitation clause in the NDA, and meanwhile you guys have been talking to Kenji about a job."

Jim, ever calm and collected, responded, "Yes, I just found out about our reaching out to Kenji today. I just think that people should be free to work wherever they want to." I said, "Sure, Jim, and I agree with you on that. It's just that we shouldn't be trying to hire the other company's employees while we're in a serious negotiation." He agreed in a roundabout way. "Well, he's staying at Serious Eats anyway, so this is all moot." We agreed to leave it at that. I eventually even signed the Vox NDA without the nonsolicitation clause. That's how badly I wanted to sell Serious Eats at that point.

I knew that Jim Bankoff wasn't doing anything illegal or immoral. In the business realm he's known as a straight shooter, and rightfully so. He was doing what he thought was best for his business, no more and no less, and he wasn't breaking the rules. But what he was trying to do with Kenji was just straight-up shitty. As I had learned over and over again, people conduct business as they see fit. There are no hard-and-fast rules. This was no one-on-one basketball game in my driveway. Jim Bankoff knew how to play for keeps. And he was really good at it. I admired and I still admire what he's been able to build at Vox. Dealing with him made me realize that I just didn't have his skills. When I hung up the phone I had to acknowledge that I was still unable to view business as a dispassionate blood sport. Business was and still is extremely personal to me. That's probably never going to change.

With that not-all-that-little snafu settled, I started engaging Jim's designated negotiator, Josh, in serious talks. First we exchanged numbers and other confidential information. I had already learned from my previous encounters with corporate entities that the potential acquirer reveals almost nothing. It was no different this time. Josh got a lot of information from me and I got very little from him.

Josh and I met for coffee a few weeks later, and he gave me Vox's initial thoughts. They would pay off all our debts (which were almost $1.75 million at this juncture) and give us $3.5 million worth of Vox stock to distribute to me and my investors, along with a little cash. All the Serious Eats employee stock my staff owned would be rendered worthless.

I asked Josh the two key questions Peter would have asked if he had been there. First: "How are you valuing the Vox stock?" Josh: "Your Vox stock would be based on a $500 million valuation for our company."

I was puzzled about the $500 million number. "But, Josh, three months ago you raised some money at a $380 million valuation. What's changed?" "Well," he replied, "we're growing like crazy, and Jim is very comfortable with that $500 million number." I thought to myself, *I'm sure he is*, but I didn't think my savvy investors would be comfortable with it, knowing about the previous recent valuation. They could use Google too. As we got up to leave, Josh suggested, "Why don't you sleep on this offer and talk to your investors about it. We can talk again in the morning."

The next day we spoke on the phone. "Josh, this deal is not going to get done on the terms we discussed yesterday." Josh said, "Okay, let me go back to Jim and see what we can come up with." Josh called me a few days later. "Jim says we can increase the Vox stock amount by a million and a half dollars at the same valuation and add a little more cash. He is not willing to budge on the Vox valuation."

The more I thought about it, the more this deal sucked. My Serious Eats employees, my second family, would get nothing. My investors, who had placed their faith and trust in me, and I would get Vox stock at an obviously inflated valuation, with no way to sell the stock.

When you are paid with stock in a privately held company, the only way you realize any money from that stock is if and when the acquiring company is sold. And being a tiny minority shareholder in a privately held company like Vox would mean we had no say in when it was sold or for how much.

I thought the deal sucked, but my desperation overruled my analysis of the deal. I sent Josh an email the next day: "I'm very excited about the prospect of this deal becoming a reality. Really. Ed." I heard nothing in return. I followed up with another email: "I left you a message. I mentioned one issue that is outstanding, the nature of the conversion of all the Vox stock we own. The second issue we need to clear up sometime soon is whether you pay my employees something for their Serious Eats stock. They deserve to be compensated for all the time and effort they have put in for me. I think if you do both of those things it will make the deal much easier for my employees, my board, and my investors to accept. Anyway, I'm confident we'll figure all these things out. We are excited to be joining the Vox family of media brands. It's a particularly distinguished group that we are proud to be with. Onward and upward. Ed." I was flattering them, Peter Cohen style, but I was having a hard time summoning Peter's no-nonsense, tough-sounding banker persona.

I talked to Peter and Mike about the deal. I also talked to the management committee at Serious Eats and our board of advisers. Nobody liked the deal. Everyone thought Vox was trying to squeeze us after looking at our financials, and they clearly were. But even Mike thought that, given the lack of options, we should take the deal. "I think this deal sucks for everyone but Vox, especially me, but I don't see any alternative. And at least you and Vicky will get out from under all that crushing debt. I think the only way out of it is to find another bidder. That would change the dynamic completely."

Josh was taking his sweet time actually producing a term sheet for me to sign (I guess he thought I had no other options), so that gave me a chance to try to scare up another bidder or two. If nothing else, I would see whether the Vox price was indeed what the market was willing to pay for Serious Eats.

Chris knew another West Coast–based digital publisher—a low-end one, to be sure, which goes shallow at every opportunity—that was in acquisition mode. We had a couple of meetings with them and they offered about the same amount of cash with the added advantage that the stock we received would be preferred stock, so that if and when they did sell the company, we would get paid first. They also offered to pay back all our debt. The debt was turning out to be an albatross around our necks. In the course of any negotiation, people immediately saw how much debt we had and smelled our desperation. We didn't give them a definitive "no" right away, but we really didn't see their offer as a credible alternative to Vox's.

Though I was sick of waiting for an actual term sheet from Vox, I became resigned to taking its offer. It certainly wouldn't feather our retirement, my investors would no doubt be seriously displeased, and my employees would be pissed, but Vicky and I would get out from under the debt. I'd have a pretty good job, at least for a couple of years. I couldn't believe that this was the position I found myself in.

While waiting for the term sheet I got an email from Cliff Sharples, who with his wife, Lisa, and a former investment banker friend, Ben Sternberg, had started Fexy, a digital media company. Cliff and Ben had reached out to me a year earlier, saying that he and his partners were raising capital to buy a few high-quality sites like Serious Eats. That was their overarching strategy for building Fexy Media. It's known as a roll-up. Roll-ups build scale and its accompanying revenue growth via acquisition.

Cliff's brother had built the home vacation rental site HomeAway by buying up more than twenty smaller competitors. It proved to be a successful strategy. He sold the business to Expedia in 2015 for a reported $3.9 billion.

In 2014 I had responded, "It sounds interesting, Cliff. Let me know when you raise your money."

This new email, dated February 26, 2015, read: "Hi Ed, Hope all is well in your world. It's been awhile since we last spoke, and I thought I would check in with you on how things are going at Serious Eats. We formalized our company last year, making our first set of acquisitions. I'd love to fill you in on what we're up to, and see how things are progressing with you. I am coming to New York the week of March 9th, and if you're in town, it would be great to drop by. Let me know if you have any time in your schedule. Look forward to catching up! Best, Cliff."

Holy shit! Cliff's email could not have come at a better time. But if he was just sniffing around without serious intentions, it couldn't have come at a more nerve-racking time. I calmly responded, "Hi Cliff, nice to hear from you. Glad you're up and running. There's a lot going on here right now, and if you're seriously interested in acquiring Serious Eats we need to talk sooner than the week of March 9th. As in either today or tomorrow. Let me know if that's possible. Thanks in advance. Ed"

Cliff responded: "OK, I'm always up for an adventure! I'm open at 5 p.m. your time, or most of tomorrow AM. Let me know!"

We spoke the next day. Cliff is a disarmingly effective salesperson, but I wanted to get right down to business. "Cliff, we're looking for two to three times our average 2013–2014 revenue, and for a new company like yours the majority of your offer would have to be in cash, as your stock value is very difficult to calculate." Maybe I *had* learned something from Peter Cohen.

At dinner at the terrific Upland on March 9 Cliff made me a verbal offer: they would assume our debts, which had grown to $1.75 million, and pay us $3 million in cash, $1.5 million dollars in Fexy stock, and a $500,000 retention-bonus pool that I could allocate to my employees. I told him I appreciated the offer and would get back to him in the morning. "I've got to talk to my brother," I explained to Cliff. "He's in Tibet right now, so he's going to be hard to reach." I didn't end up talking to Mike, but I didn't need to.

In the morning I channeled Peter and Mike and called Cliff at 8:00 a.m. "Cliff, you made a fair and reasonable offer, but it's not going to get it done. I need you to get to $7 million in total, with more cash included in the deal. And I need a term sheet by the end of the day." I hung up the phone and let out a primal scream. Had I in fact just said that? I had. Move over, Peter Cohen. There's a new investment banker in town.

The West Coast outfit from which Chris had solicited an offer had said they would beat any other offers we received, but I didn't really believe much of what Bruce (not his real name), the company's founder, said. I thought he was probably just trash-talking and posturing. Even if he was serious, I didn't want to sell Serious Eats to him. I was holding out hope for a better savior.

On March 12 we got the term sheet we wanted from Fexy. I realized that the only answer to the question of how much a business is worth is the same for everyone: it's what another company will pay for it at any given moment in time. Standard multiples are routinely thrown out the window in business transactions. Not in every case, but certainly in mine, and probably in any business in a category in which change is the only constant.

Josh and Vox were still MIA, so I emailed him about getting together ASAP. Josh responded with an email asking what the agenda of our meeting was going to be. I immediately responded, letting him know about Fexy's offer.

Amazingly, Josh didn't respond immediately to my email. Instead he sent me a term sheet the next day that was unchanged from the terms he had given me verbally a couple of weeks before. The total value was $7 million, but it was still mostly in stock.

Finally Josh and I spoke. "Ed, I thought we had a deal. You've sounded so upbeat and excited about the prospect of working with us."

"I was excited, but first of all, that's my natural enthusiastic MO, and secondly, just because I sounded excited didn't mean we had an agreement. We're not in high school arguing about who is taking whom to the prom. I have investors, and I have an obligation to both them and my employees to get the best deal I can before signing on the dotted line. And the offer we received is simply much better than yours in almost every respect."

Josh seemed totally taken aback: "So now what do we do?" I immediately answered, "Well, you need to sweeten your offer and get it up to $8 million, and it has to include more cash and less stock. So get ahold of Jim and see if he's willing to go there. And you have to do so by tomorrow morning, because I'm getting on a plane to San Francisco with my wife to meet my son, and when I get to our hotel, I am going to sign somebody's term sheet." Josh replied, "I don't know if I can get ahold of Jim right away. He might be traveling."

I smiled and said, "I'm pretty sure he has a cell phone, Josh. I'll talk to you tomorrow."

Josh called when I was on the plane waiting to take off. Based on my JetBlue experience during the Mountain View debacle, I let it go to voicemail. When we landed in San Francisco I called Josh.

He said, "Jim said he's willing to sweeten the stock offer, but the cash portion of the deal is not going to change in any meaningful way."

"Okay, Josh. I'll let you know what I decide."

I hung up and we hopped into a taxi. I thought about what had just transpired and what my history of dealings with Jim Bankoff and Vox told me. For Vox, Serious Eats was a "nice to have" company, but it was definitely not a "need to have" company. For Fexy the opposite was true. It needed to have us if its strategy was to grow its business through acquisitions. We were the linchpin of its strategy.

When I got to the hotel I signed the Fexy deal.

Vicky and I went out to dinner to celebrate. In the middle of the first toast I realized that we were celebrating prematurely. All I had signed

was a *nonbinding* letter of intent (LOI). We were a long way from the finish line.

In fact, the process was just beginning, because we were now negotiating binding contractual terms. I called Mike. "Wow, this post-LOI process feels like a business proctology exam that might last ninety days." Mike laughed and replied, "Welcome to the real world, bro."

A few days into the process I realized I needed someone beside me who could take on Fexy partner Ben Sternberg, a former investment banker, and Fexy's principal investors, a well-regarded private equity firm, so that we would be on relatively even financial footing during these final negotiations. These were some tough-minded hard-core business folks, and I needed someone who could match their toughness and experience. Having Peter Cohen on speed dial was not going to be enough. Providentially, a few months earlier I had hired a temporary controller—a "CFO in a box," I called him—from a company that rents out such people, to get my numbers in order for the hoped-for sale.

Jeff was a big, soft-spoken dude from rural Oklahoma who was a human HP 12c, the calculator of choice at Columbia Business School. He spoke acquisition-ese so fluently I thought it might be his native tongue. Jeff may have been soft-spoken, but he was as tough as the worst beef jerky and utterly unflappable. Jeff never raised his voice, no matter how freighted the financial talk got or how dire the situation appeared to be.

Jeff had a day job as the CFO of a technology company, and sometimes when I called him he would tell me that he would be unavailable for a few days because he had to raise $15 million in seventy-two hours in order for his company to meet payroll. He would say this in the same tone that someone else might say, "I'll be home in half an hour. I have to get some bananas and milk at the store." I think he was freelancing because he thought it was fun—and probably lower stress than his day job.

Jeff's acquisition-speak fluency played a crucial role in my negotiations with Fexy. He would often spend hours on the phone with Ben Sternberg and Fexy's investors in the little WeWork space I had rented down the street from our offices to conduct these negotiations. It would be just him and

me in a four-by-eight space with two desks, two chairs, a lamp, and a phone. I usually had very little to add to these conversations, which was a good thing, because as far as I was concerned, they might as well have been speaking in tongues.

Jeff could parry every thrust from his counterparts, armed with his encyclopedic knowledge of the financial world. Every time an issue was raised, Jeff handled it with great aplomb, never losing his cool. The terms we ended up with were very close to the nonbinding terms of Fexy's initial offer, thanks to my man Jeff. Even Ben Sternberg once called me for no reason other than to tell me, "Your man Jeff is pretty good." Coming from a financial adversary, that's really high praise.

Jeff was aided in his efforts by Serious Eats' lawyer, Andy Beame. Andy was equal parts lawyer, confidant, and psychologist. Andy could talk to the Fexy guys in one breath and the private equity guys in the next, and then talk me down from the ledge when I went into catastrophe mode as the negotiations hit a snag. Andy had been a rock for me his entire eight-year tenure as our lawyer.

Andy was not only an excellent lawyer with tons of experience in negotiating acquisition contracts, but he was also an incredibly empathetic fellow who would help me through any nonlegal issues. This was a typical phone call I would have with Andy, usually from the front table at the Red Mango yogurt shop next to the office. Me: "I can't believe these motherfuckers. They're trying to screw me. I don't want to deal with this anymore. I'm done." Andy's reply: "Are you finished? Because if you are, now we really have to figure out what you should do."

Andy was like a marriage counselor for Mike and me and a work therapist for everyone else. I could even talk to him about Vicky. In his own interactions with all of these people, Andy had gained everyone's trust, which was not easy to do. Andy was so good at this kind of counseling, he could have sent me two separate hourly bills, one for legal fees and one for therapy hours, and I wouldn't have complained. Andy and Jeff were my final saviors on a journey filled with them.

Once a contract was drawn up, all two hundred pages of it, Andy took

over. It was basically Andy, a partner at a medium-sized New York law firm of fewer than two hundred lawyers, against a team of Fexy's lawyers from Latham & Watkins, one of the largest law firms in the country. The amazing thing is Andy more than held his own. He held those folks to a legal draw.

There was no yelling, no screaming, no harsh words or traded accusations. There were certainly a couple of contentious moments, which I couldn't even describe here because of my lack of financial and legal expertise and experience. But Jeff and Andy just kept their cool and worked through them methodically.

I was keeping Mike abreast of all the action as best I could, and Vicky as well. I was a nervous wreck. Although we had never gotten this far with any other company, my frame of reference flung me back to all the incomplete negotiations. So whenever I discussed the situation with friends, I convinced them that these negotiations were going to end up like all the others.

We visited our friends Tom and Joan in Long Island one weekend in the middle of the negotiation. I brought them an entire loin of beef for a story I was working on for Serious Eats. I threw myself into cooking twenty pounds of steak while I told Tom about the situation. Tom's response: "I can see why you've a nervous wreck, and as a documentary filmmaker I don't know shit about this process, but it seems to me that this one is going to happen." *Easy for him to say,* I thought to myself.

Finally, on Memorial Day weekend of 2015, I was driving Vicky crazy up on Martha's Vineyard. I must have had twenty conversations with Andy and another twenty conversations with Andy and the Latham & Watkins lawyers. I had to take calls in the middle of dinner parties. I had to beg off social invitations I really wanted to accept. Finally—I believe it was the Sunday night before Memorial Day—I called Andy to see what outstanding issues there were to be resolved and to find out if the deal was ready to be signed. He told me he would call the Latham & Watkins lawyers to find out the status of the last two minor sticking points. He said in the meantime we should read the salient points of the contract out loud to each other. We did so over the course of two hours. We were good.

Five minutes later our phone rang. I was lying on our bed in the master bedroom, computer, as always, on my lap. I answered.

All Andy said was "Check your bank balance."

I logged onto our account. The balance was a higher number by many millions than had ever been in there before.

"We did it! we did it!" I cried out repeatedly. I started to scream. Vicky heard me and came in and gave me a big hug. I said to her half a dozen times, "It's over, Vick. It's really over. Peter Cohen always said, 'It's over when the check clears.' The check has cleared. The money is there. Nobody can take it away from us."

Somehow, some way, I had fulfilled my promises to Vicky and Mike, and to myself. This insane thrill ride through business, born of a need to control my own destiny, was finally over.

The potential of the blogosphere had been realized, at least for this one barbecue- and pizza-loving scribe. I felt more relieved than triumphant, maybe because I had never put so much on the line. Next to meeting and marrying Vicky and having Will as a son, this was the greatest thing that had ever happened to me in my adult life. And it didn't just happen to me. I made it happen, with a lot of help along the way and a fair amount of luck.

In our bedroom that night, staring out at the star-filled sky, all I could feel was an overwhelming sense of relief. The check had cleared. As part of the deal, I had to agree to stay on for two years. I was looking forward to running Serious Eats without the stress that came with desperately trying to keep the business afloat.

I could finally exhale.

Chapter 20

THE AFTERMATH

I drove home from the Vineyard feeling euphoric, singing old Motown songs the whole way. I was Levi Stubbs, the lead singer for the Four Tops: "Sugar pie, honey bunch. You know that I love you." I felt like Philippe Petit, that guy who successfully walked on a high wire thousands of feet above the ground between two buildings of the World Trade Center complex. Vicky, usually my co–lead singer, was strangely silent. I took the subway to the office, a shit-eating grin on my face the whole way, and immediately convened a Serious Eats management committee meeting. I told them about the completed negotiations and the specifics of the deal. I exchanged high fives with every one of them.

We paid off all our debts; my investors, including my brother and my friends, got 90 percent of their money back in cash, along with some Fexy stock. The cash was a return on an investment that most of them had totally written off years earlier, so everybody was thrilled to take such a small loss.

Mike sent me an email the following day: "You have gotten to pursue a dream and realize it more perfectly than the world usually permits. You have even made a few bucks in the process. Not a bad run so far." I treasured that email then and every day since.

We kept our apartment—whew—and Vicky and I even made some money. By the time I repaid all the debts, paid my investors and my employees, I had made enough money to feather our retirement. It wasn't a

Silicon Valley–like score. Far from it. Every successful tech entrepreneur or venture capitalist would have laughed at what Vicky and I made from the sale. It would have been walking-around money for them. Still, it was enough for us.

The Serious Eaters were just as happy as everybody else, at least initially. Everyone in our little tribe cashed in their Serious Eats stock. It didn't make any of them rich, but I think it made them feel like they had gotten something tangible from sticking with me through the joyride.

Vicky? That first week she was calling all her friends with the good news. She was doing some serious exhaling herself.

Fexy wanted me to stay on and play to my natural strengths, to be Serious Eats' creative director, spiritual leader, and den mother, both for continuity's sake and for the overall good of the company. They took the checkbook away, and all financial functions—a wise move for what are now painfully obvious reasons.

So not only did I have some cash in the bank, but I finally had my dream job, the job I had started Serious Eats to do, the job I had been trying to create for myself since I'd published *New York Eats* in 1992—and with none of the boring, stressful distractions. It was all bonus, no onus.

So why wasn't I happy?

I'd gotten off a nine-year roller-coaster ride seemingly unhurt, with my faculties intact. But in the weeks after the sale, once the high wore off, I couldn't avoid noticing that my constant anxiety and the accompanying stress I felt hadn't abated. If anything, they were worse, as though I was suffering from a form of business PTSD. I couldn't shake the cumulative effects of the thrill ride; instead of being calmed by Fexy taking over the business aspects of Serious Eats, I found myself feeling more and more anxious. I was sure that another catastrophe would come out of nowhere to befall us at any moment.

At the same time, I noticed a not-so-subtle shift in both the way Vicky talked about the sale and her attitude toward it. From her tone of voice when we spoke, it was clear that the sale hadn't completely resolved everything that had been so difficult between us.

Mike was the first one to notice my extreme discomfort. Over a terrific brisket and beef rib lunch at Hill Country Barbecue, a few blocks from his house, he expressed his puzzlement. "I just don't get it. You should feel really good about this ending. You dodged a bullet. Hell, you dodged a hail of bullets. Think of the alternatives you narrowly avoided. Yet you're as stressed out as ever. Get a grip, bro." Mike was always trying to get me to mainline reality.

I wasn't ready to. Change was coming fast, and although I've had to deal with a lot of it in my life, I'd never learned to like it. I tried to sort through my feelings, to figure out why this event that I had worked so long and hard for had failed to give me the satisfaction I craved.

First of all, now that the company was sold, I was seen as "the man." The Serious Eaters felt like I'd put our whole family up for adoption. They resented me for doing that. The problem was that I felt that way too, and could relate to their bristling resentment, even while I felt powerless to do anything about it.

The Serious Eaters were also worried about how the culture of the company would change, and rightfully so. The us-against-the-world mentality, the David-versus-Goliath attitude that bound us, would definitely have to change. Like it or not, we were the big guys now. Or at least, we were bigger.

There were no layoffs, but each member of the Serious Eats staff had to sign an offer letter from Fexy detailing his or her job description, title, and salary. No more loosey-goosey Ed Levine management. Some rebelled and pushed back on the size of the salary increase, but there wasn't anything I could do about their complaints. The checkbook was no longer in my hands. Given my experience, you'd think I would have welcomed the freedom. But it made me feel impotent instead of liberated.

Fexy did force out our GM, Chris, a blow to the Serious Eaters, who had learned to trust Chris despite his occasionally brusque management style.

I spoke almost daily with Lisa Sharples, one of Fexy's founders, who said she was going to temporarily assume Chris's GM role. Lisa is a formidable presence and a really experienced operator, so she had lots of ideas for us to implement at Serious Eats. "Everywhere I've worked we've had KPIs, and I would like to set up Serious Eats KPIs, working with your whole team," she said to me over a fine breakfast bowl at Egg Shop on Elizabeth Street. "What's a KPI?" I asked haltingly. "Key performance indicators," she replied, "numbers you and your team have to hit. Once we get everyone to buy into them, they give everyone a common set of goals that they can work toward, knowing their bonuses depend on reaching them."

I told the management committee about the KPIs. They asked the same question I had: "What's a KPI?" asked our VP of product and chief developer, Paul Cline. I call Paul my silent assassin. He is a man of few words, but when he does talk he's invariably saying something smart and thoughtful. The management team didn't really seem to mind the actual KPIs themselves. But they felt their new stepparents were turning out to be much more strict than good old had-to-be-loved-at-any-cost Ed. They felt as if they were losing their freedom.

I may not have given my employees a sense of security, but I did give them an awesome, creatively free place to work, bounded only by their own curiosity and energy levels. The people who were attracted to Serious Eats were people like me—not clock punchers. So it made sense that my own anxieties were reflected back to me by the Serious Eaters.

My fears about people leaving Serious Eats and feeling abandoned when they did were once again haunting me. A few people did leave, so my worst fears were being realized. The Fexy folks expected this to happen. I should have as well, but I didn't. I desperately needed the family to stay together; every time someone left it felt like a death in the family.

Our brilliant designer and front-end developer, Tracie Lee, left for a great job at the *New York Times*. Our supremely competent and ever-smiling overall head of production, Chrissie Lamond, left for a job at *Fast Company*, displeased by the new role Fexy had designated for her.

One set of anxieties and stresses had been replaced by another. I had thought I would welcome not having bottom-line responsibility. Instead I felt constrained and bridled under Fexy's control.

Mike was right. I did need to get a grip. For me, for Vicky, for the Serious Eaters, for Mike, and for Fexy. I had to stop fighting the changes that were coming fast and furious. I needed, in the words of Joseph Campbell, to find—or in this case relocate—my bliss. I also needed to lead my tribe to the next phase of Serious Eats. But at that moment I was lost, with no compass, no road map, and no GPS.

I have felt lost many times as an adult, and good psychotherapists have often helped me find myself. After many hours talking with my blessed therapist, I finally figured some things out. I know therapists usually don't play much of a role in entrepreneurial memoirs; maybe if they did there would be fewer unhappy entrepreneurs. Or maybe I'm just more neurotic than your typical entrepreneur. Someone else can collect the data and make that determination. After months of good therapy, and just letting the dust settle, something dawned on me. The money was a relief, but despite what I'd told Vicky and Mike, it had never been about that. It had always been about building a family of like-minded people who shared my passion and sense of purpose, and who made me and Serious Eats better every day. Not that we obsessed about the same things. Max knew everything there was to know about tea, much of which I didn't care to learn for myself. What mattered to me was that he was obsessive, had a deeply curious mind, and was an engaging storyteller. It had been the same story with Kenji; I didn't know the first thing about food science and frankly had never even thought much about the subject before. But Kenji made me care. Serious Eats was all about providing a home base for people like Kenji and Max, one without the gatekeepers who had irritated me so much as a younger writer, and trusting them to do their thing. Serious Eats was personal. It had always been personal.

I had, of course, convinced myself that building my own company was all about money, that Serious Eats was a surefire path to financial security for two entrepreneurially minded people with a need to feel secure. It was an absurd and naive notion, that starting a group food blog with an untried financial model would pave the way to a comfortable retirement.

But that misbegotten notion had given me the permission I needed from the two most important people to me, Vicky and Mike, to embark on my insane journey. So it wasn't surprising that the sale hadn't made me happy. Fexy, Lisa, Cliff, and Ben were great. They had saved us and done right by us throughout the entire agonizing acquisition process. But now I realized that getting out of financial jeopardy had created trade-offs I had never anticipated. Serious Eats had always been about the people, and the people weren't happy. No wonder I was anxious.

Armed with all these realizations, I committed myself to giving up the ghost of Serious Eats past. I would try to embrace the changes that came with the new owners taking charge, and to find compromises that would make us all happy. I was still a people pleaser.

Fexy did impose a lot of structure. Cliff and Lisa and Ben all came from conventional digital publishing backgrounds, so they believed in the business practices they had all employed and succeeded with, practices I was almost allergic to.

For example, Fexy wanted us to fully embrace the idea of sponsored content or native advertising. Native advertising is content created and paid for by brands. This content is written in the voice of the site the advertiser has bought advertising on. It is usually created by a separate team within a site or by freelancers. The whole idea is that native advertising doesn't look like conventional advertising, so readers are more likely to look at it.

On sites like Serious Eats, and on most other high-quality websites, it is always clearly differentiated from actual editorial content by being marked as "partner content." We had created sponsored content before Fexy bought us, but we had never fully embraced the concept. Kenji, his chief lieutenant Daniel Gritzer, and I all came from traditional media backgrounds, where the editorial team was walled off from the business types— the suits, as they were derisively called.

The Fexyers thought that we were ideological purists, that we almost resented the business side of the equation, that we didn't understand how the line between editorial and advertising was becoming increasingly blurred in digital media. The laws of supply and demand, the fact that there was an ever-larger glut of digital ad impressions available, meant the advertisers had all the leverage.

They weren't wrong.

I had to calmly explain to the Serious Eaters that this was indeed the new reality in the digital publishing realm. If the *New York Times* embraced native advertising and sponsored content, which it did, we were just going to have to be down with it as well.

Today we have found a way to do native advertising Serious Eats style, without feeling as if we have sold out. Do the Fexy-hired salespeople occasionally ask us to do things that we are uncomfortable doing in the realm of native advertising? Of course they do. That's their job. Sales folks are paid on commission. But we can and do say no to many of their requests, and the Fexy management team backs us up just about every time. Sometimes the Serious Eats editorial team comes up with their own ideas for how to create sponsored content that doesn't compromise our integrity and editorial freedom. They have become first-rate creative businesspeople.

In hindsight, much of our collective resentment was misplaced. Serious Eats was a business that Fexy paid handsomely for, and Lisa, Cliff, and Ben were going to create a company based on their previous experiences and their values, the same way I did when I started Serious Eats.

Even I had to admit that most of the changes were necessary, and really good for the company. The staff liked having structure and formalities like salary and performance reviews and a clearly stated vacation policy. It turns out that the Sex Pistols–like punk band that was Serious Eats had to turn into a real band with a professional manager and sufficient funds to stay in nice hotels on the road. Sho Spaeth, Serious Eats' features editor, once drunkenly said to me that he missed the halcyon, punk-rock days of the site. I reminded Sho that it had not ended well for Sid Vicious and the Sex Pistols.

I did finally accept the fact that I had sold Serious Eats, and the Serious Eaters came to realize that Fexy gets us. They were happy that the company was on firmer financial footing, though I was proud that I always made payroll. I accepted and even loved the fact that I didn't have to live on the edge anymore. I could feel good about having steered the Serious Eats ship into a safe harbor.

But there was still some unfinished business.

With the deal really done, I had to take stock of the collateral damage Serious Eats had done to my relationships with both Vicky and Mike. The fight to keep Serious Eats alive had been a grueling nine-year battle and, like most battles, it had left some wounds that still hadn't healed.

I mistakenly thought at the time that the proceeds of the sale would wipe away all of Vicky's conflicted feelings about the whole Serious Eats saga. The rewards were worth the risks, weren't they? But I couldn't wipe the slate clean. Why? Because when I learned about the relationship between risk and reward in business, no teacher at Columbia Business School spoke to the collateral emotional and psychological damage associated with the risks you take to reap the rewards. That damage, it turns out, is really difficult to repair.

Vicky thought I didn't give credit where credit was due. She was wrong—maybe one of the only things she's been wrong about in thirty-five years of marriage. It was true that I couldn't entirely admit how instrumental she'd been. And it's true that I was too dumb to really give credit where it was due. But it's also true that I literally can't imagine what it would have been like to do this without her, and I am keenly aware that it wouldn't have worked if she hadn't been on my side.

In fact, the most harrowing details I've had to relive in writing this book have nothing to do with financial security, only the terrifying knowledge of how close I came to doing real damage to the relationship that made it all possible.

For the nine long years that it took to get Serious Eats off the ground (in fact, long before that, and after) I relied every single day on Vicky's solid judgment, her business savvy, her good counsel, her sense of humor, and her preternatural calm. Her unwavering belief in me was—and is—humbling. I do not for a moment downplay the difficulty of the situations I put her in, or the tremendous sacrifices she had to make.

Which isn't to say that I was any good at communicating any of this at the time. So we kept fighting. More than a year after I sold the business, we had yet another argument that ended without a resolution, neither of us giving an inch.

I got on my bike and rode to Tiffany. I had never been inside Tiffany, so I had no idea what to do when I went through the revolving doors. I asked the person stationed right inside the door where I could buy pearl earrings for my wife. Vicky had been talking about how much she wanted a pair of pearl earrings for years, even before Serious Eats.

A kindly saleswoman showed me a variety of diamond-and-pearl earrings. I picked a pair out for Vicky. It's not a bad metaphor: a piece of grit in an oyster shell—a lot of work to make something that looks so effortlessly beautiful. She opened the box like a kid opening a present on Christmas morning. Vicky grinned from earring to earring as she walked over to a mirror to try them on. I almost started to cry, mostly out of frustration at myself. Why had it taken me so long to get to this place I obviously needed to be? Pride? Stupidity? Stubbornness? No matter. I made it. Let the healing begin. It continues to this day.

It was easier for Mike and me to put the Serious Eats sale behind us. Though our many confrontations were hard on both of us, he didn't live with the day-to-day Serious Eats stress in the same way Vicky did. Mike didn't have to confront a seemingly inconsolable spouse (that would be me) almost every night. And he was never at risk of losing his apartment and his marriage.

This allowed Mike to be the proud father of Serious Eats more easily right after the sale. His daughters told me that Serious Eats was all he talked about—other than, of course, the state of the world, the airline business, cars, and hi-fi equipment. And to me directly, Mike's first comment after the sale was "I'm proud of the part I played, however large or small it was, in Serious Eats' success. Now, with the sale out of the way, I hope I retain my right to call you for restaurant reservations." I would have happily gone myself to any restaurant to secure a "Mike" table—that is to say, quiet, comfortable, and not near the kitchen. And I would have made sure the restaurant's staff made a not-so-quiet fuss over him, because nobody liked that more than Mike.

Right around the time of the sale, Mike's kidneys started to fail, just as my dad's had. He was dying, yet his emails about the "state of play," as he called his updates on his health, were filled with optimism. Mike really did love life, maybe because he was so delighted and surprised that he had lived longer than both of our parents. Mike was convinced he would not make it out of his fifties. He used to say that every year past fifty-three (our mom's age when she died), and then fifty-seven (our dad's when he died), was a bonus. He made it to seventy-five, so that's a lot of bonus years. He took advantage of each and every one of them.

With our dad having died of kidney failure in the days before dialysis, this malady was particularly resonant and painful both psychologically and physically. Mike was reluctant to undergo dialysis because he thought it would cramp his style and limit his movements. Of course, he could barely move at that point anyway.

As a result of his illness, Mike couldn't keep his weight up, a not-so-gentle irony for a man whose gargantuan appetites had had him weighing 310 pounds before undergoing an early and radical form of bariatric surgery in 2002 that removed part of his small intestine. His weight throughout the Serious Eats years fluctuated between 165 and 175 pounds. As he got sicker, he couldn't keep any weight on.

After the sale we could stop being business partners and resume what had become a deep and abiding kinship and, yes, friendship. In that last year and a half of his life, I was gratified to be able to return some of the comfort and love he had supplied me when I was in desperate need of them fifty years earlier. I could take care of him the way he and Carol took care of me.

He still wanted to eat with me, everything from foie gras to pastrami, and drink good champagne and good wine with the food while I drank iced tea. When he died, the dude had pounds and pounds of foie gras and Wagyu beef stored away in an oversized freezer in the basement of his house in New Haven. It was such a source of pleasure for both of us to enjoy each other's company again without the Serious Eats conflicts getting in the way.

Almost a year to the day after I sold Serious Eats, I was inducted into the Who's Who of Food & Beverage in America by the James Beard Foundation at the Lyric Opera House in Chicago. I don't mean to brag, but it was pretty cool. It was the first time the Who's Who judges had recognized someone involved in digital media. The blogosphere had successfully stormed the gates.

At the time, Mike had three fractured ribs sustained in a fall. He was not well at all. Yet Mike and Carol insisted on coming to Chicago for the ceremony. He even came to the dinner afterward, held at the opera house, and to a few of the after-parties, although he could barely walk. Of course, Mike being Mike, at the dinner he ended up sharing a plate of Aaron Franklin's incomparable brisket (Franklin Barbecue in Austin is one of those bucket-list items for any food lover) with a Yalie friend of mine while having an animated discussion about the John C. Calhoun controversy on the Yale campus. These conversations were what Mike lived for, so when I looked over and saw him in animated conversation with my friend the food writer Corby Kummer, I was practically in tears. They would have been tears of joy *and* sadness—joy because Mike was still capable of being Mike and sadness because I knew that wouldn't be the case for much longer.

We went out for dinner the night before, and in typical Mike fashion, he rejected a couple of tables before we were shown a suitable one. No matter what his physical condition, Mike was still Mike.

Mike died nineteen months after I sold Serious Eats. He was down to 125 pounds by then. It broke my heart to see him like that, pale, painfully thin, and practically devoid of the restless, relentless energy that was his lifelong trademark. Mike was taken by ambulance to the hospital three times in the last six months he was on this earth. Vicky and I would go visit him each time. No matter how sick or weak Mike was, whenever I walked into his hospital room or his house in New Haven, his face lit up like the neon sign at Papaya King. He really was the proud papa of me and Serious Eats, and he took enormous pleasure in our success. And I was the proud and heartbroken younger brother/son/close friend.

A month before he died I brought him and Carol an official Ed Levine brunch from New York: Gaspé smoked salmon and scallion cream cheese

Onion Bialys

STELLA PARKS

I had my first bialy while sitting across from Ed and Vicky in their living room, trying to hash out an idea for my book. It was chewy and crisp but tender—loaded with lightly caramelized onions and a sprinkle of poppy seeds. I honestly have no idea what we were talking about exactly; all I can remember was that perfect bialy, and the sense of family between us.

YIELD: Twelve 3½-inch bialys

For the Flour Paste:

6 ounces water
(about ¾ cup)

3½ ounces bread flour
(about ¾ cup, spooned)

For the Dough:

12½ ounces bread flour
(2½ cups, spooned),
plus a pinch for dusting

½ ounce white sugar
(about 1 tablespoon)

⅓ ounce salt (volume will
vary by brand; about 2½
teaspoons for Diamond
Crystal kosher salt)

⅛ ounce instant dry yeast
such as SAF, not rapid rise
(about 1¼ teaspoons)

6 ounces water
(about ¾ cup)

For the Filling:

2 small-to-medium-size
yellow onions (about
16 ounces)

1 tablespoon neutral oil

Salt, to taste

Poppy seeds, to taste

1. In a 10-inch skillet, whisk the water and flour together over medium heat, cooking until the mixture comes together in a thick, mashed potato–like paste, about 2 minutes. Scrape onto a plate, spread into a 1-inch layer, and cool to approximately 75°F.

2. Place the flour, sugar, salt, and yeast in a food processor fitted with a metal blade, and pulse once or twice to combine. Add the remaining water and the prepared flour paste, then process until silky smooth, about 90 seconds. Turn the dough into a lightly greased bowl, cover, and set aside to rise for about 3 hours at cool room temperature.

3. Meanwhile, prepare the filling. Peel, halve, and dice the onion into ¼-inch pieces. In a large stainless steel skillet, heat the oil over medium heat until shimmering. Add the onion and cook, stirring frequently, until softened and pale gold, about 45 minutes. Adjust the heat as needed to prevent the onions from turning dark or caramelizing too fully. Season to taste with salt and set aside to cool until needed.

4. Scrape the proofed dough onto a clean, lightly floured surface, and divide into 12 even portions, just over 2 ounces each. With lightly floured hands, flatten each into a disk, and use your fingertips to create a wide indentation in the center. Continue shaping, and gently stretching if needed, until each portion is about 3½ inches across and ¾ inch thick around the rim, with a thin, indented area about 2 inche across and less than ¼ inch thick.

5. Transfer to a parchment-lined half-sheet pan that's been generously dusted with polenta or grits, and arrange the bialys on top. Divide the filling evenly among them, spooning it into the center of each. Cover with plastic wrap and set aside to proof at cool room temperature for about 2½ hours, or overnight in the fridge.

   Adjust an oven rack to the middle position and preheat to 400°F. Sprinkle the bialys with poppy seeds, and bake until pale gold all over. The timing will vary depending on the starting temperature of the dough, but expect 30 to 45 minutes.

6. Cool 15 minutes before serving. Leftovers can be kept up to 3 days in a paper bag, then rewarmed in a 350°F oven for about 5 minutes to crisp before serving.

from Russ & Daughters, bialys from Hot Bread Kitchen, bagels from Absolute Bagels, sturgeon from Barney Greengrass the Sturgeon King, babka from Breads Bakery. He loved every moment of it, though he could manage only a bite or two of each item.

I gave one of the eulogies at Mike's memorial service, held at an auditorium in the fine arts building at Yale. I recited the note that Mike had sent me after Serious Eats was sold: "You have gotten to pursue a dream and realize it more perfectly than the real world usually permits. You have even made a few bucks in the process. Not a bad run so far." It takes one to know one, my brother.

When Mike was in his element and healthy and doing one of the million things he loved to do, he used to grin broadly at me and say, "It doesn't get any better than this, Ed. Enjoy it while you can."

In one of his novels the late, great writer Jim Harrison, most definitely a serious eater, once wrote of a character: "He's literally taking bites out of the sun, moon, and earth."* That's a pretty apt description of Mike. And I miss the hell out of taking those bites with him.

---

* Jim Harrison, *The Beast God Forgot to Invent* (New York, NY: Grove Press, 2000), 89.

Chapter 21

A DAY IN THE LIFE OF
THIS SERIOUS EATER (2018)

E d, I can tell from your question that you're one of these people who doesn't understand the appeal of turkey in general. I love turkey breast meat. You know, there's a difference between subtle and bland. White-meat turkey is most definitely the former."

It was a cold, gray day in New York in early November of 2018. Kenji was schooling me from his house in San Mateo, California, while we recorded the Thanksgiving episode of the Serious Eats podcast, *Special Sauce*. What else is new? I laughed into the mic and was about to proceed to the next emailed question from a Serious Eats community member when Stella Parks, who was on the phone from her house in Lexington, Kentucky, chimed in, "I'm with Kenji. I'm a white-meat and gravy girl." Now they were ganging up on me on my own podcast! I loved it. It might as well have been a Serious Eats editorial meeting.

Though Kenji is no longer Serious Eats' managing culinary director, he is still our chief culinary adviser and considers Serious Eats his online home. Stella is on staff as our resident pastry wizard. They may not work at our gleaming new offices in Brooklyn with two kitchens (one for prepping food, the other for producing videos—and both, miraculously, up to code)—but they are both members in good standing of the Serious Eats tribe. (And Stella does come up one week a month to work with our visual director, Vicky Wasik.) They have also both published *New York Times* bestsellers in the past few years: Kenji's *The Food Lab: Better Home Cooking Through Science* and Stella's *BraveTart: Iconic American Desserts.*

M y day had started early. For breakfast I had a sour-cherry, whole-milk, super thick and creamy Persian-style White Moustache yogurt sprinkled with crushed pecans. Kenji's worthy successor, Daniel Gritzer, had turned me on to White Moustache. It's so naturally creamy and thick and seriously delicious that it's the only yogurt I can eat. When I ate my first spoonful, I thought to myself, *Oh, that's what yogurt is supposed to taste like.* Plus it comes in really cool glass jars. Check out White Moustache founder Homa Dashtaki's episodes on *Special Sauce.* She has an amazing story to go along with her incomparable yogurt.

I had gone to those gleaming new offices in the morning to meet with Fexy co-CEO Lisa Sharples, who was in from Fexy's corporate offices in Mercer Island, Washington. Lisa came into my office, which has floor-to-ceiling windows overlooking the Brooklyn-Queens Expressway, a Dunkin' Donuts drive-through, and Green-Wood Cemetery, a tree-filled patch of green in Sunset Park, Brooklyn.

"Let me show you a couple of things, Ed," she said, pulling up a chair, her laptop cradled in one arm. "First of all, let me show you where we are in terms of Q4 direct advertising and the year overall advertising. We are already at 141 percent of goal for the quarter, which we're only halfway through, and we are at 71 percent of goal for our entire fiscal year, which doesn't end for another eight months almost. That's good news." I corrected Lisa: "That's great news. I can tell you we never hit those numbers when I owned the company."

This is what Serious Eats is like circa 2018. Not only is it profitable and a much more professionally run operation, but the sound of laughter still fills our offices pretty regularly. We moved into these light-filled new offices with views of the Verrazzano-Narrows Bridge and the East River three months after I sold the company. People I felt really close to have come and gone in the three years we've been in the space, but unlike before, I was okay with their leaving. People come and people go. That's the nature of business, not family.

But in Serious Eats' case, just about every person who leaves stays in the Serious Eats tribe. Our parties are filled with Serious Eaters past, present, and probably future.

The current Serious Eats management team is managing culinary director Daniel Gritzer, who is as curious as he is talented; visual director Vicky Wasik; managing editor Niki Achitoff-Gray; VP of product Paul Cline; and marketing director Ariel Kanter. Vicky had started as Robyn Lee's successor as house photographer and has grown into her role as SE's visual director. Niki had started as an intern at SE in 2012 and here she is, six years later, as our whip-cracking and whip-smart managing editor. Ariel had come on board as SE's liaison to ad sales, helping create proposals, and now she is Serious Eats' director of marketing. They are all talented, smart as hell, passionate about what we do and how we go about doing it, and insanely curious about the food culture and the way we cover it. Paul in particular became my rock, the new Alaina. He is a man of few words, but he makes every one of them count. When Paul speaks at our management meeting everyone listens. That's because he really knows his shit. When we switched content management systems from Movable Type to WordPress, we were told it would cost us a hundred thousand dollars to hire an outside firm to do it over the course of a year. Paul did it in three months while performing all his regular duties. He's always thinking about the business holistically with the future in mind. The whole new management team upholds the Serious Eats hiring tradition I started: find the smartest, best people for the job, give them the creative freedom they probably couldn't find anywhere else, and trust them to do the right thing.

But thankfully, it's not quite so personal. Most everyone who works at Serious Eats these days thinks of it as a business first and then, perhaps, a calling. Some people who work at the company may just think of their job as a really good gig. I'm okay with that. Maybe that's why Serious Eats is doing so much better as a business. Serious Eats is growing up. And that's okay. So have I.

At the studio, associate producer Grace Chen and I met Marty Gold-ensohn, our insanely talented *Special Sauce* producer, who has been school-ing me in audio storytelling for more than twenty-five years now. I still do the podcast every week; it features real conversations about the joy and pain of putting your passion to work with food and nonfood people alike.

The ability to reconnect with people like Marty, who worked with me at WNYC on *Dish* and my short-form audio stories twenty years ago, is yet another reason I love Serious Eats. Marty is a genius editor and audio story-teller. "Audio storytelling," Marty says, "is all about narrative structure, beats, and rhythms." Marty has been working with Grace for about a year now, and that's how Serious Eats works. We bring smart people together from different backgrounds and they learn from each other. In doing so the site evolves organically.

After the *Special Sauce* taping I headed down to a book party for former Serious Eats managing editor Carey Jones's new book, *Be Your Own Bar-tender*, written with her mixologist husband, John McCarthy. Carey had started as an intern at Serious Eats in the summer of 2006, before the site even existed. You might remember how bereft I was when she and her co-managing editor, Erin Zimmer, left almost simultaneously in those tumul-tuous months of 2011. Erin now lives in New Orleans with her husband, Andrew, and their new baby. We went to their wedding in the Big Easy, and boy, was I proud when Erin's father mentioned in his toast that Serious Eats was the job that changed her life. Maggie Hoffman couldn't make Carey's party. She was busy promoting her own book, *The One-Bottle Cocktail*.

Be Your Own Bartender is Carey's second book. Carey is obsessive, driven, and very smart. She is a quintessential Serious Eater, just like Erin. Carey pursued her cocktail obsession when she worked at Serious Eats, even though I only like drinks with umbrellas in them.

When I arrived, Carey's agent—guess who?—was reading the riot act to a bookseller who had failed to get copies of the book to the party on time. Carey and John gathered in awe of the spectacle; for the first time, they were seeing the iron fist my wife hides in that velvet glove. Of course, I've known what a badass she is since the day I met her.

A few minutes later I left Carey's party to go to another one, hosted by Max Falkowitz. When Max left in 2014, four years after he arrived, to work as *Saveur* magazine's digital editor, he walked into my office and said, "I know I'm leaving the best job I'll ever have, but I have to find out what it's like to work somewhere else."

Max left *Saveur* in 2015, but while he was there he cowrote *The Dumpling Galaxy Cookbook* with Dumpling Galaxy founder Helen You. If you listen to Helen's episodes of *Special Sauce*, you'll learn that she would bring homemade dumplings to her imprisoned father in China. The journey took eighteen hours by foot and bicycle. She then came to New York by herself and became an accountant while also opening a dumpling stand in one of those subterranean food bazaars/courts sprinkled throughout Flushing, Queens, now home to the largest Chinese population in New York. If you are a fan of dumplings with delicate, translucent skins and fresh, imaginative fillings, go to Dumpling Galaxy. Helen's done so well and worked so hard that she moved out of the basement to a gleaming space on the ground floor of a brand-new office building in Flushing. Helen is most definitely a serious eater too.

Max's party was at Kalustyan's, New York's best ethnic ingredient store. The shelves are lined with foodstuffs from around the world, everything from kaffir lime leaves from Thailand to tomato couscous to mango pickles. The pungent and unfamiliar smells that emanate from every aisle are a powerful sales tool. Every time I go there I end up buying stuff I don't even use.

The party was to celebrate the launch of Snuk Foods, an online catalog for hard-to-find, exquisitely sourced ethnic ingredients. Max was doing a lot of the sourcing and all of the writing for the site, as well as editing *Caravan*, Snuk's print magazine. It was a perfect gig for Max, who loves nothing more than to take deep dives into seemingly obscure foodstuffs and get people excited about them. Max gave me a warm hug. We chatted about Snuk and *Caravan*. I could tell how excited he was. Max was beaming. He was doing what he was put on this earth to do.

Matt Danzer, the cochef (with his Thai-born wife, Ann Redding) of the Michelin-starred Thai restaurant Uncle Boons, was serving the seriously delicious leafy tidbit miang kham at the party. According to Max, "miang kham is a traditional Thai and Lao snack served on a betel leaf (or something similar). It's basically a bunch of spicy, crunchy stuff, usually fried shallots or garlic, roasted coconut, dried shrimp, peanuts or cashews, and chunks of lime (including the peel). You can get it on the regular Uncle Boons menu and at a few Thai places here in Queens."

A few feet away I saw Ethan Frisch, who runs a single-origin spice company called Burlap & Barrel. I met Ethan through Max, when they would collaborate on obsessive ice cream columns. Ethan implored me to smell and even try a number of his spices in plastic containers. I smelled the cumin. It was so intense. It was like smelling cumin for the first time. Next he had me try black lime powder from Venezuela. He explained, "It's just dried whole black limes. Those limes were probably picked a week ago."

As I left Max's party, I couldn't help thinking about what I had wrought. I had hired Kenji and Stella and Carey and Max and Erin and so many others and given them the runway, the opportunity, to spread their wings. Serious Eats' resident skeptic, Sho Spaeth, once asked me how I knew to hire Kenji and Stella. "I know you," he said playfully. "I bet you didn't make one of their recipes before you hired them." I replied, "You're right, Sho. I didn't. But after spending five minutes talking to Kenji and Stella about food and life, I knew they were put on this earth to work at Serious Eats."

In a magazine interview Max once aptly described Serious Eats as "deliciously anarchic." In that same story he said, "I was lucky to start working for a place where you were encouraged to pursue your obsessions. . . . At most publications, you're not encouraged to do your own thing—Serious Eats, it's their entire business model. Getting crazy people to talk about stuff they know about."*

Whenever I'm at a Serious Eats–related event, I think about Mike. I can't help it. He will forever be associated with the company in my mind. Mike would have loved Max's party; the food, the passion, the knowledge,

---

* Abby Carney, "Max Falkowitz, *Saveur*'s Executive Digital Editor," *Edible Queens*, June 9, 2017.

the obsessive intelligence on display. All of it. I watched Mike pursue his passions with a ferocity that inspired me to pursue mine. God, I miss my brother.

It was a perfect Serious Eats day. Eating great food, talking food with people I can learn from, giving my own take on the state of the food culture, and basking in the reflected glory of my tribe's accomplishments.

I trust there will be many more of these perfect days in the years to come, thanks to passionate deep dives by people like Kenji, Stella, and Daniel, who is as thoughtful and talented a successor to Kenji as we could have hoped to find. Stella recently made some mind-alteringly delicious homemade Klondike bars in our new kitchens. I'm afraid I polished off a half dozen of them. Please don't tell Vicky. Daniel just wrote a five-thousand-word post on mortars and pestles from around the globe. Kenji is being an extremely attentive stay-at-home dad to his impossibly cute two-year-old daughter, Alicia; there is no talking to Kenji when Alicia is awake. Kenji being Kenji, during her naps he found the time to write a lovely children's book that celebrates Alicia's multicultural food discoveries. Oh yeah—he also finds time to work on the successor to *The Food Lab*, coming to a bookstore near serious eaters everywhere in the near future. And he and his partners have opened Wursthall, a popular restaurant an easy bike ride from Kenji's house. Remember, the dude sleeps only four hours a night.

I'm not going anywhere anytime soon either. I just cowrote (with another former Serious Eats managing editor Adam Kuban and pizza tour operator Scott Wiener) a five-thousand-word post on the site, "State of the Slice," so if you want to know where to find a serious slice of pizza in New York City, you can still find out on Serious Eats. If you're ever in New York, head up to Mama's TOO! at 105th and Broadway for a square pepperoni slice. It's very possible that the Mama's TOO! square pepperoni has replaced the Spicy Spring slice from Prince Street Pizza in my heart. I'm not fickle, I'm just flexible.

Serious Eats, a business born of great loss, has resulted in a gain for serious eaters everywhere. That's the biggest win of all. In twelve years Serious Eats managed to go from surviving to thriving, with many ups and downs in the joyride that it became. But we somehow made it across the finish line, at least for the time being.

Damn, it feels good.

ACKNOWLEDGMENTS

Writing *Serious Eater* really did take a village. First I depended on my own inability to discard any emails. As I am typing this, I have 269,070 emails on my laptop. But those weren't nearly enough. I spoke to family, friends, and colleagues from every stage of my life. They filled in more holes than I knew existed.

To my spectacularly loyal, brilliant, and beautiful wife of thirty-seven years, Vicky, who courageously allowed me to tell the Serious Eats story. I hope all the ups and downs were worth it. It's rare to find a spouse willing to bare the inner workings of her marriage in a book (especially one you're still married to). The SE saga put our love to the test, and thanks to your strength, your belief, and your sagacity, we passed with flying colors. You really do have the patience of a saint. To my late brother, Mike, whose story is so central to this book, as you know if you have gotten this far.

To my sister-in-law Carol: Carol, you have provided shelter from so many storms over the last fifty years, I can never thank you enough. You also filled in so many gaps in my memory. To my old college buddy, Portfolio publisher Adrian Zackheim, who over lunch decided the SE story was worth committing to paper.

To my wunderkind editor Merry Sun—how is someone so young, so wise, so supportive, so smart, and so damn talented? I really did hitch my wagon to a star.

To Laura Tucker, brilliant writer, thinker, and SE fan, my "book therapist," recommended to me by, who else, Vicky. Laura, you made me believe I could actually tell this story. Your support, suggestions, fearless critiques, and perceptive observations based on the hundreds of thousands of words I sent you made this book better in so many ways.

To Kenji López-Alt, who, in the words of Hall and Oates, helped in a major way to make my dreams come true. Your loyalty was tested many times along the way, and yet you stood by me and Serious Eats every time.

Thanks too, Kenji, for the lovely foreword to *Serious Eater* and the seriously delicious original recipes you contributed to the book. To Stella Parks, aka BraveTart, for your extraordinary book recipes (a special shout-out for the original hot fudge and bialys) and for making Serious Eats a destination for dessert lovers.

A special shout-out to my oldest and closest college friend, Bob Rosen, who spent hours if not days talking me off the ledge, convincing me that somehow SE would make it. Our fifty-year friendship has meant so much.

To Meg Hourihan, David Karp, Adam Kuban, Alaina Browne, Robyn Lee, Erin Zimmer, Carey Jones, Maggie Hoffman, Max Falkowitz, Nick Kindelsperger, Tracie Lee, and Zach Brooks, the original SE tribe, you made me believe and gave me hope. I trust you all survived the ups and downs without any permanent damage (maybe just a little motion sickness). I'd share a foxhole with any and all of you anytime. It's been thrilling to watch all of you follow your dreams.

To the rest of the current Serious Eats tribe, who bring this crazy person's idea to life in ways I never imagined: Tim Aikens, Kristina Bornholtz, Miranda Kaplan, Maggie Lee, Sasha Marx, John Mattia, Joel Russo, Elazar Sontag, Sho Spaeth, thanks for keeping the dream alive. For the Fexy crew in Mercer Island, especially founders Cliff and Lisa Sharples and Ben Sternberg, I trusted you with my brainchild and you have proven to be wonderful stewards of Serious Eats. And to the Fexy sales team, headed by Jalaane Levi-Garza, who supply a lot of the oxygen we need.

For all of the investors: the aforementioned Mike and Carol Levine, Marc Lasry, Steve Trost, Beryl Snyder, the late Harold Snyder, Bob Rosen, Henry Cornell, Jack Heyrman, Harriet Seitler, Stephen McDonnell, Tom Douglas, Chandler Bocklage, Sol Kumin, Louisa Baur, and Nelson Heumann, all of whom believed in me and Serious Eats, thanks for taking a huge chance on me by putting your money where your mouths were.

For Peter Cohen, investment banker and friend, you were my rock and were incredibly generous and always available—and thanks to Peter's Blackstone crew, Jordan and Anthony, who crunched more numbers than I knew existed. Andy Beame, lawyer and consigliere, and family therapist when needed, par excellence. And for Jeff Driskill, whose financial acumen and preternatural calm were invaluable down the stretch.

To my late parents, Morris and Sara Levine, who instilled in me the values that carried Serious Eats across the finish line.

To my late mother-in-law, Hilda Bijur, whom I knew much longer than my own mother, who eventually came around to see that knish-loving can be a profession, too, and became a true maternal presence in my life.

To our group of steadfast and supportive friends (you all know who you are), who had never-ending faith in my ability to tell and write this story even when I didn't. To Kirk Citron, Tom Keiser, and Paul Slavin, friends and invaluable business sounding boards, who never failed to give me a reality check when I desperately needed one.

And to the rest of the crew at Portfolio, Chris Sergio, Will Weisser, Alyssa Adler, Madeline Montgomery, and Margot Stamas, all consummate professionals, you all truly made this particular publishing experience such a pleasure. To Gail Hochman, the agent for this book who so ably pinch-hit for Vicky in these extraordinary circumstances.

And of course to my son, Will, who went from toddler to creative professional and critical reader in seemingly an instant. Your mother and I are the luckiest parents in the firmament. You make parenthood a joy and an unadulterated pleasure, and it's been that way since the moment you arrived on this earth thirty-two years ago.

To jazz's Little Giant Jimmy Heath, for teaching me the true meaning of living a creative life. To the chefs and purveyors who have opened up their hearts and their lives and their kitchens to me. To Cindy Franklin and Therese Steiner, brilliant strategists and dear friends who were invaluable guides to the mysteries of management and team-building. To Marty Goldensohn, my audio storytelling guru and podcast production wizard, who actually makes it sound like I know what I'm doing on *Special Sauce*. To Dr. Lawrence Sandberg, who helps me make sense of what is happening in real time. To my writing heroes, Calvin Trillin and the late Nora Ephron, breaking bread with the two of you has definitely been among the highlights of my life. To Gina Kaiser for her more than fifty-year-old Cedarhurst recollections. Impressive, my old friend. And finally to Howie Klar, one of my closest friends and steadfast supporters who died (much) too soon to see Serious Eats come to life. You would have loved it, Howie.